Stepping
through
Origins

Irish Studies
Kathleen Costello-Sullivan, *Series Editor*

Select Titles in Irish Studies

Avant-Garde Nationalism at the Dublin Gate Theatre, 1928–1940
Ruud van den Beuken

Fine Meshwork: Philip Roth, Edna O'Brien, and Jewish-Irish Literature
Dan O'Brien

Guilt Rules All: Irish Mystery, Detective, and Crime Fiction
Elizabeth Mannion and Brian Cliff, eds.

Literary Drowning: Postcolonial Memory in Irish and Caribbean Writing
Stephanie Pocock Boeninger

Modernity, Community, and Place in Brian Friel's Drama, Second Edition
Richard Rankin Russell

Politics, Culture, and the Irish American Press: 1784–1963
Debra Reddin van Tuyll, Mark O'Brien, and Marcel Broersma, eds.

The Rogue Narrative and Irish Fiction, 1660–1790
Joe Lines

Science, Technology, and Irish Modernism
Kathryn Conrad, Cóilín Parsons, and Julie McCormick Weng, eds.

For a full list of titles in this series, visit
https://press.syr.edu/supressbook-series/irish-studies/.

Stepping *through* Origins

Nature, Home, and Landscape in Irish Literature

JEFFERSON HOLDRIDGE

Syracuse University Press

Syracuse, New York 13244-5290

First Edition 2022
22 23 24 25 26 27 6 5 4 3 2 1

∞ The paper used in this publication meets the minimum requirements of the American National Standard for Information Sciences—Permanence of Paper for Printed Library Materials, ANSI Z39.48-1992.

For a listing of books published and distributed by Syracuse University Press, visit https://press.syr.edu.

ISBN: 978-0-8156-3746-2 (hardcover)
978-0-8156-3732-5 (paperback)
978-0-8156-5533-6 (e-book)

Library of Congress Cataloging-in-Publication Data

Names: Holdridge, Jefferson, author.

Title: Stepping through origins : nature, home, & landscape in Irish literature / Jefferson Holdridge.

Description: First edition. | Syracuse, New York : Syracuse University Press, 2022. | Series: Irish studies | Includes bibliographical references and index. | Summary: ""Stepping through Origins" addresses the place of the aesthetics of nature, landscape, and family in Irish literature, aiming to show how nature is associated with a complex web of Original Sin, colonial conquest, and Oedipal guilt, and how finally some contemporary writers in their acknowledgement of the ecological movement have moved beyond this construction"— Provided by publisher.

Identifiers: LCCN 2021000134 (print) | LCCN 2021000135 (ebook) | ISBN 9780815637462 (hardcover) | ISBN 9780815637325 (paperback) | ISBN 9780815655336 (ebook)

Subjects: LCSH: English literature—Irish authors—History and criticism. | Nature in literature. | Landscapes in literature. | Environment (Aesthetics)

Classification: LCC PR8722.N3 H65 2022 (print) | LCC PR8722.N3 (ebook) | DDC 820.9/9415—dc23

LC record available at https://lccn.loc.gov/2021000134

LC ebook record available at https://lccn.loc.gov/2021000135

Manufactured in the United States of America

Contents

Acknowledgments

❦ No work of research is possible without the help of many people. To return to the beginning, I acknowledge my great debt to my deceased parents, Anne (Tallarini) and Norman Holdridge, who, though they did not attend university themselves, created a home in which learning was valued, politics addressed, and the arts and sciences elevated. I miss them both dearly and am grateful for it all.

I would like to thank my brother John Holdridge for lifelong brotherhood and love of literature and sport, as well as my sister-in-law Ruth Harman for being an intellectual companion and a sister in arms. My oldest brother James set an example in ways he may not guess just by being an artist when the rest of us were playing catch. My good friend Matthew Gaddis has been a presence in my life, though in recent decades we have lived far apart, and so I thank him for many years of shared devotion to literature, music, and art. Appreciation goes out to a similarly distant-in-space, near-to-my-heart friend, Arthur Lipner, who since childhood has taught me the meaning of jazz and of attention to the craft. The critical eye, linguistic and theoretical depth, and unfailing love and support of my wife, Wanda Balzano, deserve as much gratitude and affection as I can ever return. I warmly embrace my daughter, Sofia, for being her lively self and for keeping me grounded since the very day of her birth.

Last, as this book is academic, I would like to thank my mentor from my undergraduate days, Daniel J. Langton, who lectured in the old-fashioned way with unceasing enthusiasm for poets of all types and nationalities. In terms of Irish poetry, he first brought my attention to Seamus Heaney, Eavan Boland, and Derek Mahon, as well as Richard Murphy, John Montague, and Thomas Kinsella. I will always feel the gravitational pull of Declan Kiberd, whose work, person, intellect, and teaching style still carry me in their orbit. Scholars Anne Fogarty, Tony Roche, Christopher Murray, Brian Donnelly (who drew my attention to "Admiring the Scenery"), Angela Bourke, Terence Brown, Edna Longley, Gerardine Meaney, Moynagh Sullivan, Stephen O'Neill, Lucy Collins, Catriona Clutterbuck, Margaret Kelleher, Malcom Sen, Katherine O'Callaghan, Derek Hand, and P. J. Mathews continue to inspire. So do newer acquaintances Marjorie Howes, Matthew Campbell, Eric Falci, Brian Ó Conchubhair, Ruben Moi, and others.

I would like to extend gratitude to all of my colleagues in the English Department at Wake Forest, especially the five serving chairs, Gale Sigal, Claudia Kairoff, Eric Wilson, Scott Klein, and Jessica Richard, for providing a creative intellectual environment for my work. Colleagues from Wake who have been of great help and have also been good friends are Dean Franco, Melissa Jenkins, Judith Madera, Erica Still, Mary Deshazer, Susan Harlan, Rian Bowie, Gillian Overing, Anne Boyle, Barry Maine, Jim Hans, Phil Kuberski, the late Bill Moss, and my former colleague John McNally. Special thanks go to Ryan Shirey for co-teaching a course on Scottish, Irish, and Appalachian literature, folklore, and song. I would like to thank Eric Wilson for reading the proposal and supporting the project, as well as Omaar Hena for the years of sharing thoughts, reading my essays, and talking about poetry, theory, and all aspects of literature, as well as sharing the pleasures of minor-league baseball. I will always thank Dillon Johnston, one of the most exemplary critics of Irish poetry, as well as Guinn Batten for her evocative combination of theory and poetic insight. My thanks extend to Scott Claybrook for his help with technology. Last, my two colleagues at Wake Forest University Press, Candide Jones and Amanda Keith, have been boons to my life as well as to the life of Wake Forest University Press. I thank them for both.

I would like to thank the editors of journals and books in which some parts of this book were published. They are in no particular order David Holdeman, Ben Levitas, Marc Conner, Anne Fogarty, David Valone, Christine Cusick, Daniel Carey, François Boulaire,

Carlo Bigazzi, Wayne Chapman, Catherine Paul, and David Gardiner. This book would have been immeasurably poorer without the unstinting work of Deborah Manion and Kate Costello-Sullivan of Syracuse University Press. I also appreciate the work of the outside readers whose critiques and comments were fundamental to the book's improvement. I would also like to acknowledge the support of the Office of the Dean (Deans Debbie Best, Jackie Fetrow, and Michelle Gillespie) and the Provost's Office (Provost Gordon through the present provost, Rogan Kersh) for the Reynolds Research leaves and Archie Travel Grants I was granted over the years of this book's composition. They all enabled me to bring it to completion, if not perfection. Any mistakes herein are mine and mine only.

Chapter 7 contains excerpts from *The Last September* by Elizabeth Bowen, copyright © 1929, copyright renewed 1952 by Elizabeth Bowen. Used by permission of Curtis Brown Heritage and Alfred A. Knopf, an imprint of the Knopf Doubleday Publishing Group, a division of Penguin Random House LLC. All rights reserved.

Chapter 8 contains excerpts from *The Collected Stories of Seán O'Faoláin* by Seán O'Faoláin. Published by Little, Brown. Copyright © Seán O'Faoláin. Reproduced by permission of the author c/o Rogers, Coleridge & White Ltd., 20 Powis Mews, London W11 1JN.

Chapter 9 contains excerpts from Louis MacNeice, *Collected Poems*, Faber & Faber. © Estate of Louis MacNeice, reprinted by permission of David Higham.

Chapter 10 contains quotations from the poems of Patrick Kavanagh, reprinted from *Collected Poems*, edited by Antoinette Quinn (Allen Lane, 2004), by kind permission of the Trustees of the Estate of the late Katherine B. Kavanagh, through the Jonathan Williams Literary Agency.

Chapter 11 contains excerpts from Seamus Heaney, *Opened Ground*. New York: Farrar, Straus and Giroux, 1999. By permission of Faber and Faber Ltd.

Chapter 11 contains excerpts from "Clearances" and "A Peacock's Feather" from *The Haw Lantern* by Seamus Heaney. Copyright ©

1987 by Seamus Heaney. Reprinted by permission of Farrar, Straus and Giroux. All Rights Reserved.

Chapter 12 contains excerpts from Paula Meehan, *Geomantic*. Dublin: Dedalus Press, 2016. By permission of The Dedalus Press.

Stepping *through* Origins

Introduction

Palimpsests of Conquest

Roy Foster artfully delineates the historical significance of the house of the colonizer as one that displays its barbaric roots despite its claims to civilization: "From 1600 there is a discernibly Irish style of house, though far less elegant and coherent than it would become. The English or Scotch 'imported' styles to be found in plantation areas are less interesting and lasted less well. The castle would take a hundred years to become the country house; even then, the name 'castle' would sometime misleadingly linger on, affording the English some contemptuous amusement at Irish pretensions. But the derivation is often manifestly demonstrated even today, in the modest eighteenth-century farmhouse grafted on to the shell of a late medieval keep: a palimpsest of conquest."[1] The home as "a palimpsest of conquest" extends down from houses like the ones Foster describes through Captain Boycott's house on Achill Island, County Mayo, to the simplest cottage in the village. It is apparent from Maria Edgeworth's *Castle Rackrent* (1800) to Yeats's *The Tower* (1928). Many of the books examined in the present study bear the mark of stepping through Ireland's dark origins and reflect the complicated life of the home, as well as the family and its allegiances. Moreover, conquest takes many forms, psychological as well as political. Yet in some ways, the most potent symbol of family given in the concrete image of the house is those famine homes in which the windows were sealed with stones to keep the ignominy of dying of starvation a family secret.

Whether castle or cottage, home often exists in isolation, but remains defined by the surrounding landscape, whether the dark encroachments of nature around the Big House or the bogs, raths, and wells that inform the lives of the peasantry. This book's subtitle, "Nature, Home, and Landscape in Irish Literature," is meant to illustrate how home stands between nature and landscape, remembering that, as Schama writes in *Landscape and Memory*, "landscapes are culture before they are nature; constructs of the imagination projected onto wood and water and rock."[2] Landscape is a humanized version of nature, where the human hand, and often with it a version of home, is always evident. Nature, on the other hand, is wilderness; it is the lack of human habitation or the human touch, but it is also the primitive forces, the threatening wilderness or beast within us. In many texts this force, this wilderness, underlies the Oedipus complex, for Lévi-Strauss believes that the taboo against incest releases us from the sovereignty of nature.[3] When nature erupts from the unconscious, it breaks or at least threatens that taboo. In this instance, raw nature disrupts the acculturated aspect of the psyche. The breaking of this taboo threatens the family and therefore threatens the home.

The aesthetics of landscape dominate the scene in Irish and European history, while nature reflects barbarism and savagery and bears little of the promise of the American wilderness until the late nineteenth century, when the reclamation of the wilderness of waste places at the heart of the Irish literary revival is seen as a force for renewal. In recent years, discussions of nature have taken a different, more ecologically minded shape. Nature should be protected and understood on its own terms. The essays, or chapters, will chart how nature erupts throughout Irish history, whether politically, as in the burning of Wildgoose Lodge in William Carleton's story of that name (1833), Allingham's epic poem (1864, 1890), Bowen's *The Last September* (1929), MacNeice's *Autumn Journal* (1939), or Heaney's *North* (1975); or religiously, as in the "rough beast" of Yeats's "The Second Coming" (1919–20) and Kavanagh's and Ní Chuilleanáin's poetry; or violently, as in the attempted patricide in Synge's *The Playboy of the Western World* (1907). In short, the eruptions of nature are Oedipal, animal, erotic, ecological, or varying combinations of these categories.

Nature has been central to the Irish worldview since before the days of colonization. Whether that relationship was pre-Western or merely pre-Cartesian,[4] it most certainly relied on a sense that the borders between human and animal were fluid. Helen Waddell, for instance, notes of medieval attitudes toward nature that there are "mutual charities between saints and beasts."[5] Such sympathy was often coupled with a hermit's rejection of society. It resurfaces at various times in Irish literature. Between the eras of medieval saints and of contemporary writers, the history of the Irish view of nature and, with it, the acculturated version of nature that we call landscape have altered in numerous ways, with the changes reflecting violent shifts in the history of the country. After colonization, English perceptions of the Irish consigned them to nature as symbols of barbarism. They were the "wild Irish" because the bogs and woods offered shelter to Irish rebels and provided a space to explore historically fraught colonial tensions and social struggles.[6] When the Irish forests were destroyed, at least in part because they gave shelter to Irish rebels, their felling became symbolic of the fall of the Gaelic order—though in a coded way that only those people of a shared culture would understand. From the eighteenth to the nineteenth centuries, we move from this coded use of landscape as symbol of the Irish condition to a romanticized one. As Julia Wright notes in *Representing the National Landscape in Irish Romanticism*, the national characteristics of the Celts were tied "to a fundamental relationship with the land." With romanticism, the symbols of Ireland—the harp, the shamrock, the Emerald Isle, and the wild landscape—became points of fascination in the United Kingdom and on the Continent.[7] Yet the divisions in Irish society, which become increasingly apparent in the years after the Act of Union (1800–1801), are mirrored in what are often sectarian views of nature.

By the nineteenth century, such sympathy with nature, as expressed by the early Irish monks, was derided in the Catholic peasantry, perhaps because it had become an emblem of their barbarousness, their wildness.[8] In this light, Seamus Heaney's use of the "bog" becomes an act of restitution. The apparent disregard for nature (as overstated as it may be), examined by Seán O'Faoláin in "Admiring the Scenery," remained set in opposition to the aestheticizing or scientific objectivity of Protestants in general or, in the case of the above story, educated Catholics, but in particular to the upper class, that is, the Anglo-Irish gentry. The most celebrated example of Catholics disregarding nature may be the attitude of other peasants toward Christy Mahon in J. M. Synge's *The Playboy of the Western World*, who is seen as simple because he dwells happily among the fields and finches. The love of nature is still taken as a sign of simplemindedness in Patrick Kavanagh's *The Green Fool* (1938) and *Tarry Flynn* (1948), "corroborating the Syngean picture," as J. W. Foster observes.[9] The change from the medieval period may be owing to the combined effects of colonization, which led to the Great Famine of the 1840s and made the "blasted heath," exile, and "the deserted village" the signs of Irish subjection.

From the eighteenth to the twentieth centuries, landscape has played complex psychological and political roles in the narratives of Irishness, entailing questions of family and home from Jonathan Swift's *Gulliver's Travels* (1726) to the work of many contemporary writers. Throughout this history, the idea of family supplies a micronarrative of the state, and landscape serves as a palimpsest for both family and country, connecting personal with collective memory, particular places with their regions, individual with national identity. The family has always been troubled by the opposing needs of security and freedom, duty and desire, with all of the political implications of these oppositions and all of their repercussions in memory through the formation of identity as it is reflected in landscape, nature, and home.

Before beginning with the chronological discussion of the main themes of the book, it is important to consider how the roots of later views of landscape, nature, and the Oedipus complex (and with it the importance of family), themes of animal and human, pagan and Christian, can be found in the ancient myths and folktales of Ireland. It is important, because this interconnection is why myths and folktales became the basis of the literary renaissance that accompanied cultural and political independence in Ireland. The interest in these themes begins with the antiquarian movement in the eighteenth century and culminates in the work of Yeats, Gregory, Synge, and Heaney, among others. Yet the themes themselves are apparent in other modes in Irish literature from earlier periods. In addition, it should be noted that our first relationship with nature, as with the idea of the divine, is mythological. Our first relationship and perhaps our last, but certainly the most fundamental as in the emotional arc of mythic thinking, myth explains the suddenness of our being in a world for which our conscience seems ill fit. This relationship is the subject of the first chapter, "Stepping through Origins: Myth, Nature, Home, and Landscape."

The second chapter, "Tumbling Down into the Sky: Jonathan Swift, Edmund Burke, and Oliver Goldsmith," examines eighteenth-century ideas of landscape in Ireland. For most of the history of Irish literature in English, nature and culture are marked by disjuncture, by the monstrousness of personal and national perception, the unveiling of our animal natures, and their divergence from the conventions of English culture. Landscape functions as a bridge between nature and culture. In this view, Jonathan Swift is one of the first and foremost definers of Irish convention. Swift counters Alexander Pope's landscapes of the beautiful with sublime ruins meant to mirror the historical catastrophes of Ireland's past.[10] Even the aesthetics of nature, as outlined by Edmund Burke's *A Philosophical Enquiry into the Origin of Our Ideas of the Sublime and Beautiful* (1757), mirror the differences between Irish and English conceptions of nature and culture, as well as the need for redefinition and subversion of convention. Burke is keenly aware that terror has a political relevance in Ireland, which it does not immediately have in England. Burke's influence means that the ruined Irish landscape is also used emblematically in the work of Oliver Goldsmith, Maria Edgeworth, and Lady Morgan. In Goldsmith's *The Deserted Village* (1770), we begin with the type of conventional image of the beautiful, which Swift avoided: "Sweet Auburn! Loveliest village of the plain, / Where health and plenty cheered the labouring swain"; however, Goldsmith's subversion later in the poem would be more subtle. Artificial or real ruins on the land were used in England for authenticity or emblems of wealth, but in Goldsmith, whether intentional or not, they become a form of political protest against the psychological consequences of colonization. Ruins in Irish literature gradually become an expression of the inner sense of defilement, the arising of the uncanny and the Oedipal, the sense of the original sin of conquest; private and public intermingle in the conjunction of landscape and body.

In the next chapter, "Great Hunger, Unspeakable Home: Lady Morgan's *The Wild Irish Girl* (1806) and William Carleton's *The Black Prophet* (1847)," nineteenth-century figures of the landscape, as reflected in nationalist myth and landscape, are brought into focus. Irish writers in English are overwhelmingly preoccupied with an originary violence (often coded as "original sin," owing to the Judeo-Christian context of their writing). In some texts such as *The Wild Irish Girl*, this violence erupts in the breaking of cultural taboos such as intermarriage between English and Irish, which in turn is aligned with taboos against incest. The eruption of colonial violence often reflects the eruption of the Oedipus complex. This eruption compels writers to take a number of different stances and adopt different aesthetic strategies in changing historical contexts. In Lady Morgan's *The Wild Irish Girl*, there is a blending of landscape and body similar to that in Goldsmith, only now the Irishness of the subject matter is self-consciously displayed rather than coded carefully within the text, as it was in Swift and Goldsmith. This change is owing in part to the rise of landscape aesthetics, the growth of antiquarianism, and the importance of the Celtic periphery after the publication of James Macpherson's *Fragments of Ancient Poetry Collected in the Highlands of Scotland and Translated from the Gaelic or Erse Language* (1760).

At the heart of Lady Morgan's project, the allegory of union between Englishness (mirrored in the ordered, harmonious landscape of the beautiful) and Irishness (mirrored in the ruined or wild landscape of the sublime) combines with sexual guilt, ideas of original sin, and palimpsests of conquest. One of the most interesting aspects of this period is the increasing split in attitude toward nature between the Irish peasantry and the Anglo-Irish: only the latter could achieve and indeed welcome aesthetic distance from the historical catastrophe that was embedded in the landscape. Edmund Burke's notion of aesthetic distance, taken up by William Carleton's short story "Wildgoose Lodge" (1830), provides the reason for this lack: when you are in the midst of terror, the exalted qualities—the compensation of the sublime—are lost. In "Wildgoose Lodge," nature, culture, and the historical pressures on house and family during the Great Famine and land wars lead to a house of an informer being set on fire and all those individuals within being burned alive.[11]

The wilderness has literally reentered the house in the appropriately named "Wildgoose Lodge" and either abolished all aesthetic distance or created a greater need for it (much as it would later in Elizabeth Bowen's *The Last September*, 1929)—a need also discussed in the chapter "Some Fragments Like a Hippogriff: William Allingham's *Laurence Bloomfield in Ireland* (1864)." For Samuel Ferguson and William Allingham, the love of the land allows them to be culturally nationalist about folklore, landscape, and literature without a correspondent political commitment that would compromise their unionist stances. Sometimes, as for Allingham (or Edgeworth or Morgan, for that matter), marriage is the solution to the standoff between nationalism and unionism, even if it is merely marriage between the earth and the Anglo-Irish landlord who must "husband" the land. Nature in this scenario is to be controlled, to be suppressed as the taboo against incest suppresses the Oedipal urge, or as good husbandry pulls out the "poison-weeds" (which Allingham calls Irish dissidents in book 7, line 22) of rebellion. For J. C. Mangan and William Carleton, on the other hand, the dark necessities of nature and history contribute to the antipastoral mode of the Great Famine. In the biological treachery of the Great Famine, as the naturalist Michael Viney has noted, "nature was disgraced."[12] Although such a disgrace has not been completely erased, the reclamation of waste places was undertaken by the Irish literary revival. Even if the first attempts are notably made by such Irish Protestant writers as W. B. Yeats, Synge, Lady Gregory, and G. B. Shaw, a similar if more personally and skeptically poised attempt at reclamation would be made by Catholic writers such as James Joyce, Austin Clarke, Kavanagh, Montague, Heaney, and others.

For Irish writers from Swift to Heaney, not only has the Irish landscape remained a reflection of Irish troubles, but, much like aesthetic experience, it may also offer unmarked fields in which the bitterness of family or national life can be understood, if not, alas, entirely overcome. In all these writers, revelations or discoveries of the relationship of place (remembering, of course, that the aesthetics of landscape is an eighteenth-century development) open into demonstrations that remembrances and cures for familial or social relationships are coterminus, if not easily achievable.

The next chapter is "A Sterner Eye: W. B. Yeats, Nature, and the Inhuman and Nonhuman." One could say that the arc of Yeats's career begins in the early volumes (from what became known as *Crossways* [1889] until *The Wind among the Reeds* [1899]) with images of the inhuman within the realms of myth, landscape, folklore, and religion (Christian and pagan). The inhuman subsequently moves through questions of history (inchoate in *In the Seven Woods* [1904] and *The Green Helmet* [1910], becoming palpable in *Responsibilities* [1914]) and then blossoms into questions of aesthetics and philosophy as Yeats creates the geometrical system of *A Vision* in the late 1910s and 1920s. By the twenties, his interest in the psychoanalytical (the unconscious in particular) also begins to burgeon and to create a series of inquiries for him about the nature of self and cultural creation that deepen his poetry of the period.

The Oedipus myth at the end of *The Tower* (1928) and *The Winding Stair and Other Poems* (1933) is a prime example of the blending of themes, of becoming either the Oedipal figure of the artist struggling to uncover the source of damnation or the image of a saint praying to the divine for redemption. Yeats's major period is perhaps the greatest indication of the significance of the role of the inhuman, especially its divine expression, as so much of it revolves around questions of transcendence and immanence, of the blessing and the curse of nature.

The next chapter is "Bleeding from the Torn Bough: Challenging Nature in James Joyce." If nature reminds Joyce of exile and suffering in the image of the "torn bough," then landscape provides the common ground for love and escape. The amorous ambitions of Joyce's entire oeuvre, full of betrayal and the sense of sin, combine with their national significance to place Joyce within the tradition of Irish landscape writing in which original sin, the Oedipus complex, nature, and Irish society are inextricable. Joyce is facing his own uncanny ghosts through landscape, love, and evasion, much as Bowen, O'Faoláin, and later writers would have to do, though in different ways.

The following chapter, "Like Splintered Darkness: Nature, Home, Landscape, and Rebellion in Elizabeth Bowen's *The Last September* (1929)," shows how Lois, the protagonist of the novel, must avoid the family intrigues of the Anglo-Irish in order not to be psychologically injured in the historical struggles between the Big House (signaled by the culture of landscape) and the Irish Rebels (signaled by the dark forces of nature that encircle and ultimately destroy the house). "Through Tightly Closed Eyes: History, Guilt, and the Aesthetic in Seán O'Faoláin" examines how, in a country where history is so psychologically invasive, so radical in nature, landscapes that are barren or fertile (or both) mirror the complexities of experience in unconscious ways. All four of the early stories considered ("Fugue," "Midsummer Night Madness," "Admiring the Scenery," and "A Broken World") center around the intersection of landscape and nature, the inheritance of Irish history, and the burdens of memory. In all these stories, there is a sense that the desire for belonging, the need for community, is in tension with the loneliness and solitude of the landscape, which itself provides an aesthetic perspective and a record of history. The aesthetic perspective points the way toward reconciliation, however partial and deferred, however imbued with longing and suffering.

Landscapes are a series of personal secrets waiting to be unlocked, as we see in "Solving Ambiguities: Family Feeling in Louis MacNeice" and "The Rising Sap: Oedipal Burdens and Christian/Pagan Ecstasy in Patrick Kavanagh." The writers in these chapters established the essential polarities between an urban internationalist view and a pastoral parochial one that describe the major outlines of contemporary Irish literature. For MacNeice, landscape offers a mode of reflection on family and nation, whether that image entails Ireland in its move toward independence or Europe on the verge of World War II. For MacNeice, the personal sufferings of his own nuclear family and the breakdown of his marriage become political in subtle and articulate evocations of culture and nature, mind and body, in Ireland and Europe at large. Nature is more redemptive than eruptive, except in some psychological senses and usually in political manifestations. For Kavanagh, on the other hand, agricultural Ireland ties the peasant to the land and family in Oedipal bondage. It is only through a mystical often Christian or pagan, and sometimes both pagan and Christian, connection to nature that an individual may find redemption. The penultimate chapter is titled "Beneath Tilth and Loam: Seamus Heaney's Journey to the Underworld." Heaney's exploration of landscape, nature, home, and family is a conclusive focus of the Oedipal/Christian narrative of this book because it is so much a part of his vision of life and death, closing his career, as it does, in various confrontations with the ghost of his father and the idea of the transcendent.

The use of the Oedipus complex in this book is straightforward, though no use is without its contradictions and complexities. It figures mainly as unbridled desire: nature at its rawest, most destructive. It also connects with mythical as opposed to religious thinking and so stands on one side of pagan and Christian attitudes toward nature, a dichotomy that is a consistent concern of Irish writers from Synge to Heaney. Heaney's comments in his essay "The God in the Tree" makes the juxtaposition if not opposition of these views evident: "On the one hand, there is the *pagus*, the pagan wilderness, green, full-throated, unrestrained; on the other hand, there is the lined book, the Christian *disciplina*, the sense of a spiritual principle and religious calling that transcends the almost carnal lushness of nature itself."[13]

The Oedipal, of course, has its Freudian as well as Sophoclean roots. It revolves around the incest taboo and what Freud so evocatively calls the family romance. The mythic precedes the Freudian and, as Buchanan illustrates in *Oedipus against Freud: Myth and the End(s) of Humanism in Twentieth-Century British Literature* (2010), continues to be as important as the Freudian, if not more important, to many writers. There also is a connection between the Oedipal and the founding murder (Oedipus's killing of his father) and the guilt associated with concepts of original sin. The connection arises most obviously in Lady Morgan's *The Wild Irish Girl* (the founding murder of colonization and the idea of marriage between Glorvina and Horatio's father), and in W. B. Yeats's *Purgatory* (in which the father, driven by disgust at the idea of his conception, kills his own father and his son). It also figures in J. M. Synge's controversial drama of 1907, *The Playboy of the Western World*, in which Christy's father wants him to marry a woman who suckled him (which is one reason Christy tries to commit patricide).[14] For this project, the injunction against incest at the heart of the Oedipus complex (a term first used in 1910)[15] is what draws a line between nature and culture, a line figured in terms of landscape aesthetics by the term "landscape" itself, which is a cultural construct of nature, as Schama and others have shown. When the Oedipal erupts, it is as though wilderness disrupts the harmony of the landscape and threatens to remove the humanizing element that makes it landscape rather than raw nature. Yet this observation is not to say that nature, as well as its intermediary landscape, is always negative or destructive.

As the quote from Heaney's "The God in the Tree" conveys, the purely luxuriant beauty of nature, untouched by human culture, has redemptive capacities. In this light, pagan and Christian are contending visions of redemption, as represented in the dueling visions of the Saint and Martin in Synge's *The Well of the Saints* (1905):

> SAINT: Did you never set eyes on the summer and fine spring in the places where the holy men of Ireland have built up churches to the Lord, that you'd wish to be closed up and seeing no sight of the glittering seas, and the furze is opening above, will soon have the hills shining as if it was fine creels of gold they were, rising to the sky?
>
> . . .
>
> MARTIN DOUL: [fiercely] Isn't finer sights ourselves had a while since and we sitting dark smelling the sweet beautiful smells

> do be rising in the warm nights and hearing the swift flying things racing in the air [Saint draws back from him], till we'd be looking up in our own minds into a grand sky, and seeing lakes, and broadening rivers, and hills are waiting for the spade and plough.[16]

This conversation echoes that between Oisin and Saint Patrick in Yeats's *The Wanderings of Oisin* (1889). If pagan nature has its positive manifestations, so does Christian nature, in spite of the latter's harshly repressive presence in Irish culture. In the above exchange, the Saint's vision of nature leads toward the sky and transcendence, while Martin's pagan vision leads toward the immanence of the plow and the earth.

Sometimes the positive dimensions of Christian (or let us say divine) and natural (let us say pagan) incarnations work in unison. For Yeats, this point is where the idea of the inhuman (the divine) enters history, and with it the nonhuman (or animal). In certain cases, as in "Leda and the Swan," "The Mother of God," or "The Second Coming," the inhuman and nonhuman are the same: the rough beast of "The Second Coming," the Dove of the Annunciation, and the "strange heart" of the swan/Zeus in "Leda." Yet Yeats is not the only writer to figure the inhuman/nonhuman in his work. We see it in Swift's tale *Gulliver's Travels*, in which the nonhuman horses are the embodiments of a supreme, almost inhuman—that is, divine or supernatural—form of reason. Buchanan is right in this instance. The Oedipus myth is a story of the limits of reason, the limits of humanism, but also of the necessity of reason and humanism, however muted our expectation should be: "The assimilation and repulsion that characterizes modernists' [here we can say Irish literary] treatment of Freud [or proto-Freudian thought] itself paradigmatically re-enacts an Oedipal aspect of humanism itself; a determination to escape from fate whether it be ordained by the gods or encoded in one's unconscious desire, produces an assertion of independence, followed by a tragic recognition of one's own blind spots, a violently antisocial reaction, a period of exile and confusion, and a return to a more modest but nonetheless compelling vision of humanistic continuity, even if this continuity is merely formal."[17] Yet where Buchanan would reiterate the concerns of humanism, however humbled, for many Irish writers coming from a religious society this dilemma often craves some sort of divine intervention.

There are two ways in which the sublime encounter is given a religious rendering. One is the encounter with the divine, which I will call the inhuman; the other is with the animal, which I will call the nonhuman. Sometimes, as noted above, the two are one and the same, as in Yeats's poem "Leda and the Swan" in which Zeus appears in the form of a swan. The inhuman or nonhuman can also appear as the irrational, or the instinctual, a disruptive force rebelling against the rule of reason, as we see in Allingham's *Laurence Bloomfield in Ireland* and MacNeice's *Autumn Journal.* In Joyce, Kavanagh, and Heaney, the advent of the inhuman or divine is a type of mediation that borders on remediation. It can be the descent of grace. Likewise, in O'Faoláin, the religious and aesthetic seem to blend in his presentation of Christ's mystical answer to Oedipus. For Yeats, the advent of inhuman/nonhuman is the turning of the gyres. It is the beginning of a new era, a new divinity, whether dove or swan, Christian or pagan, Christ or Oedipus.

What I say of one author in this study can often be said of another. Though this book follows chronology, there could just as well be thematic groupings. For example, the lens applied to Carleton, Bowen, and O'Faoláin is largely if not solely political, while the lens applied to Lady Morgan, Yeats, Kavanagh, and Heaney is largely religious and Oedipal. I am endeavoring to point out the trends. The chapters that follow attempt to do justice to each author's engagement with family, sometimes but not always in the Oedipal and Christian dynamic, as seen through the lens of nature, landscape, and home, where resides the romance at the heart of both the human (Oedipal) family and the Holy Family.

There are many works devoted to the subject of nature and landscape in Ireland and elsewhere, and many have been critical in the development of mine, from the aesthetic to ecocritical discussions of nature. Several studies examine the confluence of literature, landscape, and history in Irish literature. The focus of these works, however, is largely on twentieth-century texts. Moreover, the majority of these studies invoke an ecocritical lens through which to read the cultural construction of landscape. Books such as Eoin Flannery's *Ireland and Ecocriticism: Literature, History and Environmental Justice* (2015) and Eamonn Wall's *Writing the West: Ecologies and Traditions* (2011) focus on twentieth- and twenty-first-century texts with a specific eye toward their implied ecological consciousness. Similarly, Donna Potts's book *Contemporary Irish Poetry and the Pastoral Tradition* (2011) examines elegy in relation to nature, but focuses explicitly on contemporary poetry. *The Ordnance Survey and Modern Irish Literature* (2016), by Cóilín Parsons, examines literary modernism, positioning its evolution as a dialogue with the colonial mapping project of the Ordnance Survey. It too is focused on a specific point in literary history rather than the more general study of this book. Similarly focused on a compressed period of time, and more grounded in study of the materiality of landscape, Derek Gladwin's *Contentious Terrains: Boglands, Ireland, Postcolonial Gothic* (2016) is significantly more limited by genre, terrain, and natural history. Oona Frawley's *Irish Pastoral: Nostalgia and Twentieth-Century Irish Literature* (2005) is one of the studies that more closely touches on the themes of collective and personal memory connected to colonization, but Frawley's text is also a one-century study and less concerned with the tensions between nature and landscape than is the present discussion.

Tim Wenzell's compelling work *Emerald Green: An Ecocritical Study of Irish Literature* is probably closest in scope and intent to the present work, and like J. W. Foster's invaluable *Nature in Ireland* it has provided important corroboration and eloquent and probing insight. Its ecocritical focus is different, however, as are the authors that are covered in its pages. My emphasis on the dialectic between the Oedipal and Christian also sets it apart from Wenzell's work, as does the importance of myth, among other relevant themes. Moreover, Wenzell takes an anachronistic approach to the ecocritical that in this study is avoided, though admitted as a just-enough point of view. He sees it as a strain of thinking that is evident throughout Irish history. The medieval Irish view of nature, the landscape aesthetics, the reclamation of the wilderness in the Irish literary renaissance, and the antimodernist and antitechnological strain of Irish culture in the past can be seen as ecocriticism before the advent of the term. Yet the periods are different, and "ecocriticism" is a contemporary word in which nature is respected on its own terms. Therefore, the argument here is weighted in favor of a chronological approach to the differences in the historical periods that move from the medieval period through the aesthetics of landscape and the romantic valorization of nature to the modern. In the end, nature writing, especially in the ecocritical tradition, is a relatively new but growing field in Irish studies. This book is less about environmental literature, though it references it as a more recent phenomenon.[18]

Stepping through Origins: Nature, Home, and Landscape in Irish Literature is meant to fill what is generally a palpable gap in the field by both expanding the terms of the discussion (to nature in sharper contrast to landscape, for instance) and broadening the historical periods as well as authors that it covers. In the briefest possible expression, this study aims to address the place of the aesthetics of nature, landscape, and home (family), from the eighteenth century to the present, in order to show how nature erupts throughout the history of Irish literature in terms that are Oedipal, animal, religious, political, erotic, ecological, and sometimes a combination thereof. In order to achieve the historical overview and to emphasize the importance of nature, home, and landscape in Irish literature, there is a certain amount of harking back to earlier writers and themes throughout the chapters. Wenzell states that *The Field Day Anthology of Irish Writing* (under the general editorship of Seamus Deane) paid little attention to nature writing as such.[19] This lack is because of the oft-stated political aim of the anthology to outline unionist and nationalist positions. The politics of the ecocritical are not the same as the politics of Irish history in this regard. If nature was outside the purview of the anthology, so controversially was women's writing, at least in the first three volumes. Perhaps for the same reason, the political dimensions of women's writing and nature writing challenge historical preconceptions. The last chapter of this book, "In Defiance of Human Frontiers: From Landscape to Ecology in Eiléan Ní Chuilleanáin and Paula Meehan," reflects on how these contemporary ecologically minded authors have moved beyond the constructions hitherto discussed, but that topic must be the subject of another book and will only be outlined in the work of these exemplary poets.

1

Stepping through Origins

Myth, Nature, Home, and Landscape

Like wilderness or utopia, myth is where the a priori aspects (both instinctual and idealist) of human nature may, at least partially, surface on the map. Myth provides a mode of reflection on historical questions of identity, exile, colonization, and family life. Even in the transhistorical figuration, however, the subconscious character of our encounters with nature, and with nature's eruptions, no matter how skeptical the age in which they occur, continues to unveil the historical injuries to person and to culture. It also highlights the desire for illuminated forms of restoration, until that desire and form begin to seem like second nature, like the instinct for art itself. For example, many of Heaney's poems "arise out of the almost unnamable energies that . . . hovered over certain bits of language and landscape."[1]

Mythic awareness places us in the world and is at the base of human consciousness, conducting its "raid on the inarticulate," as T. S. Eliot notes in "Burnt Norton" of the *Four Quartets*, in a phrase that Heaney borrows in the just-quoted essay.[2] These different types of knowledge, one of body (emotional, nonrational, intuitive, or figurative) and one of mind (cerebral, rational, deductive, logical, or literal) have a long and complicated relationship, but in the Age of Empires it has taken on political significance.[3] First, the epistemological debate.

In the words of W. B. Yeats, "Science is the criticism of Myths; there would be no Darwin had there been no Book of Genesis."[4] In terms of literary discussions, a meaningful extension of the epistemological debate between science and myth is the one between history and myth. Yeats, for one, believed that myth underlies many a major turn of events. There would be no history without myth, no Thucydides without Herodotus. History, like science, is also a criticism of myth.

In Ireland, it seems, national history attends even the transcendent realm of trooping fairies and banshees; there seems to be no escape on the magic winds of the transhistorical that does not set one squarely down on the grounds of the real. Through the language of the grass and skies, the bitterness of family or national life can be understood and tested by the facts of social construction, and perhaps overcome or escaped in the legendary realms that nature provides. Any ideal landscape provides both "prospect" and "refuge,"[5] that is, a protected place from which to appreciate the vista. Politically (both personally and socially), these terms translate into freedom and security, respectively. Heaney charts this transition from the personal to the political, recording how wilderness (and, with it, read nature) enters the home and probes the landscape of the domestic in the poem "Kinship":

> I step through origins
> like a dog turning
> its memories of wilderness
> on the kitchen mat . . . [6]

This poem is a testament to the mythical sexual power of the mother-goddess in Irish literature, landscape, and history. In nature, writers (and readers) often seek a personal as well as a national myth, which together speak as much of despair and repression as they do of fulfillment and liberation—for, as Heaney notes in "Kinship," the "goddess swallows / our love and terror."[7] Nature in Irish literature contains references of historical proportion and instinctual bodily significance, savoring of individual, familial, and national history.

Giambattista Vico's (1668–1744) ethnology of myth, seeing myths as keys to a nation's cultural stages, proves useful in this regard.[8] Irish myth could be used to affirm precolonial unity or to reflect the disjunction and violence of colonial history. For instance, the early Celtic and medieval inheritance moves Irish writers such as Frank O'Connor and Seamus Heaney. The god in the tree, as Heaney describes it in an early essay,[9] makes the conception of the natural world a ritualized extension of community (with pagan fertility and Christian spirituality at its contested center) rather than an escape from it into the wilderness. For other writers, including Heaney in another mode, myth is self-image and mirror of historical progress. The national importance of the story of the Children of Lir attests in a transhistorical manner to the political power of ancient myth: the exile of the children, resulting from the cruelty of the stepmother, the interloper in the family romance, resonates in the minds of the Irish across the barriers of time and place. In the "Garden of Remembrance" in Dublin's Parnell Square, the Children of Lir are linked to the political martyrs of the Republic. In Thomas Moore's rendering of the legend of the Children of Lir ("The Song of Fionnuala"), the personal and national dilemmas are indistinguishable. Fionnuala not only feels the bitterness of her exile from human form, but after long years of contentment with her father is "impelled by her cruel stepmother Aoife's curse" to the Sea of Moyle, "a stormy band of water between Ireland and Scotland," far from home, thereby making her exile complete. Her story acts as poignant background to the character Lenehan in Joyce's story "Two Gallants" who more keenly feels the pang of his own exile from humanity after he has heard a harpist play "Silent O Moyle" (as "The Song of Fionnuala" is more commonly known).[10]

Once he has introduced the dilemma of Lir's lonely daughter, who will only find peace in death, Moore situates Fionnuala's image of national and personal redemption in a commensurate landscape of the afterlife:

> Silent, oh Moyle, be the roar of thy water,
> Break not, ye breezes, your chain of repose,
> While, murmuring mournfully, Lir's lonely daughter
> Tells to the night-star her tale of woes.
> When shall the swan, her death-note singing,
> Sleep, with wings in darkness furl'd?
> When will heaven, its sweet bell ringing,
> Call my spirit from this stormy world?

Sadly, oh Moyle, to thy winter-wave weeping,
Fate bids me languish long ages away;
Yet still in her darkness doth Erin lie sleeping,
Still doth the pure light its dawning delay.
When will that day-star, mildly springing,
Warm our isle with peace and love?
When will heaven, its sweet bell ringing,
Call my spirit to the fields above?[11]

The poem speaks of personal and by implication political fulfillment after a period of dehumanizing suffering. Similarly, Johan Gottfried Von Herder's (1744–1803) conception of myths as expressions of the freedom-loving but suppressed emotional life (he is thinking of James Macpherson's *Ossian* [1760]) helps us to understand the union of landscape, history, and myth. His idea of myth as emotional expression parallels that concept of landscapes as delineations of communal ideas (the *sensus communis* of the beautiful) or states of mind (the subjective judgment of the sublime).[12] In many myths, the emotional life is social and archetypal rather than individual and psychological. Literary use of myth complicates this formula, of course; Yeats, Synge, and Joyce, for instance, use myth to psychologize character. Thomas Moore does not, but makes the landscape communal, and personal emotion coincident and inseparable. Even if not always so inextricably linked, in much Irish myth and folklore communal awareness is as important as individual consciousness.

Myth and folklore illustrate how nature is not consciously separate from culture, or they are indicative of the impending split between nature and culture, as in the story "Deirdre of the Sorrows," where Deirdre can be said to represent nature and Conchubar culture. One also thinks of the "autumnal myths"[13] (such as those from Hellenic Greece or the "Silver Age" in Rome, the myths of Orpheus, Cupid and Psyche, Hero and Leander) that seem symptomatic of a changing epistemology or a shift in personal consciousness—and sometimes both, such as, for instance, when the primitive associations of the Cuchulain saga provided Yeats with a mode of modern self-inquiry.

Seamus Heaney found a similar mode in his translation *Sweeney Astray*: "Maybe here was a presence, a fable which could lead to the discovery of feelings in myself which I could not otherwise find words for, and which would cast a dream or possibility or myth across the swirl of private feelings: an objective correlative."[14]

Heaney's comment highlights the idea of myth as an objective expression of instinct and submerged feeling. Landscape often seems the most obvious objective correlative. In *Sweeney* there are many examples of this linking:

> I am the madman of Glen Bolcain,
>
> wind-scourged, stripped
> like a winter tree
> clad in black frost
> and frozen snow.[15]

Such metaphorical links (in this instance man as tree) are penitential mortifications of the flesh, rather than celebrations of the natural world, with Sweeney's renowned praise of the trees being an important exception. When Sweeney delivers his encomium, he has just been falsely told that his children are dead, and so his celebration of the trees must necessarily combine sensual delight and mourning in high homesick refrains to the lost pleasures of familial and married love. Heaney is a defender of the mystification of the pastoral even as he invokes the antipastoral in his verse;[16] his skepticism does not keep myth and landscape from continuing to have a hold over his imagination and his conception of the modern imagination in general.

In "Midwife to the Fairies," Éilís Ní Dhuibhne deftly juxtaposes the urban imagination, reflecting upon itself through television, and the rural imagination, reflecting on itself through dark ancestral memories aligned to folklore and myth. A midwife is on her way to help a young woman give birth to an unwanted child, whose birth the midwife doesn't report and who in turn ends up being discarded in the garbage. Ní Dhuibhne intersperses this narrative with excerpts from the story of a woman being taken away by the fairies. The seeming remoteness of the place where both are taken (which ironically is close to Bray and therefore to Dublin) brings these stories of illicit sexuality to their proper wilderness (as distinct from landscape), as the main narrative describes it:

> All I could see were headlights and now and then a signpost: Enniskerry, Sallygap, Glendalough. And after we turned off the main road into the mountains, there were no headlights either, and no houselights, nothing except the black night. Annamoe is at the back of beyond, you'd never know you were only ten miles from Bray there, it's really very remote altogether. And their house was down a lane where there was absolutely nothing to be seen at all, not a house, not even sheep. The house you could hardly see either, actually. It was kind of buried like at the side of the road, in a kind of a hollow. You wouldn't know it was there at all until it was on top of you. Trees all around it too.[17]

Here is a carefully wrought image of the subconscious: absolute darkness, isolation, sudden and insufficient awareness of the scene's effects on the mind, a rising irrational force that the rational mind tries to keep in check with folktale and myth, yet one that also continues to threaten modern rationality. Ní Dhuibhne is very sensitive to the need for folktale, and is a prominent scholar of it, but she is very suspicious of the ways such stories, like the vicarious experience of illicit sexuality on television, mask rather than reveal the sources and patterns of human cruelty. Folklore and myth reflect the psychological sources of behavior so taboo that it often has no recorded history, referring first to permanent forces of nature and then to the cultural conditions connected to landscape. One has only to look at Samuel Ferguson's "The Fairy Thorn" to see that even for an artist who wanted to repress the darkly unfamiliar (especially the political threats that myth and folklore reflect in the countryside), the lone hawthorn tree, which smells of death and hints at forbidden sexuality, proves too powerful. It cannot be contained by the poem without a direct appeal to communal values of some sort, which in this case is to universal sympathy for the girl, Anna Grace, who has been spirited away.[18]

It is not surprising—indeed, it is one of their most satisfying traits—that nature and myth in literature bloom with sexual meaning. As Yeats rather cryptically attests, "Sexual desire dies because every touch consumes the myth, and yet a myth that cannot be so consumed becomes a spectre."[19] The sexual relevance of myth is one of its most apparent elements, as we see from *The Odyssey* to *The Táin*, and has its place in the unfolding of family and nation. In *The Burning of Bridget Cleary*, Angela Bourke makes the relationship between sexuality and mythologized landscape function on a linguistic as well as a physical level and shows how they contrast a rationalized modern system of farming with more organic ancient patterns of belief.[20]

Of course, we don't have to resort to myth to play with landscape in this way, to go "up the airy mountain and down the rushy glen,"[21] but throughout her book Bourke makes clear the sexual significance of the murder of Bridget Cleary and the simultaneous misapprehension of folklore that seems driven by class, marginality, conflicts between tradition and modernity, as well as issues of gender and nation. In the end, violence should be avoided in folk belief, even siphoned off, rather than indulged.[22] She also highlights the importance of the landscape that provided the setting for the tale: "As he was being driven eastward up the Anner valley in the failing light, the journalist's first impression was romantic—and literally colourful: 'I beheld the vapourish clouds proudly hurling around the purplish peaks of Slieve-na-mon, and the darkness beginning to obscure the green fields and brown bogs that lie on the slope of the mountain.'" She concludes that in spite of the fact that Cleary's house was habitable, then as it is now, "the newspaper coverage at the time of Bridget Cleary's death had made much of the mountain's mythic history and of 'the remoteness and isolation' of Ballyvadlea."[23] The erotic or instinctual source of myth in nature finds its parallel in landscape until it becomes a need of the urban imagination to keep the two absolutely linked regardless of the truth of their relationship—even if only to express the beauty and sexuality of the pastoral that has been displaced by the overdeveloped world.

Sometimes the landscape has obvious sexual, instinctual, or just deeply physical symbolic reference, as, say, in the pillar stones of *The*

Táin. In the Ulster sagas, the landscape and the bloody force of the warriors become indistinguishable, except for someone like Fergus, who is a type of redemptive phallic embodiment and is granted particular insight. The symbolism of the text is murky and shows how embedded the landscape is within the emotional web of the myths themselves, exposing the clannish aspect of the society it details. First Ailill notes that, while expecting the men of Ulster, he is unsure of what he sees on the plain of Muirthemne:

> I studied the plain before me and saw a dense fog filling the valleys and hollows, so that the high places in between looked like islands in a lake. I made out sparks of fire through the thick fog, and a world of different colours, of all kinds. Then I saw flashes of lightning, with uproar and thunder. Though there is only a light breeze out today, a great wind came that flung me down on my back and all but swept the hair from my head.[24]

Then he asks Fergus what he sees. Fergus replies:

> I know well what it is. The men of Ulster have risen from their pangs. It is they who entered the forest, great heroes thronging in might and violence; and they who shook the forest and sent the wild animals fleeing onto the plain. The dense fog you saw filling the hollows, that was the breath of those fierce men filling the valley until the hills in between looked like islands in a lake. The flashes of lightning and the sparks of fire and all those colours . . . those were the warriors' eyes, so bright you thought they were sparks of fire. The thunder and thudding and turmoil you heard, that is the humming of their blades and their ivory hilted swords, the uproar of arms, the clattering of chariots—horse-hooves hammering, fierce chariot-fighters—the outcry of an army.[25]

What drives the men of Ulster is the same force of nature that held them under constraint after their ill-treatment of the pregnant Macha, daughter of the Ocean (they made her run despite her condition). Macha subsequently curses them so that they are stricken with birth pangs when Ulster is in trouble. Some have seen this curse, along with Queen Medbh's leadership in war, as testament to a battle between matriarchy and patriarchy, or as an example of an upheaval in the hierarchy of values or of the "dangerous potential of the sovereignty goddess."[26] This battle and disorder are fundamental to the experience of the Oedipal crisis in the family romance; Cuchulain, who as fosterling hero will unwittingly kill his own son, has been said to stand for the violence that ensues when culture and nature, custom and instinct, become embroiled in such a contest.[27] A similar entanglement of nature, culture, custom, and instinct accentuates the deep sense of sexual despair in Yeats's early poem to Fergus, "Who Goes with Fergus?" It also makes the primal landscape of the wood as richly figurative of sexual loss as is the "Dry timber under that rich foliage" from Yeats's later poem "Her Vision in the Wood." The word "drive" in the first line of the former poem takes on extra psychological significance in this context. Fergus's druidic mastery of wood, sky, and sea is rooted in the sexual derivation of his name ("virility").[28] Yeats's personal feeling of sexual frustration is given even fuller national expression, is given a poetic landscape from the "deep wood's woven shade" to "the white breast of the dim sea."[29]

The story titled "The Enchanted Deer: The Birth of Oisin" contains many similar expressions of the instinctual, sensate side of our understanding. In the beginning, Bran and Sceolan, hounds with human aspects who have human origins, corner a beautiful doe; Finn is amazed to see "his two best hunting dogs frolicking around her. Instead of wounding and killing her they were licking her face and neck and patting her limbs."[30] When the doe has turned back into a woman, once she is safely within the threshold of Finn's house, she explains her past and the recognition of her human nature despite her animal form. She is later tricked by the Druid, the magician of the beast/human metamorphoses, into crossing the threshold of the house and is turned again into a doe. She is deluded by a false likeness to Finn, and for some reason she realizes the true nature of her foe too late. The child of Finn and the woman (the enchanted deer) is later born into the world of the Druid. When Finn and his men find him, he is encircled by the dogs, and only Finn's hounds Bran and Sceolan hold the other dogs back.

Though in human form, Oisin, which means "the little deer," seems a wild animal to the other dogs. Identities of human and animal are blurred, as are culture and nature. Oisin then describes his upbringing with a wealth of natural imagery that illustrates how myth negotiates the terms of the relationship between nature and culture:

> He had been looked after by a gentle doe, he said, who had protected him and sheltered him and whom he loved like a mother. They lived in a wild lonely place, ranging together through valleys, over rocky slopes, drinking from the streams, hiding in the dark woods. During the summer he had fed on berries and fruit and in the winter provisions were left for him in a sheltered cave. A dark-looking man visited them from time to time. He would speak to the doe, sometimes gently and persuasively, sometimes in a loud, threatening voice, but, however he addressed her, the doe shrank away from him with terrified eyes, every limb trembling with fear. The man always left in a great rage. Though the deer and the child were free to roam this mountain park they couldn't leave it. It was surrounded by high peaks and sheer cliffs so that there was no escape.[31]

Here we have the landscape of family romance as political parable as well as the threatened subject woman, encased in her otherness, who will not be released from such a definition of self by her tormentor, unless she succumbs to his desire. There is also the young boy whose name bears the mark of the beast, whose Gothic genealogy is apparent in this eruption of nature and who, if we read anachronistically, uncovers the Oedipal nightmare behind the social and political manifestations of family life under an oppressive regime—what has been called the "gothic family romance," a term used by Backus for an Anglo-Irish phenomenon but that could be applied more broadly.[32]

The sublime setting of high peaks and sheer cliffs, which could in some instances offer safety but here only promises constraint, physically represents the dangerous memories of what occurs within their confines:

> One day the Dark Druid arrived and cornered the doe. First he spoke tenderly, coaxing her to come with him. Then he harangued her, threatening her in a loud harsh voice. He kept up this treatment for a long time but the doe still shrank away from him shivering with fear. At last the Dark Druid took a hazel wand and struck her with it. She was powerless then to do anything but follow him, but as she was led away, she kept looking back at the boy, bleating and calling out with heartbroken cries. The boy made desperate attempts to follow her but he, too, was enchanted. He sobbed with fear and grief but try as he might he could not move a limb. He heard the deer's cries grow fainter and more desperate and he was so overcome that he fainted and fell to the ground.[33]

With the realization of the long-feared ending to the scene, the surrounding landscape significantly disappears: "When [Oisin] woke up, the hilly region where the doe and he had lived so happily had gone and though he searched for days for the high mountains and cliffs he could not find them."[34] The "high mountains and cliffs," even though they were images of his capture, were also images of fondly remembered home, and so his attitude toward them is mixed. This ambivalence is at the uncanny heart of the landscape of home.

2

Tumbling Down into the Sky

Jonathan Swift, Edmund Burke, and Oliver Goldsmith

The history of nature writing could be said to be divided between the objective and subjective views of scientist and poet of nature, respectively. This dialectic is a culmination of views in the history of nature writing that began in the eighteenth century, when it was not so much a question of science versus nature as an initiatory series of descriptive catalogs of the natural world with hints of the aesthetic, political, and social crises at hand, from Gilbert White in Selborne to Hector St. John de Crèvecoeur in colonial America. The utterance of our relationship with the natural world has become central to literature in Britain and the United States for some time, but its history in Ireland is more recent in terms of ecocriticism and more problematic in its cultural development.

It is a subject that sets one to thinking about the question of connections to the land, Anglo-Irish withdrawal and aestheticizing, Irish-Catholic denial of the land, of nature, and so on, as sectarian and troubled as such reflections might be. The editors of *The Irish Poet and the Natural World*, Lucy Collins and Andrew Carpenter, note that conflicting cultural identities historically influenced the view of nature in Ireland:

> Few of the poets in this volume would have shared Alexander Pope's vision of an unproblematic "we" responding to nature and the universe with shared insight and intention; instead the power of man over nature—or, indeed, that of nature over man—is mediated in varying ways throughout this anthology across a spectrum

> of practical, political, ethical and philosophical positions. In Ireland between the Tudor conquests and the Romantic period, these variations are especially complex, due to the layered—and sometimes merging—cultural and political dynamics of Gaelic Irish, Old English and New English communities living in and on the land. Individuals from the various tribal, linguistic or sectarian sections of Irish society held diverse attitudes towards the natural world around them; attitudes shaped by their differing intellectual, religious or ethnic traditions and lived experience.[1]

The political ramifications of Irish nature writing have troubled it from the start.

Robert Lloyd Praeger, Northern Irish Protestant, is considered the father of Irish nature writing. The author of *The Way I Went* (1937), he subtitles his magnum opus "An Irishman in Ireland," and throughout the book he makes a studied attempt to depoliticize the landscape, writing, "If St Patrick had banished from Ireland politics, instead of snakes, he would have conferred a far greater boon, and this lovely land would have had peace and charity, as well as faith and hope."[2] In response to the insistent surfacing of the political roots of the landscape, to the traces of conquest showing through the palimpsest, Estyn Evans, born in Shrewsbury of Welsh parentage, says rightly: "Geographers are not alone in stressing the significance of habitat and heritage in the shaping of the human experience. True, we might well be spared the facile couplings of Irish mist and Celtic mystery, of black basalts and black Presbyterians, creameries and dreameries, or indeed, you may add, of poverty and poetry, drums and drumlins." Yet Evans insists, "The manners and habits of a people exist in nature, as a function of place."[3] In the chapter on Seamus Heaney, we see Heaney take exception to Praeger's point of view and by implication to Evans's, while more recently poet Seán Lysaght challenges Heaney's position. This series of responses and counterresponses charts the changing course of Irish views of nature, of what it means to be politically attuned and perhaps risk being seen as overly subjective, of what it means to be objective and risk being seen as politically escapist.

We return with this thought to the beginning of this excursus: subjective and objective realities, an approach to landscape that is the focus of much nineteenth-century writing. The apogee of the meditation is captured in a quote from Emerson: "Not a form so grotesque, so savage, nor so beautiful but it is an expression of some property inherent in man the observer,—an occult relation between the very scorpions and man."[4] There is a fine line between nature and culture here, if none at all. Nature's alterity is ours. Yet, at least in literary practice, this thought predates Emerson, and perhaps predates nature writing itself, haunting its first incarnations in the pastoral of the ancient world.

The moment of reflection on the self serves as a developmental model for such a haunting in Irish literature. The prototype for Joyce's and Synge's cracked looking glass is Gulliver looking into the mirror, seeing the Yahoo in himself, and deciding "to behold [his] Figure often in a Glass, and thus if possible to habituate [him] self by Time to tolerate the Sight of a human Creature."[5] According to Carol Fabricant, in the single instance ("Ode to Dr. William Sancroft") "where the word 'landscape' appears in Swift's poetry, it is associated with transient shapes as well as visual distortion characterized by disproportioned and chaotic forms":[6]

> Here a pale shape with upward footstep treads,
> And men seem walking on their heads;
> There whole herds suspended lie
> Ready to tumble down into the sky;
> . . . .
> Disjointing shapes as in the fairy-land of dreams,
> Or images that sink in streams.[7]

Fabricant concludes that Swift realizes how "'official' contemporary art forms, such as neoclassical landscape painting and pastoral poetry, were inadequate for conveying (for example) the facts of Irish life as he knew and observed them on a daily basis"—inadequate for presenting eruptions of brute nature. Instead, as we know, Swift would choose "burlesque, travesty, satire and the mock pastoral."[8] Swift insists that disheveled, even savage, nature is both in and around us and we must be prepared for its eruptions. A milder, almost contrary, version is Goldsmith imagining himself as a traveler returned, a sort of foreigner, accepted back into the fold of imaginatively reconstructed village life. Having confronted the destruction and desertion of the village, the evils of industrialization and the corrupt urban setting, as well as emigration and the savagery of life in the American wilds, the speaker's image of "Sweet Auburn" reminds us that the sublime is what the beautiful aims to unveil and to cure.

In *Strangers to Ourselves*, Julia Kristeva notes that when the national was defined in terms of landscape and nature, it had to repress the foreign if it was to affirm a truly national identity. In such a move, civilization humanizes nature by endowing it with beings who look like us, but inevitably nature erupts, reminding us of the uneasy place of the foreigner within any realistic version of the national and, importantly, reminding us that in the depths of our psyche we are foreigners to ourselves. This latter demonstration is, of course, the appearance of the uncanny: "Initially it is a shock," writes Kristeva, "something unusual, astonishment; and even if anguish comes close, uncanniness maintains that share of unease that leads the self beyond anguish, toward depersonalization." This unveiling for Swift reveals the monstrousness of our animal nature, as we see when Gulliver realizes that he too is, at least in part, a Yahoo: "My Horror and Astonishment are not to be described, when I observed, in this abominable Animal, a perfect human Figure."[9] Gulliver's ensuing depersonalization is referred to above.

As for Goldsmith, after the shock of disappointment at the state of Auburn, he exclaims:

> In all my wanderings round this world of care,
> In all my griefs—and God has given my share—
> I still had hopes my latest hours to crown,
> Amidst these humble bowers to lay me down;
> To husband out life's taper at the close,

And keep the flame from wasting by repose.
I still had hopes, for pride attends us still,
Amidst the swains to show my book-learned skill,
Around my fire an evening group to draw,
And tell of all I felt and all I saw;
And, as a hare, whom hounds and horns pursue,
Pants to the place from whence at first she flew,
I still had hopes, my long vexations past,
Here to return—and die at home at last.[10]

The efforts toward humanization of nature are of an animal seeking safety after the predator's chase. The image from Ovid's *Metamorphoses* and Shakespeare's *The Rape of Lucrece* alluded to the experience of rape.[11] Here it significantly applies to the sport of the gentry, which highlights the sexual dangers to the peasantry that came with the rise of the demesne. Any effort to humanize the landscape, to "husband out life's taper," takes on political significance, even as it attempts to ameliorate the situation. One must be simultaneously cognizant of the dangers contained within nature's alterity, aware of the political and personal meanings of its dark side, and romanced by the aesthetic beauty of the landscape. As Protestants, the split in the Ascendancy mind between Swift's and Goldsmith's positions as colonizers and any social harmony they might envisage takes on political, psychological, as well as cultural dimensions. "To worry or to smile," writes Kristeva, "such is the choice when we are assailed by the strange; our decision depends on how familiar we are with our own ghosts."[12]

The ghosts of the modern Irish landscape appeared in the seventeenth and eighteenth centuries. Kevin Whelan writes in "The Modern Landscape: From Plantation to Present" in *An Atlas of the Irish Rural Landscape*:

> At the beginning of the seventeenth century, Ireland was a lightly settled, overwhelmingly pastoral, well wooded country. . . . By the end of the century, the most rapid transformation in any European seventeenth-century economy, society and culture had been

> effected. Two processes were central to this process; the initial subjugation, subsequent colonization and final integration of Ireland into the expanding English state, and the concurrent enhancement of Ireland's location within the North Atlantic commercial world. These close encounters with the emerging world economic system led to abrupt transformations in regional economies, the agrarian order and the landscape itself.[13]

In itself this observation is not news, but it is striking how well it outlines the work of Swift and Goldsmith, the reasons for their resistance to change, the political relevance of their traditional beliefs, their attempt to recognize in a changing Ireland some semblance of themselves, to humanize Irish history. Part of the effort toward humanization is most easily represented by positive portrayals of the pastoral. If the rupture reflected in the landscape is a sublime encounter with history, then pastoral harmony is the beautiful, a compensatory shift in the psychology of aesthetics. An image of the pastoral sweetness in Goldsmith is apparent in the beginning of *The Deserted Village* (1770). It is more difficult to find such an image in the antipastoral Swift.

As Jeffares notes, one must go outside the major texts, having a guiding political aim as they do: "Some of the pleasantest references in the *Journal to Stella* are to Laracor in County Meath. Indeed, one passage has a rhapsodic quality." Jeffares then goes on to quote the following passage: "Oh, that we were at Laracor this fine day! The willows begin to peep, and the quicks to bud. My dream's out: I was a-dreamed last night that I eat ripe cherries.—And now they begin to catch the pikes, and will shortly the trouts (pox on these ministers), and I would fain know whether the floods were ever so high as to get over the holly bank or the river walk; if so, then all my pikes are gone; but I hope not."[14] It is nature methodized in Horatian terms; it is in such settings that Gulliver might finally come to terms with himself and his wife and family, as Swift did with Stella. For most of the history of Irish literature in English, however, nature and culture are marked more by disjuncture, by the monstrousness of personal and national perception of identity, by their divergence from the conventions of English culture. Of these first palimpsests of conquest, Swift writes in *Gulliver's Travels*: "I could not forbear admiring at these odd appearances in Town and Country: and I made both to desire my Conductor, that he would be pleased to explain to me what could be meant by so many busy Heads, Hands and Faces, both in Streets and Fields, because I did not discover any good Effects they produced; but on the contrary, I never knew a Soil so unhappily cultivated, Houses so ill contrived and so ruinous, or a People whose Countenances and Habit expressed so much Misery and Want."[15]

Gulliver is on his way to Lord Munodi's estate, which is very similar to the Big House demesnes in Ireland. Like Swift, Munodi is a Tory Anarchist and misanthropic stand-in for the Anglo-Irish gentry, who hasn't followed the practices of the kingdom and designed his buildings and lands according to modern, innovative, and, as we see, ineffective models:

> We came into a most beautiful Country; Farmers' Houses at small Distances, neatly built, the Fields enclosed, containing Vineyards, Corngrounds and Meadows. Neither do I remember to have seen a more delightful Prospect. His Excellency observed my Countenance to clear up; he told me with a Sigh, that there his Estate began, and would continue the same till we should come to his House. That his Countrymen ridiculed and despised him for managing his Affairs no better, and for setting so ill an Example to the Kingdom; which however was followed by very few, such as were old and wilful, and weak like himself.

Then for all of the beauty and symmetry of his home, we see that Munodi despairs of continuing along the lines he has so far laid out:

> We came at length to the House, which was indeed a noble Structure, built according to the best Rules of ancient Architecture. The Fountains, Gardens, Walks, Avenues, and Groves were all disposed with exact Judgment and Taste. I gave due Praises to every Thing I saw, where of his Excellency took not the least Notice till after Supper;

> when, there being no third Companion, he told me with a very melancholy Air, that he doubted he must throw down his Houses in Town and Country, to rebuild them after the present Mode.[16]

Of course, this discussion is part of the discourse on the quarrel between the ancients and moderns that underlies much of Swift's work and forms the heart of "A Voyage to Laputa." The juxtapositions of landscape and family, moral, aesthetic, and governmental rules define the savagely satirical intent of *Gulliver's Travels.* Goldsmith delineates a similar juxtaposition, with a similar aim to unmask bad government and the destruction of beauty and morality, albeit with a more sentimental hand.

In *The Deserted Village*, Goldsmith moves from the opening image of beautiful landscape and village life to the core of aesthetic and political happiness, contented sexuality, "secret laughter titter[ing] round the place." The erotic motif takes on added political meaning, and the "spoiler's hand" gathers new significance when compared to the Jacobite *aisling* poems of the eighteenth century, in which a ravished or endangered woman symbolizes the loss of Gaelic Ireland and the need for a Stuart avenger to come from abroad. The most telling Shakespearean phrase in this passage is "the glaring impotence of dress." When impotence is placed next to the "spoiler's hand," we have an emblem of the psychological consequences of colonization, much like Gulliver staring into the mirror in disbelief, in which all outward show, no matter how excessive, cannot hide the inner sense of defilement and failure.

The reigning trope is modeled on the idea of marriage versus defilement. This trope, of course, had been foreshadowed by the *aisling* tradition, with Ireland seen as a woman and the terrain as a feminized landscape. Both bring into focus the sexual, aesthetic, and political allegory of union as a cure for the original sin of occupation and for the pull of the family romance, as we notice in the heady Oedipal theme at the end of Lady Morgan's *The Wild Irish Girl.* As the idea of Union, and the Act of Union, became more unworkable, the themes associated with it became more monstrous when repressed (as in Ferguson's "The Welshmen of Tirawley" and "The Fairy Thorn") and more political when explored. As Catherine Nash writes in "'Embodying the Nation': The West of Ireland and Irish Identity," "This sense of love for the feminized landscape yet fear of its power is repeated. . . . [T]he sexual element of love is cast in Oedipal terms with its mixture of guilt and fear. . . . Like the Oedipal love of the mother, love of the Earth has become a source of shame. The desire for loss of self in experience of nature [finds] its echoes in Synge's account of his experience on Aran" and becomes, in a masturbatory ritual over the hearth in Kavanagh's *The Great Hunger*, "an orgasmic loss of consciousness of self."[17] In other words, it is a twentieth-century culmination of Gulliver's crises and Goldsmith's thwarted desire for the landscape of home, as seen from those individuals who felt cast out by the stony gray soil.

An image of family as both an aesthetic and a political figure is particularly common in the eighteenth century and forcefully expressed by Edmund Burke, to whom the family was a defining structure in colonial and governmental relations. A disruption in the affairs of state was similar to one in the affairs of the home. Burke believed that because the Catholic Irish wanted the privileges of the British constitution, they needed the "protection of a common father."[18] In the field of aesthetics (which studies our responses to society, nature, and art), marriage and family reveal the psychological, cultural, even sexual significance of our shared reality. Eighteenth-century Irish aesthetic philosophers such as Burke, James Usher, and Francis Hutcheson know that family manners, or the law of the heart, provide important aspects of aesthetic and social life by determining how we react to the world around us, by developing rules of decorum, pleasure, and propriety that lead to cultural improvement. If society is harmonious, so are its aesthetic representations; if it is in upheaval, its art reflects the troubles. It is not surprising that for all these Irishmen, there is a connection between social affections and the communal or familial inheritance of Irish society with its emphasis on feeling. Burke and Hutcheson are famed for their emphasis on feeling or sympathy as equal to Kant's idea of Reason in both political and aesthetic domains. Their emphasis is very much at the heart of Oliver Goldsmith's frequent, deceptively simple, and noted connection between the contented family group and the successful nation in such works as *The Deserted Village* and *The Vicar of Wakefield.*

Perhaps it is because, for Catholics, the private, emotional world of family within harsh colonial surroundings could provide forms of resistance to English rule of law, while for Protestants, as Roy Foster writes, "family alliances from the early eighteenth century often provide the subtext to political associations in later generations" of the Anglo-Irish Ascendancy. In *Modern Ireland, 1600–1972*, Foster notes the importance of "family alliances" in the period of Anglo-Irish Ascendancy. He similarly observes of Catholic Ireland: "The eighteenth-century Catholic Church was still beset by the traditional problems of Irish Catholicism: internal indiscipline, factional squabbles, often with a family orientation."[19] Most important, the figure of the family was central to how Catholic and Protestant Ireland viewed their relationship. From the Protestant perspective, marriage with a Catholic led to social discredit, while, from the Catholic perspective, Foster writes that "the apparent exploitation of [Ireland's] less developed economy, together with the continuing failure to grant Catholic emancipation, created the terms in which nationalist rhetoric denounced the Union: a recurring metaphor being that of the failed marriage." W. J. McCormack notes that nowhere do these Oedipal crises become clearer than in the conceptions of intermarriage between classes and religion.[20]

In *The Vicar of Wakefield*, Goldsmith gives the family an explicitly political setting: "The little republic to which I gave laws was regulated in the following manner: by sunrise we all assembled in our common apartment, the fire being previously kindled by the servant. After we had saluted each other with proper ceremony, we all bent in gratitude to that Being who gave us another day. This duty being performed, my son and I went to pursue our usual industry abroad, while my wife and daughters employed themselves in providing breakfast."[21] As the passage progresses, the hierarchies of class and gender increasingly attend the "little republic," yet the hierarchies betray the tension between republican and monarchist thinking that bedeviled both

Goldsmith's and Burke's essentially conservative thought. Though conservative, Goldsmith opposed older authoritarian values. As a man of feeling, his is a benevolent family, respecting rights and individuality, a just and caring model for society. The family's position in the pastoral of Goldsmith's politics is given a more conventionally aesthetic representation later in the novel, where the "place" of "retreat" is so perfect that people seldom need to visit cities or towns.

Such a painting of a gentle landscape around simple cottage life evokes images of harmonious society, of familial warmth around the fire, while, on the other hand, a painting of a wild or ruined landscape, bereft of human inhabitants, dwarfing or terrifying the individual, has quite the opposite effect. In the terminology of landscape painting, the former is known as the landscape of the beautiful, the latter the landscape of the sublime. This distinction is very important for an understanding of Oliver Goldsmith. The beginning of *The Deserted Village* provides an example of the beautiful:

> Sweet Auburn! Loveliest village of the plain,
> Where health and plenty cheered the labouring swain
> Where smiling spring its earliest visit paid,
> And parting summer's lingering blooms delayed.
>
> . . . .
>
> How often have I paused on every charm,
> The sheltered cot, the cultivated farm,
> The never failing brook, the busy mill
> The decent church that topped the neighbouring hill,
> The hawthorn bush, with seats beneath the shade,
> For talking age and whispering lovers made. (1–4, 9–14)

From this image of beautiful landscape and village life, Goldsmith moves to the core of aesthetic and political happiness: contented sexuality. The deepest springs of the aesthetic life, the world of the senses, are given affirmative social and political expression, without which society and individual alike are abused. Goldsmith reveals that there is a governing trick to it: "The bashful virgin's sidelong looks of love, / The matron's glance that would those looks reprove." It is a confluence of nature, family, and the state. In the eighteenth-century love of "natural feeling," the laws of nature are not so much laws of the jungle, or a medieval concept of original sin, but the principles of our natural sympathies, which need only gentle guidance to be understood (a guidance sometimes lacking in the mother from *The Vicar of Wakefield*). This guidance is what one may call Goldsmith's metaphysical optimism.

From line 35 onward, we learn why such loveliness has fled. The reasons Goldsmith gives have a markedly anticommercial, indeed anti-capitalist, flavor: "Ill fares the land, to hastening ills a prey, / Where wealth accumulates, and men decay." Because of the Land Enclosure Acts (which effectively allowed landowners to dispossess entire villages) in England and even more so in Ireland, the villagers have been driven to the alienating labor of the city. A sexual specter again hangs over the scene; we are told of "the spoiler's hand" as a figure for misgovernment. The narrator, "sad historian of the pensive plain," walks through the ruins of the village remembering past happiness with what Raymond Williams calls "a mixture of nostalgia and protest."[22] He recollects various village characters, beginning with the "village preacher," natural leader of this little Christian republic. He is friend to beggar, old soldier, and children and, being the unifying force of religion, remains patron of the pastoral scene, even through the sublime storm that effects such drastic change in village life:

> . . . all his serious thoughts had rest in Heaven.
> As some tall cliff that lifts its awful form,
> Swells from the vale, and midway leaves the storm,
> Though round its breast the rolling clouds are spread,
> Eternal sunshine settles on its head. (188–92)

His religion takes the terror out of the sublime. In his image of pastoral religious life, Goldsmith seeks to unify many of the characteristics of the beautiful (feminine, caring, gentle) with the sublime (masculine, judicious, strong). In fact, Goldsmith took Burke to task for overemphasizing the terror of the sublime to the diminishment of the importance of love.[23] After the parson, there is the village master, a similarly unifying figure, although here Goldsmith earns Samuel Johnson's sobriquet the "gentle master," with the gentlest satire on academic pretensions, coupled with sympathy for rustic life:

> With words of learned length, and thundering sound
> Amazed the gazing rustics ranged around;
> And still they gazed, and still the wonder grew,
> That one small head could carry all he knew. (213–16)

There follows a scene of domestic bliss and loving frugality, for which the poet is justly renowned (221–35). It ends with an image ("while broken teacups, wisely kept for show, / Ranged o'er the chimney, glistened in a row") countering commercial ideas of usefulness. It also exhibits a sensitivity for objects of the past, similar to the preacher's liking for the beggarman, which is full of arcadian longing.

Readers are given a portrayal of class harmony in a pub that leads to Goldsmith's most explicit denunciation of avarice and luxury. One theme of the poem, of course, is that art must be at the service of nature (art is "Nature methodized," as Pope writes in *Essay on Criticism* [line 88]) rather than the opposite of nature. In these lines, as we move away from the unity that the parson represents, there are increasingly fewer closed couplets, leading to an emotionally rhythmic finale, as virtue surrenders to vice:

> The toiling pleasure sickens into pain;
> And, even while fashion's brightest arts decoy,
> The heart distrusting asks, if this be joy. (262–64)

Despairingly, Goldsmith wonders in the above lines, as anyone might, if it might be true that for some to be rich, others must be poor. "The rich man's joys increase, the poor's decay" (266). And a few lines later: "The robe that wraps his limbs in silken sloth / Has robbed the neighboring fields of half their growth" (279–80). Then there is a "fair female," representative of the land, society, and custom, betrayed by avarice: "Thus fares the land by luxury betrayed" (287–302). The idea of sexual suffering as representative of social ills finds a mirror in Brian Merriman's *The Midnight Court* and in much of Jonathan Swift's satire, as well as in the *aisling* poems of the Jacobite period.

The denouement of the poem makes what is explicit in the language explicit in action. The villagers are now in hostile urban surroundings. The concluding scenario is one of the proverbial ruined maid, with "betrayal" becoming the substantive word of the poem:

> Now lost to all: her friends, her virtue fled,
> Near her betrayer's door she lays her head,
> And pinched with cold, and shrinking from the shower,
> With heavy heart deplores that luckless hour,
> When idly first, ambitious of the town,
> She left her wheel and robes of country brown. (331–36)

The "spoiler's hand" mentioned earlier in the poem is now salient. From city abandonment, we move to the wildernesses of America, where, seeking to reestablish Auburn in the New World, the people find only "crouching tigers . . . / And savage men, more murderous still than they" (355–56).[24] The ruined maid and the barbaric wilds of America lead, of course, to the destruction of family as well as village and nation. The scene of the family's destruction is sentimental. When compared with his other comic works, such as *She Stoops to Conquer* (1773) and *The Vicar of Wakefield* (1762), it nevertheless gains more power. In the former play, which also deals with similar themes of nature and art, country and city, simplicity and sophistication, such a scene of ruin is cleverly forestalled through farcical means. In the novel, when the hapless father is freed from debtors' prison, the errant daughter finally marries the squire who had "ruined" her (marries through the good services of his uncle). The reality of such ruin was perhaps too tragic for Goldsmith to portray successfully; comedy worked better. This thought makes the tragedy of the poem even more poignant. Yet the most haunting context in which one may read the close of Goldsmith's poem is biographical. The self-styled "citizen of the world" traveled widely through the Continent and England, but judging from the poem felt at home in Ireland and with his family (for Goldsmith home and family were inextricable). Like James Joyce, though he never returned home, Oliver Goldsmith continued to roam its streets.

The satire and sentiment of the eighteenth century would eventually require a more mythological response to nature and nation, landscape and family, seeking distinctly Irish cultural expression. The antiquarian movement would be at the heart of this response. Looking for something in Ireland and Irishness that would express a cultural nationalism, if not a political one—as many of the movement's proponents from Brooke to Ferguson were Protestant and often unionist—it is now a truism that myth and folklore provided the best avenues, but not surprisingly they also unlocked many of the deepest springs of cultural and later political independence.

Such a theme of the dark roots of self and family, what Burke calls "pedigrees of guilt,"[25] is carried on in Maria Edgeworth's *Castle Rackrent* (1800), in which political struggles are reflected in the family fortunes of the Big House owners and of their servants; in the divided allegiances of William Carleton, which keep Denis O'Shaughnessy from going to Maynooth; and in James Clarence Mangan, whose sufferings and identity-shifting translations make him the emblem of nineteenth-century Irish history. In the twentieth century, it can be said that the sublimated family crises of W. B. Yeats, Lady Gregory, Patrick Pearse, J. M. Synge, James Joyce, Samuel Beckett, and others have helped to reflect the struggles of the new national literature.

Since the Irish literary renaissance, Irish literature has been constructed so as to seem a testament to nineteenth- and twentieth-century experience: the land wars, the religious and ethnic strife, the woes of colonization and decolonization. Questions of identity and place have been paramount and not easily answered. In the introduction to their anthology of Irish poetry, Peter Fallon and Derek Mahon state: "The word most frequently dwelt on in this selection is probably 'home,' as if an uncertainty exists as to where that actually is." In a move indicative of modernist and postmodernist writing, contemporary Irish writers confront the vagaries of their own experience and history, whether from Northern, Southern, Eastern, or

Western regional identities. Personal reflections inevitably have public resonance, and aesthetic choices political implications. The position of the contemporary Irish writer continues to be troublesome, to be divided, as Thomas Kinsella laments in his essay "The Divided Mind": "I recognise that I stand on one side of a great rift, and can feel the discontinuity in myself. It is a matter of people and places as well as writing—of coming from a broken and uprooted family, of being drawn to those who share my origins and finding that we cannot share our lives."[26] Kinsella captures the familial, political, as well as poetic ramifications of this idea of division from the past. In the aesthetics and politics of Irishness, there is constant effort to find a way of re-creating the familiar, of healing the wounds of history with images of shared reality. Yet, as we have seen, it is in the eighteenth century that the roots for these images of a shared reality are found.

3

Great Hunger, Unspeakable Home

Lady Morgan's *The Wild Irish Girl* (1806) and William Carleton's *The Black Prophet* (1847)

❦ The destruction of the Irish forests during the Elizabethan and Cromwellian wars,[1] enacted to expose the Irish rebels, became a part of the Jacobite tradition,[2] but codes of dispossession, destruction, or neglect, as observed in previous chapters, are apparent in Swift, Burke, and Goldsmith. From the eighteenth century to the nineteenth, this coded use of landscape as symbol of the Irish condition became a romanticized vision—a shift in perspective that accompanied the movement toward reforestation from 1756 to 1845.[3] As has also been noted, the divisions in Irish society, which become increasingly apparent in the years after the Act of Union (passed in 1800 and enacted in 1801), are reflected in the view toward nature, in the efforts to balance "the blasted heath" with the "sweet village."[4] Such a background helps us to understand Irish attempts to humanize Irish history. Part of the effort toward humanization is most easily represented by positive portrayals of the pastoral. If the rupture reflected in the landscape is a strong encounter with history, then pastoral harmony is a compensatory shift in the psychology of aesthetics. Landscape aesthetics, on the one hand, insists upon continual sympathy and harmony by displaying a model of the beautiful blessed land; on the other hand, in order to reflect the opposite religious, political, and aesthetic significance, it recognizes dissonance in sublime images of cursed nature. The eruptions of wilderness and the compensations of the pleasant place are mutually defining opposites; the one is often invoked to challenge or exorcise the other.

Nineteenth-century literary figures of the landscape, particularly in Lady Morgan's novel *The Wild Irish Girl* (1806) together with William Carleton's story "Wildgoose Lodge" (1830) and novel *The Black Prophet* (1847), reflect a growing consciousness of political and social upheaval in the years leading up to and immediately following the Great Famine. Such figures of the landscape also reflect upon long-enduring problems of family life in Ireland, especially of marriage and other unions. Furthermore, the allegory of union between Englishness (mirrored in the ordered, harmonious landscape of the beautiful) and Irishness (mirrored in the ruined or wild landscape of the sublime) says as much about individual consciousness as it does about public history, as a host of critical books have made amply evident.[5] In this reading, we may ask how do nature, home, landscape, and original sin figure in *The Wild Irish Girl* and *The Black Prophet.*

In *The Wild Irish Girl*, Morgan's blending of landscape, seascape, and body in the description of Castle Inishmore has psychological and historical reverberations: "Towards the extreme western point of this peninsula, which was wildly romantic beyond all description, arose a vast and grotesque pile of rocks, which at once formed the site and fortifications of the noblest mass of ruins on which my eye ever rested. Grand, even in desolation, and magnificent in decay—it was the Castle of Inishmore. The setting sun shone brightly on its mouldering turrets, and the waves which bathed its rocky basis, reflected on their swelling bosoms the dark outlines of its awful ruins."[6] Not only does this description conflate the gendered terms of the beautiful and the sublime as laid out by Edmund Burke (beautiful equaling the feminine, the sublime equaling the masculine—a subversion Morgan displays throughout the book), but it also relies on a series of assumptions concerning landscape that serve to define the relationship of Ireland and England. The allegory of union at the heart of her project is full of such conflations, combining with sexual guilt, suggestions of original sin, and palimpsests of conquest. In Horatio's dream of the face of Glorvina as the head of the Gorgon, these themes converge. Similar to the female Yahoo in *Gulliver's Travels*, who tackles Gulliver while he is bathing,[7] sexual desire in *The Wild Irish Girl* both reveals and conceals the ugly truths of conquest and the underlying connection to nature. Both bring into focus the sexual, aesthetic, and political allegory of union as a means of redemption for the sins of occupation and incest, as we notice in the heady Oedipal theme at the end of *The Wild Irish Girl* or in the family intrigue of *The Black Prophet.* Edmund Burke had foreseen that an Act of Union without legal protection under the constitution was just fornication, suggesting the tangled roots of generation and colonization.[8] As the idea of union, and the Act of Union, became more unworkable, the themes associated with it became more monstrous as they were repressed. Finally, the original sin that threatens to undo the proposed unities at the end of *The Wild Irish Girl* bursts into the flames of political violence that consume "Wildgoose Lodge" and erupts in the crime that, once discovered, hangs the eponymous character of *The Black Prophet.*

Early in the narrative of *The Wild Irish Girl,* it is clear that the landscape is based on familial and national ideas of England and Ireland. Horatio's journey to Ireland, as Katie Trumpener notes, sets the standard for later national tales of Anglo-Irish or English gentlemen coming to Ireland in the expectation of barbarism, only to be reeducated, fall in love, and become responsible landlords.[9] Horatio's father suggests that Horatio should go to Ireland, and, even if coincidentally, this advice mingles national and social concerns in its description of Ireland's landscape: "I see no cause why Coke upon Lyttleton cannot be as well studied amidst the wild seclusion of Connaught scenery, and on the solitary shores of the 'steep Atlantic,' as in the busy bustling precincts of the Temple" (1:6). It is a knowing coincidence on the part of Lady Morgan. The "wild seclusion," of course, is the result of the historical catastrophe of the English advance into Ireland from Elizabeth's reign to Cromwell's commonwealth. Cromwell's invocation of "To Hell or Connaught" cements the connotations of the civilized invader versus the barbarian native that had been frequently used since Edmund Spenser's era.

These distinctions have a previous topographical basis in the formation of "the pale." Whether the expression "beyond the pale" derives from this area of Ireland, or from a similar one in Russia, or was merely a later rationalization (see "pale" in *The Oxford English Dictionary*, 2nd edition, 1989), its distinction between wild and civilized lands pervades the text. In a novel titled *The Wild Irish Girl*, a novel that consistently tries to recuperate the Irish from the category of barbarian, while using the best connotations of that savagery, the wild seclusion where Horatio is sent to study is perhaps all too emblematic of the rupture of raw nature. Just as the savage implies the ability to salvage, making the primitive a redemptive force, so nature in such instances is instinct with original sin and innocence. The primitive scene in Ireland, in which Horatio will live, is also described in the colonial terms of early travel books like the one Horatio consults: "I remember when I was a boy, meeting somewhere with the quaintly written travels of *Moryson* through Ireland, and being particularly struck with assertion, that so late as the days of Elizabeth, and Irish chieftain and his family were frequently seen seated round their domestic fire in a state of perfect nudity" (1:13).

Horatio secretly desires to unveil this emblem. Like a good romantic, he is seeking his nature in nature, having been unable to find it in culture. In fact, he is seeking to redeem "the *original sin* of [his] nature," which is the sin of being overly refined (1:8) and later the sin of his family's role in the colonization of Ireland. Seeing that Dublin has been Anglicized, that it is too much in the civilized sphere of European culture and history (even Dublin Bay resembles the Bay of Naples), he heads off with alacrity to his destination in the province of Connaught. As he says, "The native Irish, pursued by religious and political bigotry, made [Connaught] the asylum of their sufferings, and were separated by a provincial barrier from an intercourse with the rest of Ireland, until after the Restoration; so I shall have a fair opportunity of beholding the Irish character in all its *primeval* ferocity" (1:14). Horatio then goes on to develop this conceit within the Burkean language of eighteenth-century aesthetics:

> To him who derives gratification from the embellished labours of art rather than the simple but sublime operations of nature, *Irish* scenery will afford little interest; but the bold features of its varying

> landscape, the stupendous attitude of its "cloud-capt" mountains, the impervious gloom of its deep embosomed glens, the savage desolation of its uncultivated heaths and boundless bogs, with those rich veins of a picturesque champagne, thrown at intervals into gay expansion by the hand of nature, awaken, in the mind of the poetic or pictorial traveller all the pleasures of tasteful enjoyment, all the sublime emotions of a rapt imagination. And if the glowing fancy of Claude Lorrain would have dwelt enraptured on the paradisial charms of English landscape, the superior genius of Salvator Rosa would have reposed its eagle wing amidst those scenes of mysterious sublimity with which the wildly magnificent landscape of Ireland abounds. But the liberality of nature appears to me to be here but frugally assisted by the donations of art. (1:18–19)

Horatio even quotes Burke's idea from the *Enquiry* of "delightful horror" as the mixed basis for sublime feeling (1:19). He also nods to the prominent painters of the beautiful (Frenchman Claude Lorrain [1600–1682]) and the sublime (Neapolitan Salvator Rosa [1615–73]), insisting that the latter is the superior genius, as the landscape of Ireland is the superior landscape. It is interesting to note that Rosa's depictions of the bandits of Southern Italy had political references, as it had been a colony of Spain (and to a lesser extent France) for many centuries. The *banditti* (*sic*) were in fact the early version of what is loosely known now as the Mafia. Like the dangers of Ireland, such figures in the landscape represent the political turmoil of the period in Southern Italy. It is also a reminder of how much of Europe was colonized by other European nations and regions. The dialectic of barbaric Irish versus civilized English underlies this passage; now we know how the phrases "wild seclusion," "barren heath," and "healthy pasture" will carry cultural and political significance. Nature and culture are at odds in the colonial scenario, and it is the object of civilized England to stop nature from destructively erupting in Ireland, while seeking the redemptive possibilities nature nevertheless possesses. Horatio's encounter with natural, uncultivated beauty ("here *agriculture* appears in the least felicitous of her aspects" [1:18–19]) will make him confront his own nature, as the novel seeks to reconcile English and Irish cultures and landscapes.

It isn't long before Horatio discovers his family's "original sin" of conquest. The ruined castle of Glorvina is the product of his own family's usurpation, as well as his own steward's misrule and criminal actions. He is ashamed: "It would be vain, it would be impossible, to describe the emotion which the simple tale of this old man awakened. The descendant of a murderer! The very scoundrel steward of my father revelling in the property of a man, who shelters his aged head beneath the ruins of those walls where his ancestors bled under the uplifted sword of mine!" He fully understands the theatricality of the moment: "Why this, you will say, is the romance of a novel-read school-boy." He then contemplates the biblical roots, the original sin, of murder: "Are we not all, the little and the great, descended from assassins; was not the first born man a fratricide? and still, on the field of unappeased contention does not 'man, the murderer, meet the murderer, man?'" The tangled roots of Cain and Abel have been exposed: "Yes, yes, 'tis all true; humanity acknowledges it, and shudders. But still I wish *my* family had either never possessed an acre of ground in this country, or had possessed it on other terms. I always knew the estate fell into our family in the civil wars of Cromwell, and in the world's language, was the well-earned meed of my progenitors' valour; but I seemed to hear it now for the first time" (1:128–29).

Confronted by the gravities of his original sin (which can only be understood in person and by implication not by absentees), Horatio deploys the logic of colonial occupation to alleviate his conscience and to fend off any ideas of the humanity of the other: "I am glad, however, that this old Irish chieftain is such a ferocious savage; that the pity his fate awakens is qualified by aversion for his implacable irascible disposition. I am glad his daughter is *red headed*, a pedant, and a romp; that she spouts Latin like the priest of the parish, and cures sore fingers; that she avoids genteel society" (1:130). Glorvina's red hair makes her particularly barbaric, like the redheaded Yahoos of *Gulliver's Travels* who are especially lascivious. In the end, Horatio fears that Glorvina's beauty and accomplishments will challenge the colonial assumptions of superiority that support his hereditary political claims. Of course, such deployment of the colonial logic is sure to be undone through Horatio's aesthetic appreciation of the scene, not to mention the sexual attractions of Glorvina herself, who is always perceived as part of the natural landscape of Ireland. The aesthetic is a foundational or subversive experience (or both), political, philosophical, or artistic, as Horatio's journey through the countryside on the way to Glorvina's home, Castle Inishmore, makes clear.

The sublime scenery of his journey unites the sensible world to the supersensible moral sphere and so potentially undoes all the threatening contrarieties of the Gothic encounter on which the colonial suppression of the physical primitive world is based. This concrete description of the sensual world is elevated to the abstract level of the spiritual. Irrational fears vanish under the influence of the rational and moral intelligence:

> Such were the sublime objects which seemed to engage their attention, and added their *sensible* inspiration to the fervour of those more abstracted devotions in which they were so recently engaged. At last they reached the portals of the castle, and I lost sight of them. Yet still, spell-bound, I stood transfixed to the spot whence I had caught a last view of their receding figures. . . . While I felt like the victim of superstitious terror when the spectre of its distempered fancy vanishes from its strained and eager gaze, all I had lately seen revolved in my mind like some pictured story of romantic fiction. (1:151)

Horatio then hears Glorvina's voice ("Glorvina" coming from the Irish for "the sweet voiced"), after his encounter with the aesthetics of nature has prepared him to see her and fall (both figuratively and metaphorically) into a new form of consciousness. He asks himself: "Was it the illusion of my now all awakened fancy, or the professional exertions of the bard of Inishmore? Oh, no! for the voice it symphonized—the low wild tremulous voice, which sweetly sighed its soul of melody o'er the harp's responsive chords, was the voice of *a woman*!" (1:152).

Horatio quickly decides to call himself Henry Mortimer and to pose as a landscape painter so as to gain admittance to the house without anyone knowing his guilt; however, guilt will unsettle both his waking and his sleeping dreams, as he is confronted by the original sin of desire for conquest: "I fell into a gentle slumber, in which I dreamed that the Princess of Inishmore approached my bed, drew aside the curtains, and raising her veil, discovered a face I had hitherto rather guessed at, than seen. Imagine my horror—it was the face, the head, of a *Gorgon*!" He then wakes to a vision of the real Glorvina, which cures him of the nightmare: "Awakened by the sudden and terrific motion it excited, though still almost motionless, as if from the effects of a night-mare (which in fact, from the position I lay in, had oppressed me in the form of the Princess) I cast my eyes through a fracture in the old damask drapery of my bed, and beheld—not the horrid spectre of my recent dream, but the form of a cherub hovering near my pillow—it was the Lady Glorvina herself! Oh! how I trembled lest the fair image should only be the vision of my slumber: I scarcely dared to breathe, lest it should dissolve" (1:186–87). The monstrous Glorvina is an image of Ireland shaped by the colonial logic with which Horatio first attempted to ease his conscience. It proved that the Irish were barbarians who could be monsters unless vigorously ruled. The sexual register of the dream is significant. The rest of the novel is in some way an attempt to cure himself of the monstrousness of his Gothic dream as the beautiful face of the real Glorvina had done; it is an attempt of the beautiful to unveil the sublime and to cure the murderous original sin of colonization, if not of Gorgon-like desire itself.

The princess is continually described in natural terms. Yet, as Horatio finds himself drawn to her, she is seen as art and nature balanced. Morgan embodies in her the link between the natural and the national. The road ahead for Horatio is to find a way to woo and win her, and that road, of course, is attended by various successes and failures. What is most important at the early juncture of the novel is that Horatio is going through a mystical experience: in order to return to the world a new man, he must be estranged from it

(2:120–23). In short, like a good romantic, he must return to blessed (rather than cursed) nature, the abode of the princess: "It seemed to me as if I had lived in an age of primeval simplicity and primeval virtue—my senses at rest, my passions soothed to philosophic repose, my prejudices vanquished, all the powers of my mind gently breathed into motion, yet calm and unagitated—all the faculties of my taste called into exertion, yet unsated even by boundless gratification." He must reject his former self: "The past given to oblivion, the future unanticipated, and the present enjoyed, with the full consciousness of its pleasurable existence. Wearied, exhausted, satiated by a boundless indulgence of hackneyed pleasures, hackneyed occupations, hackneyed pursuits." He must also admit the redeeming influence of his new consciousness: "At a moment when I was sinking beneath the lethargic influence of apathy, or hovering on the brink of despair, a new light broke upon my clouded mind, and discovered to my inquiring heart something yet worth living for. What that mystic something is I can scarcely yet define myself; but a magic spell now irresistibly binds me to that life" (2:124).

Glorvina has this influence because, through his love of her, Horatio may reconcile the sublime and the beautiful, the etiological (Glorvina coming from the line of original rulers of Ireland) and the standard of sense (the reason and decorum of English rule), the monstrous and the lovely, nature and culture. The protective mood of love surrounds the sublime origins of the landscape when Glorvina and Horatio then take a walk together: "The luxury of landscape through which we wandered, the sublimity of those stupendous cliffs which seemed to shelter two hearts from the world" (2:41–42). The cliffs are the transcendent, lofty barriers of the world, marking off beginning and end.

As the novel progresses, Glorvina takes on certain powerful characteristics of the sublime, such as reason and fortitude, while her father is increasingly enfeebled. He is emotional; she is art and mind. Horatio is not only confronted by a vision of Ireland he didn't expect, but is also witness to Lady Morgan's Wollstonecraft-like challenge to Burke's categories of the masculine sublime versus the feminine beautiful.

Lady Morgan's challenge may be less conscious or overt than Mary Wollstonecraft's, but it is nonetheless an implicit part of the novel.

Later at a funeral, Glorvina is described in terms of the unity of sublime and beautiful as she stands amid the Irish mourners: "Glorvina, whom they had not at first perceived, stood like an idol in the midst of them, receiving that adoration which the admiring gaze of some, and the adulatory exclamations of others, offered to her virtues and her charms. While those, personally known to her, she addressed with her usual winning sweetness in their native language, I am sure that there was not an individual among this crowd of ardent and affectionate people who would not have risked his life 'to avenge a look that threatened her with danger'" (2:188). At the end of this passage, Morgan quotes Burke's apostrophe to the queen of France in *Reflections on the Revolution in France.* Glorvina, like the queen of France, is the figure of the beautiful that is meant to be protected by the sublime character of the people, the strength of the king, by moral rule. The funeral that Glorvina is attending surrounds the death of a father, as we are ominously told. It prefigures the death of Glorvina's elderly father and, of course, the demise of Irish power in general.

Her position here as an *aisling* figure is very important for Horatio, for he will have to provide protection now that the power of the Irish state has been so diminished. Like Friar Laurence in *Romeo and Juliet* (a play to which the novel often alludes), Father John is one of the first to realize the potential of the love between Horatio and Glorvina: "Perhaps," said the priest, with his usual simplicity, "this sacred sympathy between two refined, elevated, and sensible souls, in the sublime and beautiful of the moral and natural world, approaches nearer to the rapturous and pure emotions which uncreated spirits may be supposed to feel in their heavenly communion, than any other human sentiment with which we are acquainted" (2:150). As in *Romeo and Juliet*, the dream of the priest eventually becomes the priest's tragedy. In *The Wild Irish Girl*, the war between the rival groups is meant to be resolved. Efforts toward resolution will entail a certain amount of cultural analysis. In particular, certain English prejudices against Ireland must be confronted, and a series of conversations must ensue.

As so often in the novel, the cultural descent of the Irish has natural analogies (2:177–78). "Landscape and morality" becomes the theme of the novel (2:189–93). The effort made throughout the narrative from now on aims to exculpate the Irish position. These conversations persist throughout the narrative, with references to Irish history meant to vindicate the nationalist position: "Nor is it now unknown to them, that in the veins of his present Majesty and his ancestors, from James the First, flows the royal blood of the *three* kingdoms united." Finally, Horatio seems convinced. The various aspects of this topic are explored, some points foreshadowing Matthew Arnold's *On the Study of Celtic Literature* (1867): "My dear Sir," he (the priest) replied, "a country may be civilized, enlightened, and even learned and ingenious, without attaining to any considerable perfection in those arts, which give to posterity *sensible* memorials of its passed splendor. The ancient Irish, like the modern, had more *soul*, more genius, than worldly prudence or cautious calculating forethought" (3:68). Other conversations, such as on the cultivated lands of the industrious North (3:198) or the question of landownership of ruined monasteries and convents (3:199), expose the long history of sectarian views. Lady Morgan's desire to convince the English of Irish values, whether Catholic or Milesian, is of primary interest to her, but for the present discussion the connections between culture and nature are most relevant. In this light, Glorvina must redeem the historical wrongs against Ireland and the failures of Irish culture through the application of her natural influences within the intricate arrangement of colonial powers.

Horatio makes this point clear when he says of Glorvina's ability to redeem our original sin: "'O Glorvina!' I passionately added, 'if even thou, fair being, reared in thy native wilds and native solitudes, art deceptive, artful, imposing, deep, deep, in all the wiles of hypocrisy; then is the original sin of our nature unredeemed . . . '" (3:210). Following this reflection of Glorvina's character, Horatio must return to the inhuman scene of the crime, the sublime origins of the original sin, rattled by the sense that all is lost, that Glorvina might be unfaithful, that there is no redemption (3:238). He fears that the family has deserted the castle. In the language of aesthetics, this encounter is not a moment of the sublime but a moment of the horrible, that is, one without any compensatory shift in meaning. "A few burning tears relieved him from an agony he was no longer able to endure; and he was now competent to draw some inference from the dreadful scene of desolation by which he was surrounded. The good old Prince was no more!—or his daughter was married! In either case it was probable the family had deserted the *ruins* of Inishmore" (3:240). The fear is that the original sin may be unredeemed. The sublime encounter may have no moral outcome.

It is a fear that will never be entirely banished from the novel. The incestuous nature of the original sin of colonization is revealed, but can it truly be considered and resolved? By usurping the fathers of the conquered land, we implicitly usurp our own, and perhaps we cannot resurrect them. The cure, or antidote, is a portion of the poison: the old father, the prince, must die in order to give birth to the new. As a consequence of the cure, nature's voice is silenced along with Glorvina. On the brink of marrying the earl, Horatio's father, she finds out the truth of the original sin of occupation, and of the relationship between father and son, and falls silent (3:226). She had wished to marry Horatio's father (who had been described as youthful at one point) in recognition of his desire to help and protect her and in order to save her own father's life and lands; now it seems that the marriage will mean the death of her own ancestral rights. The prince of Inishmore wants to know what has happened. After discovering the long history of Horatio's arrival and the earl's lineage, he dies (3:232).

Soon the history of the families, the murder, and the colonization is revealed to all (3:242). The earl immediately adopts Glorvina and makes some attempt to undo the sexual aspect of the marriage and the breaking of the taboo that was just forestalled (3:242–47). Culture is meant to refine nature, but seems to attempt merely to wish it out of existence. Is Glorvina's silence at the end of the novel meant to show that the antidote tasted too much like the poison? Critics have examined the question of Glorvina's silence from a political and feminist standpoint.[10] Like the political and feminist, the aesthetic view of the novel hangs on the shift from nature to culture that the marriage promises—and Glorvina's silence leaves it hanging.[11]

Ostensibly, the novel insists that history, and with it the very land itself, will be healed by the marriage of Horatio and Glorvina (3:250). The earl tells Horatio to be a good landlord, but the law does not preclude bad landlords. Although this novel was an attempt to introduce the English to Irish culture, there are remnants of the colonial law at work; the Irish are still subject to their feelings. Childlike, they need rational rule. The Irish still need to be husbanded, as does the land, and so the earl advises Horatio to "place the standard of support within their sphere; and like the tender vine, which has been suffered by neglect to waste its treasures on the sterile earth, you will behold them naturally turning and gratefully twining round the fostering stem which rescues them from a cheerless and groveling destiny" (3:263).

Ownership of the land is still in English hands, and the union without protection of the constitution is fornication, as Edmund Burke foresaw.[12] Will this union of Horatio and Glorvina afford the protection of the constitution? On this point, Glorvina's silence is sublime, the silence of the original sin, of the ruined castle that Horatio was horrified to think was forever empty, the silence of the barren heath. We hark back to Horatio's very first image of the castle and the conflation of the sublime and the beautiful, for it now seems prescient. Glorvina and the castle intermingled from the start. The feelings of Glorvina are like the swelling of the surrounding seas, full of foreboding and suggestive of the ruined past, but representing all and saying nothing: "The setting sun shone brightly on its mouldering turrets, and the waves which bathed its rocky basis, reflected on their swelling bosoms the dark outlines of its awful ruins" (1:136). In the end, it is the sea and landscape that are most articulate, for they carry signs of harsh memory so visibly that words are no longer necessary. The historical scars would be carved only more deeply as the nineteenth century progressed.

☙ ☙ ☙

The topography of Ireland finds its cultural as well as cartographic equivalent in the Ordnance Survey of the 1830s,[13] when landscape and place-names became the map of national aspiration. The roots in late-eighteenth-century ideology are apparent in the landscape, that is, the "Wearing of the Green" and the "Tree of Liberty." Yet there is an increasing split in attitude toward nature and landscape between the Irish peasantry and the Anglo-Irish throughout the nineteenth century. "In either kind of Irish Romantic literature," notes J. W. Foster,

> there was under the circumstances, little celebration of Irish nature for its own sake, none of the self-rewarding sensuousness of Keats or the personal enrichment or pantheistic spirit Wordsworth found in the Lake District. There are no Irish poets of the time to whom we might refer as "nature poets" in the way we might refer to Wordsworth and John Clare as nature poets. (The words "nature," "landscape" and "scenery," in fact, have among the bulk of Irish people to this day a somewhat effete connotation and evoke an Anglo-Irish worldview.) Nor was there that interest in cutting-edge experimental science we find in Shelley or Coleridge.[14]

The real or mere Irish could not objectify or appreciate nature as could the Anglo-Irish.

For Catholics, nature became "symbolic"; for "Dissenters it became objective," and so attracted them to science, J. W. Foster avers, though one may suspect that he overstates it.[15] Edmund Burke's notion of aesthetic distance, taken up by William Carleton in "Wildgoose Lodge" (1830), may provide a reason for the complexities and political and sectarian components of Irish views of nature and landscape: when you are in the midst of terror, all the exalted qualities, the compensation of the sublime, are lost. In Carleton's riveting short story, the struggle between nature and culture in the midst of the historical pressures on house and family during the famine and the land wars result in such an eruption of nature that, as noted previously, a house of an informer is set on fire and all those people within are burned alive.

In the narration, as if to remind us of our position as readers, and of the then primarily English readership, Carleton is concerned with aesthetic distance, in a way similar to Swift's questioning of conventional ideas of landscape.[16] The aesthetics of landscape is corrupted, as is the home that is set therein. When the narrator states, "After this we dispersed every man to his own home," we must wonder what type of return this could be.[17] The wilderness has reentered the house in "Wildgoose Lodge" and abolished all aesthetic distance. For Samuel Ferguson, the psychological split toward the land takes the form of the divide between his cultural nationalism and his political unionism, a split in which the landscape is "objective," neutral ground, which only rarely, as in Ferguson's "The Fairy Thorn" and "The Welshmen of Tirawley," allows the darker possibilities that James Clarence Mangan and Carleton reveal. In Mangan and Carleton, the dark necessities of nature and history lead to the antipastoral mode of the Great Famine with all of its political reflections. One of the most extended expositions of the antipastoral mode is William Carleton's *The Black Prophet* (1847), a story of an Irish village that revolves around the original sin of a murder, a crime that seems to give utterance to the social catastrophe of the famine, to the attending historical incidents of colonization, and to the landscape, as well as images of nature, that serve as backdrop. *The Black Prophet* was written in the midst of the "Great Famine," but is based on memories of the famines of 1817 and 1822.[18] The novel's plot essentially revolves around three families, the Sullivans, the Daltons, and the family of the Black Prophet, known as the McGowans for most of the novel until, near its end, the Gothic genealogy of the family is revealed. Condy Dalton is supposed to have killed one Bartle Sullivan. This murder is the original sin of the novel that provides a raison d'être of sorts for the Great Famine itself. As God demands that the blood of the murdered man be accounted for, the suffering of the starving populace calls out for its own blood to be acknowledged. These two scenes of original sin as a cause for suffering parallel one another throughout the novel.

It is said that the famine victims "with cadaverous and emaciated aspects had something in them so wild and wolfish, and the fire of famine blazed so savagely in their hollow eyes, that many of them looked like creatures changed from their very humanity by some judicial plague, that had been sent down from heaven to punish and desolate the land."[19] The murder was committed some twenty years before, in the year of the 1798 rebellion, and the Black Prophet is fittingly a United Irishman. The political aspect of the original sin is therefore not in question, only who is guilty of what crime. It is at the setting of the gray stone of the glen, where the murder is said to have taken place, which is the rock of the haunted church of Irish consciousness, so to speak, that nature most truly speaks its symbolic truths of sin and suffering, revealing a vast web of familial intrigue that mirrors the political intrigue of the country.

The first description of the natural scene, by emphasizing its unsocial atmosphere ("Neither bird, nor beast, was seen or heard, except rarely") and by placing it within the memory of the childhood of the narrator, highlights, through sheer juxtaposition, its place within the social fabric of the landscape, which is why the narrator remembers seeking the wider social world after viewing the dreary place:

> At all events the glen was said to be haunted by Sullivan's spirit, which was in the habit, according to report, of appearing near the place of murder, from when he was seen to enter this chasm—a circumstance which, when taken in connection with its dark and lonely aspect, was calculated to impress upon the place the reputation of being accursed, as the scene of crime and supernatural appearances. We remember having played in it when young, and the feeling we experienced was one of awe and terror, to which might be added, on contemplating the "dread repose" and solitude around us, an impression that we were removed hundreds of miles from the busy on-goings and noisy tumults of life, to which, as if seeking protection, we generally hasted with a strong sense of relief, after having tremblingly gratified our boyish curiosity.[20]

This encounter is as framed by notions of rebellious curiosity, both personal and political, as it was for Wordsworth. It also has important familial and social echoes.

Family, nation, and the blasted heath are particularly intertwined, or intertwined in a particular way, in Irish literature and history, starting from Burke's idea of the family as a "little platoon" or Goldsmith's of the family as a "little republic."[21] The family that the novel sets forth as one that represents Ireland wronged and righted is the Daltons, who suffer unjustly, both economically and physically, because of their wrongly accused father (and it is seen by all as their original sin and cause of their downfall).[22] They are redeemed through romantic love, as well as by a knowing agent of the Crown, one Mr. Travers (the bad former landlords, the Hendersons, are suitably dispatched). As noted, the father is supposed to have murdered one of the Sullivan family, whose daughter in turn is in love and loved by one of the Dalton sons. This love works to redeem the original sin, at least as far as the plot would have us believe. The family that truly represents the Irish nation, however, is that of the Black Prophet, whose daughter, it seems, no love can save and whose father is the very oracle of the famine itself. As Flanagan notes: "Carleton's imagination was most firmly engaged by the figure who gives the novel its title, [who] is the strongest link between the plot and the rich possibilities of the theme."[23] The father is driven to evil, to wrongly framing the Dalton father, among other heinous acts, because he has lost faith in the world, having suspected his wife of being unfaithful.

It turns out, in the end, that he is the murderer, having murdered his wife's brother (Bartle Sullivan survived, went to Boston, and returned just in time). That the murder occurs within the family makes it more darkly reflect Burke's "pedigrees of guilt"[24]—a pedigree that distinguishes the political reality of family life in Ireland, where informing, betrayal, or conversion to the enemy's faith or faction was too often the order of the day (the originally Catholic Carleton, for example, converted to Protestantism). The wife, it turns out, was unfaithful in spirit only; she loved another but never acted on her feelings. This latter truth is revealed to Sarah, the wild, beautiful, but good girl (she is a Glorvina of the famine, in other words) on her deathbed, whose suffering is only conventionally redeemed, but remains an unredeemable emblem of the Great Famine itself.

Julian Moynahan notes: "She is full of a self-mistrust and anger that come from growing up in an unloving household."[25] Carleton writes of her after her death:

> It is impossible to say to what a height of moral grandeur and true greatness, culture and education might have elevated her, or to say with what brilliancy her virtues might have shown, had her heart and affections been properly cultivated. Like some beautiful and luxuriant flower, however, she was permitted to run into wildness and disorder for want of a guiding hand; but no want, no absence of training, could ever destroy its natural delicacy, nor prevent its fragrance from smelling sweet, even in the neglected situation where it was left to pine and die.[26]

He might well be describing Ireland in his recitation of the relationship of landscape and nature, culture and wilderness. We may disregard Carleton's sentimentality at her death. Though Moynahan agrees with Carleton that "she redeems her humanity by sacrificing her life to save others," to the present critic this gesture seems only partially effective, as Sarah dies wild, without a stable sense of family and home. We may mitigate the force of Carleton's intentions here because colonial novels are often best read in the interstices between public consumption and private awareness; even Moynahan concludes of all the deaths: "It appears as if the very possibility of an Irish future is being liquidated."[27] We are told she has come to terms with her father and mother, but it is not believable, not even in terms of landscape or nature. The wilderness is represented by Sarah, while the pleasant place is represented by the reconstituted position of the Daltons. Sarah, in the end, is the most powerful of all because she embodies post-Newtonian ideas of nature's erupting energy.[28]

Like many of the famine victims, Sarah is left deserted in *The Black Prophet*, her family almost unrecognizable to her, her mother reduced to the word "mother" and her father reduced to grim stoicism in the face of his hanging. Here Margaret Kelleher's analysis of *The Black Prophet*, in her study *The Feminization of the Famine*, provides insight:

> With Carleton's novel a further aspect to the feminization of the famine is revealed. The characterization of famine mothers, through the associations of domesticity and natural instinct, together with

> the connotations of sin, even madness, allows the author to move the discourse on famine away from the political and economic spheres and into a moral register. The suggestion of "nature" being the special provenance of motherhood, both less and more than human, is particularly significant. As Warner and many other feminist critics have emphasized, the "conflation of nature and woman only continues the false perception that neither is inside culture, that women do not participate in it, let alone create it." The figure of woman can thus serve to restrain the challenges delivered earlier in the famine novel, through the "strange fold that changes culture into nature," politics into morality.[29]

Through Sarah, we find our better selves. If Sarah is not a conventional famine victim, because she does not die of starvation, she nevertheless dies of a disease born of famine. Even if her hunger is not physical, Sarah nevertheless dies hungry: hungry for the love of her mother (absent most of her life) and for the love of another (Condy Dalton, who loves Mave instead). As Maud Ellmann writes in *The Hunger Artists*, there is "something about hunger, or more specifically about the *spectacle* of hunger, that deranges the distinction between self and other." Even Sarah's self-sacrifice is the result of such a derangement. The moment of reflection on the self, which serves as a developmental model for such a haunting in Irish literature, is Gulliver looking into the mirror and seeing the Yahoo in himself; it is also his hunger to transcend this image. Sarah, in the end, is an image of famine; she rises from the gray stone, what Carleton calls the "stone of destiny,"[30] of the deserted houses of famine victims, a ghost of the unspeakable home of the Great Hunger.

4

Some Fragments Like a Hippogriff

William Allingham's *Laurence Bloomfield in Ireland* (1864)

Though *Laurence Bloomfield in Ireland* was published in the middle to latter part of the nineteenth century (originally published in 1864 and revised in 1890), it contains many of the manifest hopes for the salvation of the Union between Ireland and the United Kingdom that characterize the preceding half of the century. Allingham sensed that the world was changing and that Ireland was part of that change, yet he held on to the old imperial prejudices toward Ireland.[1] This contradictory movement in his thought reflects the historical tension between its writing and revision, that is, between the period following the Great Famine and the revision fewer than thirty years before the 1916 Easter Rising that would set in motion the move toward the War of Independence shortly after.

The plot of the long poem is a familiar one: a young idealistic, though somewhat aimless, absentee landlord, Laurence Bloomfield, returns to Ireland, having had his early fervent nationalism tempered by the glory of empire. Still sympathetic though condescending to the suffering of the "savage natives," he must decide what his role is in Ireland and whether to go or stay. His eventual transformation into the almost ideal landlord much beloved by his tenants is the result that in itself strains credulity, for, as Margot Backus notes, the "children of the Anglo-Irish were epistemologically disempowered by virtue of their cultural displacement."[2] The process toward idealized and culturally rooted landlord reveals the difficulties facing the prospect of its achievement. A stereotypical tenant family, the Dorans illustrate the conundrum of Irish history, which for so long eluded English attempts to find a solution. The modestly successful father works hard, though is constantly in fear of the caprices of his unjust rulers. The son, Neal, also works hard toward improving his family's lot. Seeing the historical injustice, however, he becomes increasingly radicalized and drawn to the rebellious Ribbonmen who have grown in their capacity to wreak havoc throughout the land. The eviction of a family with a mortally sick daughter and a fistfight at the fair between Neal and some rowdy tinkers combine to bring the conflict to a head. The cruel land agent Pigot is fired by Bloomfield, who restores the trust of his tenants. Later, through his wise judgment, sound managing of his estate, and model nonsectarian school, Bloomfield redeems Neal, and there is peace among his tenants at large, though this predicament is not representative of the relationship between the landlord class and their subjects as a whole, which ominously remains fraught. The allegory of union is central to the text, as the landscape is threatened by the natural world and by the Oedipal crisis that is about to erupt in the Doran household. The question remains at the end of the epic: Can Bloomfield prevent the violent eruptions of nature and rebellion?

All of it takes place against the background of the Ireland, its ruins, its mountain fastness, its uncultivated lands, that Bloomfield, in name and in deed, promises to make fruitful. Ribbonism is compared to "vagrant seeds" and "poison-weeds."[3] The landscape at the lough mirrors Neal's angry acceptance of rebellion. Later, Bloomfield's management transforms him and the landscape. The mountains, the ruins, the untilled fields combine to represent the dark forces of the wild Irish, of the Celtic temperament that Bloomfield and Allingham feel must be ruled by English reason.[4] Nature and culture, like Irishness and Englishness, stand as much in contrast as in unity. Their counterparts of folklore—myth and emotion (Irish) versus science, reason, and objective knowledge (English)—function similarly. In many texts before it, marriage represents the union of these opposites. The Augustan order of the rhyming couplets that compose this poem seems purposely wedded to the romantic views of the landscape and its ruins, in order to reflect how the work of an enlightened gentry is meant to redeem Irish history.[5] But form and content are at odds: if the rhyming couplets suggest Augustan order, the content reveals the ruins of a former culture (Gaelic Ireland) as well as the decay of the prevalent one (Ascendancy Ireland).

In the end, for all of its optimism, the long narrative poem allows for a much more pessimistic outcome, as though it foresaw, in its minor notes interspersed with its major chords, the end of the Union of Ireland and Britain and the failure of its imagined improvement. The dark, irrational forces of rebellious wilderness threaten Allingham's vision throughout the poem and at its conclusion, when Laurence's enlightened rule is countered by the mood cast by other more oppressive landlords. Those dark Oedipal forces lie in wait until the right moment arrives, as surely it did years later with rebellion and independence. When Pigot is assassinated, the unconscious forces of the text, like the unconscious of the nation, are on the verge of erupting. The darkness of the mountains descends after the fair and most probably will descend once again. The success of the young landlord and bride, and the blooming of his estate, family, and tenants, cannot be successful, considering the enmity and wilderness, both psychological and natural, that are arrayed against them.

The epic-like poem begins in book 1, "Laurence," with obvious echoes both in content and in form (rhyming couplets) of Goldsmith's *The Deserted Village*. The first lines give an idealized image of the land ("Autumnal sunshine spread on Irish hills / Imagination's bright'ning mirror fills") in the autumn sunlight, with the hero of the story presented as a returning absentee landlord quietly inquisitive about the state of his lands, meeting the curious tenants of his estate. The idealized image of Ireland is quickly undercut by the reality. We then move to an image of what life is like in Ireland, where the soil is rich but not cultivated, where animal and human cohabitate, where the landscape is denuded ("groveless"), where "wasteful acres" are "crowded thick / with docken, coltsfoot and hoary weed," where there is a "ruin'd cottage-wall" and the landscape is dotted with reminders of the folklore of the "savage natives."

Bloomfield is as yet "unaccustomed" to the poverty he witnesses: "Pigs, tatter'd children, pools at cabin doors"; he sees a land uncultivated, signs of the collapse of culture, and nature's eruptions all around. As stated previously, the return of the absentee landlord is a common theme in Anglo-Irish literature, from Morgan's *The Wild Irish Girl* through Edgeworth's *Castle Rackrent*, *Ennui*, and *The Absentee* to Allingham's own rendition.[6] Like the O'Shauglins who became the Rackrents, Bloomfield is both bound to the landscape and literally fed on the milk of Irishness. We also learn that now Bloomfield is an orphan. His family condition reflects his Anglo-Irish dislocation, but it also leaves him outside the Oedipal triangle and perhaps is one of the reasons he is not prepared for the Irish/English/Anglo-Irish family romance:

> At twelve years old his birthplace he had left,
> A child endow'd with much, of much bereft;
> Return'd a boy—a lad—the third time now
> Returns, a man, with broad and serious brow.
> A younger son (the better lot at first),
> And by a Keltic peasant fondly nurst,
> Bloomfield is Irish born and English bred,
> Surviving heir of both his parents dead.

He returns having been educated and having traveled the world, all experiences that make him like "some rich landscape," as Allingham concludes.

When W. B. Yeats was a child in England, he was teased for his Irish accent and connections. Similarly, we hear that Bloomfield was tested by his schoolmates for his devotion to the "emerald Inishfail (Isle of Destiny)."[7] "The Glories and the griefs of Erin filled [his] / Heart and imagination." In short, Laurence was a staunch nationalist:

> While thus he thunder'd, "'Tis for slaves alone
> To live without a country of their own!
> . . . .

> England, whose fraud and guilt have sunk us low.
> Speak, Irishmen, shall this be always so?"

He is therefore shipped back to England, where at Cambridge he witnesses the grandeur of imperial England and is convinced of its noble heritage, of which he believes Ireland should be part. We also discover that the narrator knows our hero at university and "could descry / Keen intellect and generous sympathy." He sees him in counter-Arnoldian fashion as the proper mix of Hibernian and Englishman. Having traveled the world, Bloomfield soon discovers a lack in himself (much like Lois in Bowen's *The Last September*). He has grown idle and has a "need in truth for work." Typical of many an absentee (Morgan's Horatio, Edgeworth's Lord Colambre of *The Absentee*, or Lord Glenthorne of *Ennui*), idleness is seen as a chief ill of the ruling class and a cause of their decadence and the subsequent disorder of Ireland. His English friends in London warn him of the "savage natives, high and low. Not unamusing for a month or so." They tell him to "take care / And don't get shot . . . or married." The fear of marriage again is linked to the savagery of the Irish and of his going native and becoming more Irish than the Irish themselves.

Arriving again in Ireland, he finds in book 2, "Neighbouring Landlords," that his own class is hoping he will be a steadfast member of the Orange order and "fight the county with a fierce Green Man." Bloomfield, however, is quietly assessing the scene, and we are therefore given a survey of the ruling class in his area. Sir Ulick, Laurence's uncle, is led by Pigot, who turns out to be the cruel land agent of the story, the Captain Boycott of the poem. As a result, he lives in splendor off the labor of his tenantry. The very landscape reflects the cruel order:

> Shut out from view a thousand vulgar fields,
> Whose foison grandeur to Sir Ulick yields,
> With many a roof of thatch, where daily toil
> Extorts the bread of man from earth's dull soil.

Ulick's motto is *Meis ut placet utens*: "Doing what I like with my own." Sir Ulick "loves to seem to reign." Bloomfield is disgusted and concludes: "A kind, just man would make the poor his friends." Sir Ulick, on the other hand, is like one of Swift's projectors, always experimenting on his lands and thereby laying them waste. The next landlord is Lord Ashton, the epitome of the reprobate aristocrat, straight out of *Castle Rackrent* and a type reappearing in O'Faoláin's "Midsummer Night Madness" in the figure of Henn. Then there are cheap and joyless Fingal, prince of Glenawn, and the shabby yet genteel Dysart, who also is a rackrenter, though he is dear to the "Keltic" mind because of his kindliness and disposition. He is dissolute but takes care to help his illegitimate brood of children. The only landlord who might inspire Bloomfield is flinty Isaac Brown, a "man elect, Wesleyan stout," for at least he runs his estates well.

Finally, there is "The O'Hara," of "princely Irish race." Like Glorvina's father, he is a remnant of the Gaelic order who is no longer able to run his estate, bound as he is to ancient wrongs ("Hates England's name") and to Catholicism's rigid religion (he helps both church and convent). Having lost his sons and made his daughters nuns, the destruction of his rule is assured. He remains "learned in forgotten troubles. . . . Proud, dyspeptic, taciturn and shy." "Secluded from the troublous world," he will be impotent to change it. The O'Hara, Glorvina's father, and Count O'Halloran in Edgeworth's *The Absentee* are some of the most interesting figures in Irish history and fiction. They are like the harpists who met in Belfast in 1792 for the Harpist Festival and whose music was transcribed by Edward Bunting (which in turn provided the music that inspired Moore's *Irish Melodies*). They are fragments of a dispossessed culture, figures of imaginative powers fading from the world. They embody the elegiac note of the mythical Celtic world that made the Celtic periphery so important to the romantic imagination, even in some ways to the ecological movement itself, standing as images of a prelapsarian wholeness with nature, which colonization had ruptured. In this light, "The O'Hara's" connection with Catholicism introduces the Celtic fluid sense of nature that resurfaces in the work of Seamus Heaney.

In keeping with this elegiac note, the second book ends with an image of autumn's harvest. It is an image that is more Death and his sickle than Ceres and her bounty, reflecting both ill-managed land and civil unrest.

> It should have been a peaceful, grateful time;
> But o'er this landscape enmity and crime
> Like shadow lay. The harvesting is done;
> The shadow stays, in spite of moon or sun.

Book 3, "A Dinner at Lisnamoy House," takes place at the home of Sir Ulick. Action will need to be taken. Talk quickly turns to how to control the natives and to priests, of whom Nassau Blunderbore (living up to his name) states: "All papists are but rebels in disguise." They discuss Ribbonism, and a story is told that reminds us of William Carleton's "Wildgoose Lodge" and the vengeance that secret societies with violent aims can inflict upon the population. Importantly, we find out that Pigot has been threatened by Captain Starlit of the Ribbonmen. Bloomfield is unsure of what to say, having had his nationalist tendencies muted, but he does insist to the vicar that wealth has its noble prerogatives, to which the vicar pessimistically replies that "philanthropic dreams / Are fine—but human nature mars our schemes!" "Nature" is the operative word, pointing, as it does, from the inner character to the maintenance of the land.

Neither set of clergymen makes out too well in the story, as they are described as adverse to conflict. This want contributes to the lack of authority that Bloomfield, the absentee, represents and is made worse by the other irresponsible and cruel landlords. Pigot, meanwhile, insists only on the rights of property. As he rides, Bloomfield feels the irrational welling around him in the

> . . . latticed moonshine . . .
> Like films of sorcery or sacred rite
> Of sprinkling by the holy priestess, Night.

Bloomfield knows something of what the other landlords say is wrong, but having known the "pain of too much freedom," he "doubt[s] his own judgment." He leaves the dinner party and rides through a landscape now harboring imagined as well as real dangers after all the talk of insurrection:

> Our young Squire heard not, or unheeding heard,
> One whispering bough that stealthily was stirr'd;
> Saw not the glitter of an ambush'd eye
> That glared upon the landlord moving by.

This experience makes him fear ambush and think of flight. In short, he does not know whether to leave or stay in Ireland. Finally, as the book ends, he must face the "crime," whether it is the crime of insurrection, of misrule, of colonization, or his own flawed personality. In this confrontation with crime, or original sin, he is like many a fictional young absentee landlord before him.[8]

Book 4, "The Dorans," takes place in the cottage of the representative Irish family of the story. We see how the Dorans must work the unyielding land to earn their keep, how their young daughter, Bridget, is symbolic of the Irish woman: beautiful but a bit too much as nature left her. We see how the father, Jack, has been worn down by his work, how the son, Neal, being intelligent and quick, is prey to subversion by the Ribbonmen. The school they frequent is vexed by Sir Ulick. They are a simple people, though perhaps misled by Catholicism and their own tendency toward folk beliefs. Allingham in this regard is both sympathetic and prejudiced. They are constantly under the threat of forces of the state, whether it be bailiffs or the landlord class. They are always on the edge of economic ruin and so fear any change that might leave them vulnerable. Though Neal wants to improve the house, and has to some degree, his father is worried that the rent will be raised as a result. This oppression drives rebellion. During the time of the Land League, radical violence threatens to engulf them (Neal especially). In the way of stories written for the English, Allingham has the peasantry turn their hopes toward Bloomfield (again, his name bears the promise of his return).

The next book, "Ballytullagh," describes the hamlet and tells the tale of the Dorans in terms of the larger community, which is still haunted by the famine. We have an "ancient woman" that is reminiscent of Goldsmith's "wretched matron . . . sad historian of the pensive plain,"[9] and of course the Shan Van Vocht. The book is concerned with showing how Ribbonism feeds off landlordism and vice versa. The focus shifts toward the Catholic clergy and how they in turn depend on the status quo for their power. Neal is described as saddened by the political turmoil, and, like Bloomfield, his view of the landscape reflects his emotions and deepens his dismay:

> And far from north to south a roof of rain
> Hangs heavily this morning; dark and dead
> The dismal view, and Neal's own heart like lead.

That it surrounds Bloomfield's "long-untenanted abode" makes clear how interwoven the stories of Neal and Laurence are. The book ends with a sermon against Ribbonism. The congregation is not completely moved, but the people are frightened. They know the "clergy have their game to play." Confronted by the social and political divisions, the book ends on a note of transcendent love ("Love / Is monarch, earthly kings how far above") that will be confirmed by the author's intentions and tested by what happens throughout the rest of the long poem.

The next book, "Neal at the Lough," illustrates the difficulty of making that wish come true, especially given the prevailing political winds. There is also a generational split. If the younger Anglo-Irish generation is more sympathetic to Gladstone's lenient policies than the entrenched older generation (as we saw in book 5), then the younger generation of the Irish peasantry has been radicalized in a way that frightens the older generation. We learn that old Jack is very cautions, while his son, Neal, is rash because he is moved by "Old Ireland's glories, and her wrongs, / Her famous dead, her landscapes, and her songs." The book is a Wordsworthian meditation on history and landscape, during which Neal's conscience is shaped and challenged. First, he is riled by lessons of the 1798 rebellion, which is reflected in the metaphors of flood and fire. Neal is then pictured in a sublime landscape (a "purple mountain-top . . . majestically simple and serene / Like some great soul above the various crowd") during a moment that will give him thoughts "abstracted heavenward." He then goes fishing in a scene that is heavily indebted to Wordsworth's *The Prelude*, when the poet remembers stealing a boat as a boy and being confronted by the fatherly voice of conscience. For Neal, stealing is not the issue (he does not steal). What bothers him is the prick of conscience he still suffers for having disagreed with his father. As in *The Prelude*, there is a link between an Oedipal confrontation, an encounter with death, and with the ruins of history that for Neal leads to further thoughts of history, beginning with the Round Tower: the Round Tower recalls the precolonial idyll of "the Isle of Saints and Scholars." Neal then thinks of the myths and peoples of ancient Ireland, the stories of Saint Patrick, Bridget, and Columkill and of their learning, famed throughout Europe. For a modern reader, the phallic significance of the Round Tower after the disagreement with the father is perhaps too obvious, but its connection to childhood as well as to precolonial Ireland is significant, and the sexual meaning, however unconscious, underlines the Oedipal nature of Neal's rebellion.

The historical references come in a flurry: the Viking invasions, the Norman entrance, and the traitorous Dermot MacMurrough ("be thy name accurst") are described next. The Elizabethan conquests follow and then the "Curse of Cromwell." William of Orange defeats James ("sneaking Shamus" [49]) and establishes the Protestant Ascendancy and the Penal Laws. Neal then faces the crime of Ireland's history, its bitter fruits, and the pall it casts over the landscape. It will make Neal amenable to the rebellion, which he confronts in the form of the Ribbonman Tim Nulty. Like a good stage Irishman, Nulty speaks in a strong brogue and has "merry-twinkling eyes." Neal then takes the oath, having been prepared by his sojourn on the lough. Meanwhile, Laurence confronts the bigotry of his uncle Ulick and the latter's support for Pigot's view that the native Irish are the foe. The reign of love, which was heralded at the end of the previous book, now seems to have no earthly rule.

In book 7, "Tenants at Will," the circumstances merely worsen. Any hope of unity in the figure of Oona meets the misfortune of the

Muldoons' eviction. The image of eviction is a scene of violated family and female sorrow:

> And soon from house to house is heard the cry
> Of female sorrow, swelling loud and high,
> Which makes men blaspheme between their teeth.

The eviction leads to a malediction against Pigot. Allingham's narrative begins to flow torrentially. We then read of Ballytullagh's destruction and of how the Muldoons go to their cousins, the Doran (Neal's family) house. There later in the next book, Rose Muldoon (ill before the encounter) dies in Bridget's arms, while a meeting of Ribbonmen and the decision to punish Pigot goes on in hideous detail. The only intercession on the ruler's part is the sarcastic "Ireland, forsooth, 'a nation once again!' / If Ireland was a nation, tell me when?" This declaration leads to a dismissal of Irish history as well as the Red Indians' and the Bushmen's. Colonial rule is all that is left. Though the book ends ominously with a meeting of the Ribbonmen, there is hope in the joyousness of a dance. Culture counters politics in a display of what Deane calls "the pathology of literary unionism," but it is an important display for the place of the aesthetic as well.[10] It is not merely a political escape; it is also a psychological one, in a counterbalance typical of the poem.

Book 8, "A Ribbon Lodge," depicts the Irish rebels as simians who "grunt a welcome," live with animals, are drunk, and laugh with derision and murderous intent. The childishness of the Dorans meets its opposite in prime stage-Irish fashion. The Irish are childlike in peace, but animallike in rebellion. Their ties to the land, their naturalness, as we saw in *The Wild Irish Girl*, are in constantly shifting descriptions, much like nature itself, which is either innocent or red in tooth and claw. Allingham insists that there are rational reasons (like the famine) for their rebelliousness, but the author isn't quite able to give them the rational capacity for understanding and for governing in a coherent political fashion. He is still depending on English rule to accomplish this—or at least Irish Protestant rule—and so the appeal to an escapist logic will haunt the text to its end.

In book 9, "The Fair," we are given a vision of the community: its innocence and potential for prosperity, on the one hand, and its penchant for drunkenness and violence, on the other. Bridget and her beau, the hardworking, abstinent Denis, represent the former, the tinkers the latter. Lisnamoy is described as "an ugly town" redeemed only by its rural surroundings and the beauty of Bridget, who *aisling*-like, represents the "country maidens" with "shapely limbs." The rival churches seem to represent the political factions at work, while the language spoken, the accents from all over Ireland, and the fact that in this trading fair "now mingle Sassenach and Gaelic tongue" give one hope for an eventual hybrid nation where all shall be one. Such hopes are quickly dashed by the tinkers, and the stage is set for conflict as Neal enters the scene. His psychology is bound to an image of changing weather and the land, while being riled by drink and his recent oath to the rebellious cause Neal is vulnerable to his fraught emotional state. A fight between Neal, his "partisans," and the "tinkers" ensues, and a

> Wider conflict rages: fierce the din,
> Loud the men's oaths, and sharp the women's screams;
> The general fair to this mad whirlpool streams.

Pigot is called to the fair, and his intransigence only heightens the mayhem until

> . . . anxious good-wives draw
> Their lingering husbands homeward; dance and song
> Grow wilder, and more bacchanal each throng
> In every street and tavern of the town;
> With darkness from the mountains creeping down.

The book ends on this ominous note of wilderness descending on the town and nature and rebellion erupting. One is sure that the belief in progress and in Bloomfield in particular will be brought to bear in the next book, "Pigot." As justice of the peace, Bloomfield "has not used his power," but now he will be forced to. At first he lets Pigot go alone, but when confronted by the fainting figure of Jack Doran, who has been evicted because of Neal's connection to the Ribbonmen, Bloomfield decides to step in, which pushes Pigot to resign (a resignation Bloomfield quickly accepts). The community of his tenants is moved by his goodwill, and it moves Bloomfield to burn the list of Ribbonmen. The wishfulness of this thinking, written during the land agitation, is apparent in these lines: "If Bloomfield were an angel from the skies / They could not hunger more with ears and eyes." There is an extended discussion of Pigot, how his wife wanted him to leave his work as agent, how Pigot was driven by habit to continue, and how his wife, "a fading woman," felt neglected by this unrefined, practical man who lacked all aesthetic sense. This description prepares our sympathy for him in the light of his future assassination, which is partly his fault, as Allingham attests, though he might have lived a blameless life elsewhere, as Allingham apologetically concludes.

The concluding books seem less historical than imagined. Book 11, "Lord and Lady," uses the image of marriage and the allegory of union as its overarching themes. Laurence Bloomfield becomes a stock character who cures his tenants of drinking; who roots out Ribbonism from his area, having convinced Neal to renounce them; and who starts a nonsectarian "model" school. We begin with a reference to Martin Doyle, a writer of the literature of improvement. Allingham realizes that he is writing a directive rather than describing a turn of events. The racial stereotyping is pronounced: "The Kelt [is] rash and wild, / Quick, changeful and impulsive as a child." It harks back to Arnold's mid-nineteenth-century version of the Celtic character. Bloomfield's fulfillment of his name is represented by his husbandry of the land. The description of Laurence's husbandry of the land recalls Swift's Lord Munodi, but without the trenchant, tragic-satirical bite, which in Swift exposes misrule as well as implies proper rule. This musing on the relationship between nature and culture, rich with Anglo-Saxon ethnography[11] and the role of empire from Ireland to India, goes on for a page and a half, ending with a lengthy vision of Irish history that Laurence Bloomfield has linked together and that shows how folk culture and conquest make music together, as long as one epistemology (myth) is guided by another (science or empirical knowledge).

Laurence lives in the eminence, the heights of "*Croghan*" (meaning heights; my emphasis) Hall with his wife, Jane, who cuts a figure of the idealized feminine, especially when compared with Bridget and Mrs. Pigot, who are both neglected in their separate ways (Bridget left too natural, Mrs. Pigot left alone). Like the properly husbanded land, Jane combines spirit and sense in perfect balance,

> Of soul and body nobly feminine.
> Instinctive wisdom, humour swift and gay,
> A simple greatness.

After such an idealization, the flaws in this reasoning perforce begin to show. Neal, for one, remains the uncanny at the heart of this sublime vision of Irish unity, for "he's the same, and not the same." By that description, Allingham means Neal is still Neal, but his rebellious ways have been removed, much as the weeds have been cleared from the land. Rebellion has been incorporated into the state of Bloomfield's affairs, but the text admits that all is not well. Other landlords remain opposed to Laurence's rule. His uncle Sir Ulick is the most important exception, as he is family and being family shows how unstable this rule is, depending on the individual landlord as it does. Even though Lisnamoy has changed for the better, as every traveler sees, it strikes this reader as ironic (if typical a usage in reality) that the new pub is called the Bloomfield Arms. Landscape and militarism are still joined. After a long passage on the need for nonsectarian education, the book ends in a dance, which in its happiness contrasts with the violent fair of before.

The final book, book 12, "Midsummer," continues with its vision of just rule and the happy society that results. As the long poem began in autumn, it ends at the height of summer, with all of the fulfillment such a season conveys. Landlords discuss the union between Ireland and England, with Laurence arguing for greater autonomy for Ireland and his counterparts insisting that "I would that Irishmen could Ireland rule. / They cannot, Irishmen are still at school." He does admit, however, that England, their "master," remains "unbeloved." This tension will be revealed in the contrasting visions of the landscape this book provides, which is central to the epic poem as a whole. They suggest the strained relationship between Christian and pagan, England and Ireland, premodern and modern, reason and emotion, order and chaos, nature and culture, science and myth; the list goes on. The opening paean of the book contains all the hope for the future that Allingham can deliver. "Rich are the warm, long, lustrous, golden hours, / That nourish the green javelins of the wheat." Here is a vision of the beautiful, of a harmonious relationship between nature and culture. We soon hear that there is no political intrigue under Bloomfield. He has broken up the Ribbonmen, using Neal as a vehicle. We learn that Neal has learned Protestant industry, after we have been given a number of very pagan anti-Catholic versions of religion in Ireland. The "poison-weeds" of Ribbonism have been uprooted and with them all morbid signs of social schism. Denis and Bridget have gotten married. Laurence and Jane have had children. He has transformed a "dreary wilderness" into a blooming field (to match his last name a little too conveniently). Nature and Ireland have been husbanded, but the military allusions do not bode well:

> A regiment of young trees stood well in rank
> To guard from swooping gale on open flank,
> And here and there with due entrenchment round,
> Green larches held the rugged bits of ground.

If not definitive of much more than the literary figures of the era, this figure of speech captures the ambivalence of the text between protection and subdual.

Though there are still bad landlords at work, the one Catholic Gaelic landlord, "The O'Hara," dies in Rome, leaving a "large bequest" to establish a nunnery and a college, "when convenient: squeezing dry / The lands and tenants meanwhile." Catholic rule is decadent and beholden to the pontiff. Bloomfield stands as a lonely exception between extremes; however, the last meaningful image of nature harbors fragments of the monstrous and mythic qualities that his moral stature is meant to subdue:

> . . . now, bright sunshine broods upon the world,
> With silence; save the boom of bee uncurl'd
> From bed of thyme; or when a marvellous thing,
> Horns, beard, and yellow eyes, with sudden spring
> Cresting some fragment like a hippogriff,
> Is gone, its goat-bleat echoing from the cliff.

It is meant to be a transcendent image reflecting the good work of Laurence and Jane, but "Sultan Serpent" nature threatens to erupt and undo all they have accomplished. Although "the landscape here is noble," Laurence says, it is not without its subversive qualities. The hippogriff, head of an eagle and body of horse, child of the griffin, which itself has a lion body and an eagle head, is suggested by the fleeting vision of a goat, "horns, beard, and yellow eyes." The goat in turn recalls the "natural" man. And so the naturalness of the wild Irish comes to the surface once again. Nature overturning culture—Oedipus convicted of his unknowing crimes. Laurence himself has doubts about his project, which only after a pregnant pause Jane tries to erase:

> "This mild green country in the western sea,
> With guardian mountains, rivers full and free,
> Home of a brave, rich-brain'd, warm-hearted race,—
> This Ireland should have been a noble place."
>
> "It will be," Jane replied.

Though history has run contrary to Jane's assurance since the book was written, at least in terms of English rule, the unachievable nature of such projected rule has already been admitted in the text. Its "joy" eludes us for we only glimpse it "as when a dead man wakes alive // In some new happy world." Such a glimpse of Judeo-Christian paradise, however, is not to be dismissed too readily. As Justin Quinn wistfully notes: "The social realism of *Laurence Bloomfield in Ireland*—balanced, sympathetic, at times humorous and acerbic—remained a resource untapped by Irish poets in the decades to come. They had other business to conduct."[12]

❧ ❧ ❧

In the mind of W. B. Yeats, the literature of the nineteenth century, the quiet century, was impeded by history, particularly the Act of Union and the Great Famine. It wasn't until the age of Parnell and the Land League that anything like a national literature began to appear, with Yeats himself at the forefront. Yeats believed that the genius of the century was the conflicted William Carleton (Irish-speaking would-be priest and Protestant convert).[13] Yeats regarded *Laurence Bloomfield* as a "failed epic," but he admired Allingham's poems for children ("The Fairies" in particular, which he anthologized).[14] Yeats felt indebted to James Clarence Mangan and Samuel Ferguson, though he wrote that his "rhymes more than their rhyming tell / Of things discovered in the deep" ("To Ireland in the Coming Times"). Much of his early interest in writers of this period, including those above, is owing to their use of folklore and myth. For the older Yeats, Bishop Berkeley (1698–1753) provides philosophical, Edmund Burke (1729–97) political, Jonathan Swift (1667–1745) social and personal, and Oliver Goldsmith (1728–74) poetic paradigms for social and political order. Together, they form the foundation of Yeats's landscape. He would use them as stepping-stones, but his use also illustrates the overarching theme of this book.

Donald Torchiana notes how Berkeley's belief "coincides with that Irish belief that finds divinity and spirituality, even heaven itself, in natural things." He proceeds to explain the relevance to Yeats: "This may also be why Yeats frequently places the Irish natural world against the world conceived, as it seemed to him, by English materialism. Rural Ireland, not cut off from the flow of tree, leaf, and rock by any rigid urban geometry, adhered to the total world, not its slim abstract remnant conceived by mechanical philosophers."[15] One imagines that Yeats was also moved by Burke's endeavors to maintain social order in such a passage as the following:

> If, however, you could find out these pedigrees of guilt, I do not think the difference would be essential. What lesson does the iniquity of prevalent factions read to us? . . . They ought not to call from the dead all the discussions and litigations which formerly inflamed the furious factions, which had torn their country to pieces; they ought not to rake into the hideous and abominable things, which were done in the turbulent fury of an injured, robbed, and persecuted people, and which were afterwards cruelly revenged in the execution, and as outrageously and shamefully exaggerated in the representation, in order, a hundred and fifty years after, to find some colour for justifying them in the eternal proscription and civil excommunication of a whole people.[16]

This passage could almost act as a prologue to the "furious factions" of Yeats's "Meditations in Time of Civil War." Such "pedigrees of guilt" inform much of Yeats's late thought. His Swiftian and Oedipal play *Purgatory* (1939) begins with the imperative "study that house," placing it firmly in the landscape tradition of the "Big House," and ends with the imperative "study that tree," making it clear that nature in the guise of the tree contains the only hope of absolution. The tree stands "there like a purified soul," and the old man does not; his "cruelty and deceit" are not "expiated in primary suffering and submission."[17] In short, Christ does not answer Oedipus. The old man hopes that when he has "stuck" his "old jack-knife into a sod / And pulled it bright again," he will be free.[18] All of it in a play where the old man, who has killed his father, is seen killing the son, in hope of stopping the tragedy of birth and the family romance from happening again. The old man is hoping that nature in the guise of sod with which he cleans the knife will cure him of guilt, but, without surrender and submission, without an anguished recognition of the Fall, it cannot. The barren landscape of the play and the eternal return of the crime betoken the collapse of the family and the recurrence of the Oedipal crises that mark Irish history. To familiarize himself with his own kind, Gulliver (like Swift and Yeats) must confront his disgust on a deeply uncanny level—disgust at procreation with his wife and disgust with nature. He must learn to lash the vice, but spare the name if he is not to be like the old man in *Purgatory* who in his sexual disgust kills both his father and his son.[19] The destruction of family leads to the disruption of the social order as Yeats conceives of them in his socially minded work of the 1920s and '30s.

The poems of social disruption "Meditations in Time of Civil War" and "Nineteen Hundred and Nineteen" when juxtaposed with the two "Coole Park" poems of cultural unity formulate a social theory. They are companion poems, just as *The Tower* and *The Winding Stair* are complementary volumes. The four poems seem beholden to eighteenth-century ideas, particularly those beliefs of Swift, Berkeley, Goldsmith, and Burke in ways that the sequence "Blood and the Moon" makes explicit. All these poems share the same meditative space: the tower and the winding stair. They are symbols of family and nation centered in a landscape, the West of Ireland, which had become synonymous with hidden and authentic Ireland from the eighteenth century on, but also with an Ireland defiled and full of the romantic ruins of its conquest.[20]

In "Meditations," Yeats questions whether the violence and bitterness of the ruling class were necessary for the conditions that gave birth to the grand order of the rich and to the poetic world it sheltered. The landscape surrounding the tower in which Yeats writes is harsh and unforgiving. The imagined rich man's house must subdue that landscape, just as in Berkeleyean fashion Yeats's poetic imagination has done. Throughout the poem, Yeats is configuring a reality based on Burke's ideas of society. The sixth part is a Burkean appeal for a return to social order, while in a countermood "Nineteen Hundred and Nineteen" records a descent into nightmare. Society is being degraded, much as Swift was "dragged . . . down into mankind" in "Blood and the Moon." The failure at the end of "Meditations" is a failure of the erotic impulse of family to create orderly and aesthetically sensitive societies, a failure that in Yeats's mind leads to civil war. Rather than bodies full "of their own loveliness," there is an "embrace of nothing." Like Gulliver, Irish society is staring into the glass, trying to recognize self, family, nation, or even the human species. The landscape has lost its transformative powers. We are cast into the wilderness at the end of *The Deserted Village* where, as in "Nineteen Hundred and Nineteen," betrayal is the dominant mood.

Yeats's Coole Park poems, "Coole Park" (1929) and "Coole and Ballylee" (1931), on the other hand, are monuments to Lady Gregory's ability to run an estate, or demesne, that maintains the social as well as aesthetic balance in a way that *The Vicar of Wakefield* does. Gregory's maternal authority is the "hidden pole"[21] of the Unity of Being and Culture. As the confluence of feminine beauty and masculine sublimity, and as the exception to Burke's rule of sublime authority and feminine partiality having specifically and solely masculine and feminine attributes, she is able to achieve an extraordinary wedding of power and wisdom.[22] In "Coole and Ballylee," Yeats meditates on how he can continue to embody the experience of the Unity of Being and Culture that he had known at Coole Park. From the embattled position of the tower, he bears witness to the signs of division as dark, barbaric forces reassert themselves. He is aware of the connection between the divisive force of the tower and the unifying force of Coole Park and realizes that the tension between them is what bears fruit; it is the space in which flows the "generated soul."

The force inside the dark womb, the antithetical psychic power of eighteenth-century Irish poet Raftery's cellar seeks to rise to Coole Park's unity in a marriage of Gaelic and Anglo-Irish Ireland. Yeats's tone is tragic, however, as the effort in this age is increasingly difficult. "Nature's pulled her tragic buskin on." The implication is that Burkean ceremony and tradition, wherein "every bride's ambition [is] satisfied," might also protect the tenuous powers of reconciliation, the soulfulness that can set "to right" what knowledge, or ignorance, had "set awry."[23] Though the soul can achieve a great deal as it climbs the winding stair (symbol of the soul's ascension), it must be protected, and Yeats, like Burke, believes that only tradition, ceremony, and custom can do so. The destructive force of the darkening flood threatens this belief, much as the terrifying force of a flood first gave Burke the sublime subject for his *Enquiry*.[24] At such moments of inhuman intrusion, or nature's eruptions, we can see why the tragic satire and ruined, savage landscapes of Jonathan Swift inspired Yeats, why the apocalyptic eloquent despair of Burke and the gentle nostalgia of Goldsmith moved him. The lesson Yeats draws is that an inhuman force is shaping history in ways the finite human mind cannot comprehend.

5

A Sterner Eye

W. B. Yeats, Nature, and the Inhuman and Nonhuman

❧ For Yeats, one suspects, prior literary uses have corrupted the word "landscape." The word does not appear in his poems, though the concept is implicit in the constituent images (trees, leaves, grass, skies, hills, shore) that are abundant. Animals are also plentiful and varied: there are hounds, birds, foxes, and fish, among other gentle and rough beasts throughout his oeuvre. The emphasis is more on animals than on nature itself, which appears only relatively few times and often either as in someone's "nature" or else as an unstable philosophical category. One of the main reasons for their frequent occurrence is that Yeats invests animals with supernatural as well as natural forces. Like the shepherds who tend the domesticated animals of Yeats's pastoral, animals are more in touch with what the poet calls supersensible rhythms, that is, they are more instinctual and therefore closer to God, to the divine.

For Yeats, however, this relationship is complicated, as God and nature are at times opposed and at times one and the same. Therefore, nature functions as a hinge between the immanent and transcendent worlds, while animals act as a natural vehicle for supernatural forces. In fact, Yeats's use of the word "nature" often swings on the distinction between the natural and supernatural (for example, "Plato thought nature but a spume that plays / Upon a ghostly paradigm of things," from "Among School Children," or "Once out of nature I shall never take / My bodily form from any natural thing," from "Sailing to Byzantium"). The more contemporary term "inhuman," often used for animals and the divine, provides a helpful lens. Rather than split the term between the two aspects, "inhuman" has been reserved for the divine, and "nonhuman" has been used to designate the animal kingdom. This explanation will serve to understand how Yeats combines the two in the "strange heart" of the swan/Zeus in "Leda and the Swan" or the Dove/Holy Ghost that is the "three-fold terror of love" in "The Mother of God." These poems are central to Yeats's idea of how the advent of the Godhead influences human history. They also illustrate what links the divine, the instinctual world of animals, and the unconscious. At times, it will be necessary to veer more toward discussions of the inhuman, leaving the human, the nonhuman, and the natural world behind, in order to understand how and why Yeats believed that "we are lost amid alien intellects."[1]

The arc of the discussion provides a number of perspectives: the religious/mythical (Christian and pagan), the psychoanalytical (desire and the unconscious), the aesthetic (the beautiful and the sublime), and the historical (violence in the formation of culture). It will attempt to record how W. B. Yeats's poetry throughout his career involves the question of the inhuman entry into human consciousness as well as into history. One of the main oppositions is the relationship between the immanent and the transcendent, a lifelong concern of Yeats's, whose handling of this theme is a potent reminder, in an age in which material culture is of paramount concern, of how we are by "that inhuman / Bitter glory wrecked" ("The Results of Thought"). The inhuman speaks both of poetic revelation and of inspiration. It brings together the various themes of this book. It is unique in its conjuring of Yeatsian images and themes and so remains at the heart of the critical enterprise.[2] At the center of this discussion lies the relationship between nature and culture, pagan and Christian, Oedipus and Christ.

For Yeats, the inhuman is also inextricable from the problem of representing, apprehending, and engaging suffering in its alterity and its constitutive basis of subjectivity. We need to register that moment when the inhuman Other meets the human self, but must also admit that the defeat of the human is what defines both sides of the encounter.[3] That very suffering is probably the greatest indicator of the force of the inhuman, as we see in Yeats's pagan and Christian advent poems. There are a number of avenues to this conclusion. The one through Yeats's work will be made clear, but it begins with Adorno's idea of the inhuman, one that has also been influential for this book. At the beginning of Jean-François Lyotard's book *The Inhuman: Reflections on Time*, the author quotes Adorno engaging in a paradox typical of the Frankfurt school: "Art remains loyal to humankind uniquely through its inhumanity in regard to it." Adorno provides an avenue of understanding in *Aesthetic Theory* that seems like a working definition of at least one aspect of the inhuman and the suffering it causes: "Suffering remains foreign to knowledge; though knowledge can subordinate it conceptually and provide means for its amelioration, knowledge can scarcely express it through its own means of experience without itself becoming irrational."[4] It is only through our finiteness that we sense the breadth of the infinite or see visible proof of the invisible ("the wind blow[ing] where it listeth" [John 3:8]).

For Yeats, myth and religion often connote the inhuman, the transcendent, the supernatural, while history, science, and biography denote the human, the immanent, the natural, though of course in any idea of advent or incarnation there is a certain amount of interaction. Following Berkeley's idealism, Yeats believed that the scientific dispensation would not last and that the eruption of nature would prove its end, as Yeats in *Explorations* makes clear. He believed that science, conceived in the seventeenth and debated in the eighteenth centuries, now understood this. Yeats observes: "Yet it may be that our science, our modern philosophy, keep a subconscious knowledge that their raft, roped together at the end of the seventeenth century, must . . . part and abandon us to the storm . . . that all it can do is, after a steady scrutiny, to prove the poverty of the human intellect, that we are lost amid alien intellects, near but incomprehensible, more incomprehensible than the most distant stars." That alien, inhuman intellect is connected to the uncanny, Oedipal encounter with nature, whether subconscious or external. It is those "monstrous, familiar images [that] swim to the mind's eye."[5]

"Every kind of humanism," Roberto Calasso writes (and quite likely Yeats would agree), "is unsuited to grasp the divine, precisely because of its bias in favour of the human." In *Tiepolo Pink*, Calasso argues that we have failed to understand the eighteenth-century Venetian painter Giambattista Tiepolo because we have not taken the mythological dimension of his painting seriously enough, and with the mythological comes animal and human imagery combined. "Who exactly are these strange effete young men, these bare-breasted women with untidy hair lounging in desolate landscapes, with smirking skeletons and grave Oriental figures and babies with cloven hooves, female as well as male satyrs, and these quizzical animals—horses, monkeys, goats, sheep, owls, but above all snakes? There are snakes everywhere, wriggling in the dust, twining themselves round sticks, writhing on mysterious slabs of stone which you expect to be inscribed but often are not. What are they all gazing at? What, or who are they waiting for?"[6]

For Calasso, the *Scherzi di Fantasia* (a series of etchings by the Venetian artist) plunge us back into the world of Chaldean magic, whose soothsaying mysteries had fascinated the humanists of the Italian Renaissance, much as Yeats's early symbolism and early interest in magic plunges into the Chaldean world.[7] Those impassive Orientals, always there, like Yeats's Magi, always watching, are the last representatives of genuine spiritual power, a power that, as Yeats believes, has always come from the East. The blurring of the line between East and West, animal and human, and natural and supernatural is an important one. Yeats, too, following myth, makes his swans emblems of a divine inhuman force, makes his eagles symbols of an inhuman perspective, his dolphins and birds figures of transmigration. He has his own divine bestiary, "human, superhuman, a bird's round eye" ("A Bronze Head") and a vision of the afterlife that could be straight out of Calasso's evocation of Tiepolo, where natural and supernatural, human, nonhuman, and inhuman richly commingle:

From where Pan's cavern is
Intolerable music falls.
Foul goat-head, brutal arm appear,
Belly, shoulder, bum,
Flash fishlike: nymphs and satyrs
Copulate in the foam. ("News for the Delphic Oracle")

To Yeats, an inhuman force underlies all human endeavor and makes us puppets of its will, forces us to act as if, to paraphrase his poem "A Bronze Head," "a sterner eye looked through [our] eye." Yeats's version of the inhuman is recognizably divine and threatening. It is also a version of otherness, both ancient and modern, that challenges identity. It is God as Augustine might have described him, and also unconscious desire (or Thing) in a way that is quite consistent with Lyotard's definition of the inhuman.[8] At the start of the second of two technologically driven, inhuman, and sublimely destructive world wars, such a blending defines Yeats's apocalyptic "rough beast," that is, both transcendent force and immanent unconscious instinct. Sometimes, as in "Leda and the Swan," it can be both at the same time, that is, we discover the transcendent in the immanent, the immanent in the transcendent, as Leda discovers the strange heart of Zeus beating in the breast of the swan. In fact, if the inhuman is God, the nonhuman is animal, then they can be triangulated with the unconscious so that at various times and in various ways all three are one and the same, as in the images of the swan and "rough beast."

The relationship between immanence and transcendence is part of contemporary philosophical discussions of religion. Both Gilles Deleuze in *Pure Immanence* and Lyotard in *The Inhuman* speak of this interdependence, but their emphasis falls squarely on the side of immanence. Deleuze writes quite baldly: "Transcendence is always a product of immanence." Lyotard writes similarly: "Elusive, impossible to grasp. Again we're back at transcendence in immanence." For them, as for many skeptics of our contemporary age, it is a strong almost counterinterpretation of the Kantian transcendental, but for Yeats, it is fair to say, giving due place to transcendence is important. Adorno says something similar when he observes that it is difficult to tell in dreams when the ego is the source of dreams or the receiver (noting the profundity in the difference of the simple phrases "I dreamt" versus "There came to me in a dream").[9]

In *Christ in Post-modern Philosophy: Gianni Vattimo, René Girard and Slavoj Žižek*, Frederiek Depoortere studies the difference between three contemporary philosophers of religion. He notes that there is a "major difference between Žižek [and to an extent Vattimo] and Girard." Žižek claims that the incarnation of Christ should be understood as the complete abolishment of God's transcendence. God is just the excess of Life projected "onto some figure of the Other." Christ frees us from this Divine Thing, and this liberation must lead to the abolishment of all (superior) transcendences. For Girard, in contrast, Christ reveals the true character of transcendence. He believes that Christ liberates us from our excessive violence. In Yeats the relationship of immanence and transcendence is not so much hierarchical as it is interpenetrating. Yeats's idea of interpenetrating gyres includes both visions of divine presence (as does R. P. Harrison's).[10] Indeed, we live in the interstices, asking questions of the inhuman and wondering whether we hear only human voices in reply.

Questions of the inhuman are asked first by the body, which is where nature erupts within us—whether it is the body when moved by its drives or rebelling against the suppression of those drives, or it is the mind seeking sublimation of those drives in art, religion, or politics. For the mature Yeats, the body awakened in the Greek era, when the statues were put before the Mediterranean and "gave to the sexual instinct of Europe its goal."[11] The young Yeats knew how the pagan inspiration of the antiquarian movement was in troubled conversation with the Christian heritage of Ireland. *The Wanderings of Oisin* (1889) is a record of the conflict between body and mind, pagan and Christian. It is a testament to the role the inhuman plays in this relationship, particularly in the boredom and anger of Oisin (whose animal lineage has been discussed), languishing and battling in paradise (icon of the restless desire of Western tradition),[12] and the glowing figure of Niamh, the "faery bride" for whose "bosom" Yeats was "starved." The long poem's formative importance perhaps lies in its early sublimation of violence and conception of imagination as an erotic zone between immortal and mortal worlds. In short, the world Oisin wants is the natural immanent one. The closing dialogue between Oisin and Saint Patrick is an early salvo in what would be the battle between the pagan and the Christian (between what in his later years he named antithetical and primary). They are irreconcilable but mutually dependent forces that wait upon the advent of the inhuman to settle the relationship. Niamh, however, is only a minor nature deity, and so not representative of advent.

In these early years Yeats has a transcendental Arcadian impulse placed alongside (and sometimes against) an urge toward embodiment that is often too infrequently expressed in the young idealist's life. The gentle folk are also minor nature deities and not that history-creating and altering force that Yeats would recognize as a sometimes immanent and sometimes transcendent vision of the inhuman. Their presence, their "inhuman misery" or happiness for that matter, influences our existence for good and ill alike, as in "The Madness of King Goll." Like Oisin and Fergus, Goll represents the body's unconscious-driven frenzy, which Yeats both admires and fears and which through poetry he is consistently trying to reconcile with a social conscience. The "little town" slumbering in the "harvest moon" is juxtaposed with the ceaseless murmuring of the leaves. It is as though nature and culture could be "married" (as instrumental voice and human voice are "married") only in the song of "inhuman misery" that is "trolled" by the mad king with his tympan (an ancient Irish stringed instrument played with a bow).

The volume *The Rose* (1893) begins with "To the Rose upon the Rood of Time," which is a repetition of some of the themes of "The Stolen Child," presenting a choice, or dilemma, between the supernatural and the natural, the inhuman (animal or divinity) and the human, the transcendent and the immanent. In many of Yeats's poems, animals are associated with immanence. What John Berger writes of ancient views of animals in *Why Look at Animals?* applies equally to Yeats: "Everywhere animals offered explanations, or, more precisely, lent their name or character to a quality which like all qualities was, in its essence, mysterious."[13] Their relationship with the supersensible, or supernatural, is one of powerful present expression and recalls the etiological uses of animals to the Greeks and Hindus. In early poems, the animals are not so threatening or spiritually evocative as they later become. They are generally associated more with the domestic. Compare the field mouse with the wild swan, the weak worm with the eagles.

Hounds run from "The Ballad of the Fox Hunter" to "Hound Voice," but they move from domesticated animal to savage beast. In the early poetry, nature is already associated with dream and vision. What moves Yeats most in the myths he chooses is how the heroes themselves embody supernatural shape-changing powers. Cuchulain's son (who in the original myth is named Conla) remains nameless in Yeats's rendering (in both "Cuchulain Fights with the Sea" and later in the play *On Baile's Strand* [1903]). It is as though the inhuman force of desire and the Oedipal crises (his mother, Aoife, has ordered him to kill his father), as well as the kinship with the great Cuchulain, cannot be named. The inhuman is tragically visible again in the "invulnerable tide" the grief-stricken Cuchulain assails after he realizes he has unknowingly killed his son. The Oedipal tragedy is an expression of the entanglement of desire, inhuman instinct, and conscience (divinely or socially inspired) that mark us both as human and as supplement to nature.[14]

For Yeats, instinct is the deepest connection we have to the inhuman (divine), the nonhuman (animal), and nature; the eruptions of our instinctual drives reveal the connections between them. Whether it is the thundering swans above (the demoniac creature), nature is not so much a reflection of our mental state, or objective correlative, as it is an influence upon us, a catalyst. Natural storms do not so much reflect as they become internal ones. So the "earth" in "The Man who Dreamed of Faeryland" takes "him to her stony care." And the song of the "lug-worm" makes it seem that "sun and moon were in the fruit." None of it is enough, however; the man craves God and nature to be reconciled, that "God burn Nature with a kiss." He desires to find no reflection in the world; he is a lover whom "no lovers miss," and this Platonic desire leaves him comfortless in the "grave." History must bear the weight of our presence, of our being, for us to be able to transcend time and exist in space beyond time (to paraphrase Rilke's definition of poetry).[15] There is a desire in the will of this lover of fairyland that remains unrequited. It is a desire for ecstasy and not serenity, for self-transcendence and not self-possession (which the later Yeats would seek), for heaven and not Eden. Beatitude is not a "homeostatic state" of reconciliation,[16] but a dynamic, intoxicating process of self-surpassing and of surpassing the human in connection with the inhuman. It is an internal palimpsest of conquest.

The inhuman in Yeats's early poetry is a combination of the transcendental and the immanent with an emphasis on the former, but the two forces seem to come together in the themes of *The Wind among the Reeds* (1899). This symbolist volume, published on the eve of a new century, displays an imaginative and erotic zone as an immanent category between immortal and mortal worlds (much as in *The Wanderings of Oisin*), emphasizing the interaction in the movement of the wind, the leaves, the sound of the crickets, the valley of the apocalyptic Black Pig. "The Secret Rose," for instance, contains all the pagan heroes, gods, and legends on its petals, but it retains its Christian emphasis. The rose is no daffodil, but rather a symbol of Christian and pagan forces. If it is a contradiction in terms, we must remember that its mystery is that it is "far off and most secret," very near and far away. This contradiction can be settled only when, again apocalyptically, the "great wind" that holds the antinomies "of love and hate" in balance blows the stars about the sky. These early symbolic uses of nature would become actualized or living embodiments of immanent forces.

Near the end of the volume *Responsibilities*, Yeats chooses an image of immanence: "The uncontrollable mystery on the bestial floor" ("The Magi"). Though about Christianity (Yeats would see the Second Coming as anti-Christian or at least Greek and pagan), this poem combines the qualities of Christian and pagan dispensations, which is consistent with Yeats's idea of interpenetrating gyres. Christ comes from the transcendent Father but is incarnate in the world. The mystery is uncontrollable because it is an animal drive, the presentation of instinct, the same one as Fergus oversees, or that lies behind Cuchulain's son and his Oedipal quest. It is the unappeasable appetite of the death drive, which seeks its own destruction and makes us "moon-accursed" in the poem "The Empty Cup." For Yeats, instinct, the force of nature, drives the violence that shapes civilization on both personal and public levels.[17]

Yeats has come to realize that we need the inhuman most when we are most resistant to it. In *Wheels and Butterflies* (1934), Yeats writes: "Science has driven out the legends, stories, superstitions that protected the immature and the ignorant with symbol." In other words, it has driven out the comfort of the inhuman. As noted above, he believed that the Enlightenment dispensation would not last and that nature and the inhuman would prove its end. Like God, nature has lost its separateness as a category beyond our comprehension and control. If the ancients looked for comforting patterns in the constellations because they were surrounded by wild and hostile nature, then we, surrounded by domesticated nature (that will soon go wild itself), must look beyond those anthropomorphic patterns. The "comfort we need," as Bill McKibben concludes in *The End of Nature*, "is inhuman."[18]

Yeats's awareness of the need for the comfort of the inhuman provided the basis for his writing of *A Vision*. Besides the personal implications of the beginnings of *A Vision*, that his newly wed yet neglected young wife faked the automatic voices in order to obtain the comfort of his attention, there is the overarching idea of desire behind the book itself: "We desire belief and lack it. Belief comes from shock and is not desired." He concludes: "Belief is renewed continually in the ordeal of death."[19] The latter ordeal is an encounter with the inhuman. In *A Vision*, Yeats has erected a complicated geometrical system meant to show how lyric moments illuminate the sexual-religious basis of psychological or historical change. It is not surprising that the mystical book was written in the shadow of World War I and foreshadow of World War II.[20] Following Nietzsche's idea of the Apollonian and Dionysian, Yeats believes in two realities that are constantly interlocked: the antithetical (subjective) reality and the primary (objective) one. They are interpenetrating, although one or another is usually dominant. When any type of balance is achieved, civilization reaches its apogee, as for example in Byzantium, when Christ is represented in the pose of Zeus and this primary love also expresses antithetical power. There are moments in history when the gyres turn and one dispensation gives way to another: normally in the form of God's descent into nature. The most prominent examples of this transformation are when Leda is impregnated by the swan (Zeus) and gives birth to Helen, Clytemnestra, Castor, and Pollux, thereby creating the age of a Greek antithetical, subjective culture. Another is when the Dove (the Holy Ghost) impregnates the Virgin Mary, who gives birth to Jesus, and so creates a primary, objective age. The privileged figure in this subject-object religious relationship is the sexual one, and the privileged vehicle is the animal world.

In *A Vision*, Yeats writes of the coming of the rough beast: "When the old *primary* becomes the new antithetical, the old realisation of an objective moral law is changed into a subconscious turbulent instinct. The world of rigid custom and law is broken up by 'the uncontrollable mystery upon the bestial floor.'"[21] Yeats in the last line is referring to his own poem "The Magi." In this moment of religious epiphany, the human gazes upon the specter of the inhuman taking human form, becoming incarnate. This moment is not the advent of humanism, but rather its opposite, the advent of the inhuman divine in the guise of the nonhuman animal (a humanistic sublime, it has been noted, is an oxymoron).[22] The breakdown of objective moral law and the rise of turbulent sexual instinct takes place in "The Second Coming" and "Leda and the Swan." "Two Songs from a Play" and "The Mother of God" depict the opposite movement: "When the old antithetical becomes the new primary, moral feeling is changed into an organisation of experience which must in its turn seek a unity, the whole of experience."[23] Christ comes in "pity for man's darkening thought" as "Two Songs from a Play" describes the advent of Christ. Morality comes again to give shape to sexual instinct; Eros is given a religious dimension.

There are no two volumes in Yeats's career that constitute the essential statement of his vision of the inhuman as powerfully as *The Tower* (1928) and *The Winding Stair and Other Poems* (1933).[24] The former is generally a portrayal of the antithetical forces and the latter one of the primary, and the two volumes interpenetrate in their conceptual framework.[25] They correspond in theme and form so much as to make them function as a single volume, or an image of thoughts being hammered into unity. One has only to look at T. Sturge Moore's contemporaneous design for each volume to see an emblem of this interaction. For *The Tower*, the tower is embossed into the cover (and on the flyleaf) above its reflection in the stream below that connects Coole Park to Yeats's tower, while on the cover of *The Winding Stair* the tower is opened for us to see the ascending stair. The mirroring and interlocking are made more than abundantly clear in the poems themselves. For just a few examples, *The Tower* ends with "A Man Young and Old," *The Winding Stair* with "A Woman Young and Old." As noted earlier, the former's poems of the role of masculine or antithetical violence in the formation of culture ("Meditations in Time of Civil War," "Nineteen Hundred and Nineteen") are complemented by the consideration of feminine culture's civilizing influence on nature and man in the latter volume's poems on Lady Gregory and Coole Park.

These tensions are apparent in the poems themselves: the violent, bitter men of "Meditations" long for such civilization; Lady Gregory's "powerful character" can keep a swallow (whether ambitious artist or violent, bitter man) to its first intent, thereby combining masculine and feminine characteristics. The comparison most germane to this discussion is that between "Leda and the Swan" and "The Mother of God," with "Two Songs from a Play" (concerned with the heart of Dionysus becoming the sacred heart of Jesus) and "Vacillation" providing the bridge. In "Leda and the Swan" and "The Mother of God," a thought (the conceptual paradigm shift of a new age) becomes an experience (the rape of Leda, the annunciation to Mary), which accords with both Yeats's and Freud's conception of dream (thought becomes experience). That "Leda and the Swan" was once titled "Annunciation" in an early version emphasizes the direct connection between these poems. Both are visions of the inhuman, of the unconscious as object of the gaze (Mary thinking about Christ's birth and life, Leda observing and being observed in a manner consistent with the Lacanian concept of the gaze).[26]

Easthope claims that for Freud, "if there is no unconscious there can be no opposition between nature and culture."[27] These poems, especially "Leda and the Swan," among many meanings, are about the distinction between nature and culture, unconscious and conscious, subject and object, human and inhuman. How is Leda to resist? Because she cannot at that moment but must in the future if she is to survive, she becomes the basis of future resistance that will define the human against this inhuman force (à la Rancière).[28] In this she is the figure for human suffering from which we dissociate ourselves only at the loss of our humanity. This status results from her trauma, as the trauma of defeat at the hands of the Persians led to the flowering of Greek culture. Remembering that "The Second Coming" is the companion poem to "Leda and the Swan," the prophecy that heralds the advent, we should note that Oedipus is implicit in the former poem. He will answer the riddle of the Sphinx, but he is as subject to the violence of this advent as Leda is. Mary, on the other hand, keeps her subjectivity intact. If Leda's story is told in the third person, Mary's is in the first, the lyric "I." What Mary suffers from the Holy Ghost in the form of the Dove, in purest Christian sympathy, is the future passion of her son crossing the human/inhuman threshold as the immanent Jesus becomes the transcendent Christ.

These examples are just the most significant of advents, but not the only ones in which the inhuman appears in animal form. There is the close of "The Tower" where the death of human presence ("every brilliant eye that made a catch in the breath") becomes the inhuman voice of the bird "among the deepening shades" of death. The bird can be said to be the symbol of transmigration from one world to the next and the first step from the human to the inhuman Otherness of God. There is the "daemonic rage," the divine spark that illuminates the mind in part 1, "My House," of "Meditations"; there is the "peacock scream" in part 3 of the same poem. In terms of the advent that Leda experienced, there are the "monstrous familiar" images of the unconscious rising to the "mind's eye," while in terms of Mary, or the ecstasy of the saint, there are the ladies on the backs of the unicorns, whose "hearts are full of their own sweetness" and bodies of "their loveliness." These exemplary instances of the daemonic otherness of the animal world show how Yeats's system gave him metaphors for his poetry, as he notably said it would. What unites many of these poems is the double vision of antithetical and primary as well as immanent and transcendent revelations, as represented by "Leda and the Swan" and "The Mother of God." The close of "Two Songs from a Play" captures the unconscious source: "Whatever flames upon the night / Man's own resinous heart has fed."

In terms of the unconscious, Yeats's evocative use of the Oedipus myth at the end of *The Tower* and *The Winding Stair and Other Poems* presents a sexual entanglement of taboos and affections. Here the human is left to his own devices and suffers from his own limitations, without divine aid, recognizing kin only in the seasons of nature. As Oedipus states in Sophocles's *Oedipus Rex*: "I am the child of Fortune. . . . She is my mother; my sisters are the Seasons; my rising and my falling match with theirs. Born thus, I ask to be no other man than that I am."[29] Yeats sees this cursed position in the myth of Oedipus as the condition of the artist, a Michelangelo, solving the riddle of the Sphinx and then confronting the source of his damnation (social and familial division) in the eruptions of nature (murder of the father and the violated maternal taboo in the marriage bed), which marriage repeatedly attempts to avoid, and religion to sanctify, but both of which move perilously toward:

> Even from that delight memory treasures so,
> Death, despair, division of families, all entanglements of
> mankind grow
> As that old wandering beggar and these God-hated children
> know.

> In the long echoing street the laughing dancers throng,
> The bride is carried to the bridegroom's chamber through
>   torchlight and tumultuous song;
>
> "From *Oedipus at Colonus*"

Yet the myth contains a prototype of Saint Catherine, in the figure of Antigone, who prays to the divine for redemption and mourns for the human condition:

> Pray I will and sing I must,
> And yet I weep—Oedipus' child
> Descends into the loveless dust.[30]
>
> "From the *Antigone*"

Yeats's major period is perhaps the greatest indication of the significance of the religious role of the inhuman, especially its divine and natural expressions, as so much of it revolves around questions of transcendence and immanence, redemption and sin.

How imperative this configuration is to Yeats as a mature poet is most powerfully expressed by the idea of writing and the question of human and inhuman sources of inspiration both in nature and in mind. In these ways, the play of mind and world brings the question of context and text to the fore and shows how much they overlap. From "Fragments" to "The Gyres" and particularly "Man and the Echo," the question of the relationship between the inhuman and poetic voice quite literally haunts the great poet. There is also something foundational here, as though we had uncovered the original root of all human consciousness, the universal guilt we felt at the thunder in the skies. This unveiling of the unitary origin of thought returns us to Giambattista Vico's notion of the age of giants and unbridled appetite before the thundering heavens awoke them to guilt and consciousness.[31] We return to the idea that, in our finite particularity, we discover the reasons for the fall and our inescapable guilt.

In Yeats's late poetry, there are ample demonstrations of his celebration of the inhuman forces of nature and romantic desire to heal the divided consciousness. In the late poems, the impersonal demands of true insight are made of hard material, and all efforts and demands come down to scrutinizing the fall from grace, the mark of the beast. One must grope with a dirty hand, that is, delve into the mysteries of nature. The beast must be lured with the symbols of savage fate and consumption. The elder poet experienced little sensual life beyond his mere witnessing of the sensual wonders of the world, but the sexual drive remains tormenting. The purifying drive is equally strong, however; Yeats is caught between the erotic drive (that most inhuman of specters) and the purifying one (that most inhuman of aims), but he is seeking synthesis in the senses. Only now he acknowledges the abject crossing of the threshold and the necessity to "grope with a dirty hand."

"The Spirit Medium" is an attempt to discover synthesis. It is a poem on the Platonic banishment of the arts, as a futile celebration of this world of shadows, but it is one that ends by paradoxically embracing the arts as an expression of Neoplatonic form. It is not the abandonment of the sensible that occurs in Kant's moral, positive sublime, for the Irish poet insists that the way to the transcendental is through the physical realm. In the face of those souls whose perception has been purified by death, the poem is a form of profane transfiguration:

> Because of those new dead
> That come into my soul . . .
> I bend my body to the spade
> Or grope with a dirty hand.

In the last stanza, the lightning from the close of "The Wild Old Wicked Man" has struck again. Like the pure realm of the soul, it is a supernatural incarnation. To be there is to abandon the known world for the inhuman one:

> An old ghost's thoughts are lightning,
> To follow is to die;
> Poetry and music I have banished,
> But the stupidity
> Of root, shoot, blossom or clay

Makes no demand.
I bend my body to the spade
Or grope with a dirty hand.

Yeats and the old man do not want to follow the lightning because they do not want to renounce the sensible world. They seek instead to embody physically that spiritual power, to unite sensible and supersensible, in "root, shoot, blossom or clay."

"Hound Voice" is Yeats's late-Dionysian evocation of the inhuman drive that comes from within, that is, nature's voice inside us. Though the gods of Greece are in exile (to borrow the idea of Heine's essay),[32] they are still very much a part of our subconscious and of our chosen wilderness. The hunt at the core of this poem is the hunt of Dionysus: "The true victims of their gruesome hunt, however, are the animals of the forest. . . . The revel rout, however, is only following the example of its divine leader, Dionysos, himself a hunter."[33] Nietzsche's description of the metamorphosis captures the very essence of the psychic ecstasy that overtakes the initiates of the Dionysian mystery cults (which is surely what Yeats's poem celebrates in all its dark intensity). Nietzsche realizes that such mythic consciousness is at the heart of artistic reverie in the forest of signifiers: "To see oneself transformed before one's own eyes and to begin to act as if one had actually entered into another body, another character. . . . Such magic transformation is the presupposition of all dramatic art. In this magic transformation the Dionysian reveler sees himself as satyr, *and as satyr in turn, he sees the god.*"[34]

As R. P. Harrison illustrates in *Forests: The Shadow of Civilization*, Dionysus is not the only god behind such scenes of carnage as the dismemberment of Pentheus. Artemis, too, demands such bloodletting, such engorging. His analysis of the myth of Actaeon and Artemis provides insight into Yeats's poem as well:

> In the Actaeon story Artemis is the agent both of metamorphosis and the guardian of nature's mysterious matrix of forms. By transforming the predator into the prey, she reveals to Actaeon in his

> person the true nature of what he has laid eyes upon: the preformed kinship of all creation. The story has an unmistakable psychological influence upon the reader, for while Actaeon is literally de-anthropomorphized, the stag that he turns into becomes humanized. Now that Actaeon has become a stag we are able to suffer its fate as if it were a human being. The distinctions collapse. The world reveals its deceptions, its *irrevocable* deceptions. Like Actaeon, we are made to see that the forms of the world are transient, illusory, and reversible. All things, whatever their formal natures, arise from a more primordial unity. This is the terrifying insight enjoyed by Actaeon that day in the forest, where he had the dubious privilege of seeing the *dea silvarum* naked.[35]

Though Yeats is invoking the insights of predation and not victimhood, the experiences of the myth and the poem are very similar. Elsewhere, as in "Man and the Echo," Yeats has paralleled the pain of animals (in that case the rabbit) with the pain of human beings. Here humans and animals (the hounds) share the same voice, the hound voice. Celtic myth also blurs such boundaries; Oisin, for example, has animal as well as human origins. Yeats has been blurring such boundaries his entire poetic career; from *The Wanderings of Oisin* through "Leda and the Swan," from the Adonis myth underlying "Her Vision in a Wood" to "Hound Voice," he has sought to look through the sterner eye, even if it meant merely to have the terrifying vision of a "more primordial unity." A glimpse of such primordial unity of the unconscious unveils a world of violent desire and shape changing, which is perhaps best rendered with full poetic force and pity in Ovid's *Metamorphoses.* The above poems by Yeats follow in that tradition. From the days of composing "The Choice," Yeats recognizes the rage, the violent possession, which is associated with writing. Though he is always thinking of context, it is this inner element underlying the act of writing that both escapes materialist historical formulation and, at least for Yeats, redefines personal and public history.

As Calasso writes in *Literature and the Gods,* writing itself contains something of the violence of "Hound Voice," as though we are embarked on a dangerous hunt for meaning, triangulated by "the hand that writes the voice that speaks, the god who watches over and compels," or as Calasso also renders them: "the I, the Self and the Divine." "Every sentence, every form is a variation within that force field," writes Calasso:

> Hence the ambiguity of literature: because its point of view is incessantly shifting between these three extremes, without warning us, and sometimes without warning the author. The young man writing is absorbed at his tablet. . . . Perhaps he has no idea who is beside him. The stylus that etches the letters demands all his attention. The head that drifts on the waters sings and bleeds. Every vibration of the word presupposes something violent. A *palaiòn pénthos*, an "ancient grief." Was it a murder? Was it a sacrifice: It isn't clear, but the word will never cease to tell of it.[36]

What is perhaps most striking in this passage by a scholar of pagan mythology and modern consciousness is how expression is adrift on suffering and speaks of the relation between subject and object, writer and reader, human and inhuman. If the reference to Orpheus at the end of the passage reminds us of the place of the excoriated artist such as Marsyas, the reference to murder and sacrifice reminds us of the common crime and Oedipal guilt. It shows us how social order is based on murder or sacrifice and how "things hidden since the foundation of the world" (Matt. 13:35) are revealed in the act of expression. The more Christian-minded Girard observes: "It is the originary scapegoating which prolongs itself in a process which can be infinitely long in moving from, how should I say, from instinctive ritualization, instinctive prohibition, instinctive separation of the antagonists, which you already find to a certain extent in animals, towards representation."[37] Or as Yeats pithily writes: "They had brought no fabulous symbol there / But my heart's victim and its torturer" ("Her Vision in a Wood").

Yeats's greatness in terms of the aims of his sacred book (which is what he calls his poems as a whole) is how he places us between the pagan and Christian, nature and culture, polytheistic and monotheistic, and immanent and transcendent experiences of the world. That is why Calasso, on the one side, and Girard, on the other, make sense. Yeats captures a spiritual need in the epistemological shift of our times. As Calasso writes in *Literature and the Gods*: "It is the anguish we feel for the absence of idols."[38] Calasso writes of how Yeats was moved by Mallarmé's conception of the trembling of the veil toward a consideration of epochal change and the coming of the "savage God," which he felt he was observing: "A century on . . . we can't help hearing in Yeats's words the striking, overheated chord of a new era."[39]

Yeats writes of the historical cycles between Christ and Oedipus: "What if Christ and Oedipus or, to shift the names, Saint Catherine of Genoa and Michelangelo, are the two scales of a balance, the two butt-ends of a seesaw? What if every two thousand and odd years something happens in the world to make one sacred, the other secular; one wise, the other foolish; one fair, the other foul; one divine, the other devilish? What if there is an arithmetic or geometry that can exactly measure the slope of the balance, the dip of the scale?"[40] That geometry or arithmetic is akin to the supersensible rhythms. Every vibration of the word echoes the transcendent or inhuman world. Art captures the rhythm of the "transitive law of gesture."[41] Yeats believes that pagan and Christian make the same gestures, whether it is Leda or Mary, Mary or Venus.[42] That gesture reveals the form of the unconscious. We may say that the force behind the gesture is the inhuman. The artist makes that perpetual gesture in memory on his torch-lit way to his Oedipal discovery. In the passage Yeats makes Christ and Oedipus interchangeable with Saint Catherine and Michelangelo. Saint Catherine is the great mystic and favorite subject of Van Hugel's great work on mysticism that influenced Yeats so deeply and tempted him at least momentarily toward Christianity.

That Yeats would instead emulate Michelangelo's profane perfection of mankind is fitting, but most importantly represents the tension between faith and self-discovery. Human history is one of impossible reconciliation between the mystic and the artist, yet it is a reconciliation that must nevertheless be sought. We return to Girard to understand the place of the unconscious and the geometry of the relationship between Christ and Oedipus. He states that when Christ asked God to forgive his crucifiers, he had discovered the unconscious *avant la lettre* and thereby brought to light the founding murder (the patricide of which Oedipus was unaware) repeated inversely (God sacrificing Christ as Abraham would have Isaac), which is thereby undone in the Crucifixion.[43] The rabbit's cry that distracts Yeats's thought in "Man and the Echo" symbolizes the same discovery of this founding murder (the rabbit's death cry was a childhood experience for Yeats that forever made him avoid hunting) and asks for the same forgiveness in a cry that imitates the death cry yet moves beyond to establish a form for approaching the gods (or God).[44] That form is art's form, "great works constructed in nature's spite," as Yeats writes in "Coole Park" (1929). All religions may make the same gesture, but there is an unfolding of religious understanding that neither negates that which precedes it nor completes it. For Yeats, we are merely characters in the post-Christian play listening for the echo, the answering voice, which helps us to understand our parts. Calasso puts it into sharp focus: "They (Mary, Joseph, the child and the donkey) are anonymous extras, *absorbed in the landscape*. The vision is still to come."[45]

James Joyce, in answer to Yeats on many levels, also responds to the heterodox vision of the elder poet with what has been called "Catholic Categories." At the end of "The Dead," the generous tears that fill Gabriel's eyes consummate his desire for Greta and become for critic Colum Power the intimation of the synthesis that takes place fully in *Ulysses*: "The perspective achieved at the end of this story is the one from which all of Joyce's work should be read, and it is the perspective that will ultimately resolve the *anima-animus* and *eros-agape* puzzles."[46] Gabriel's epiphany for Power may be multivalent, and allow for critical dispute, but it does not mean it is so suffused with ambivalence as to have no meaning at all. The snow that is general covers the "mutinous" waves of the Shannon and the crosses in the churchyard. It clearly connects the sacred and profane, the religious and political, in ways that are consistent with the uses of landscape, nature, and the family in Irish literature throughout its history.

6

Bleeding from the Torn Bough

Challenging Nature in James Joyce

❦ Any essay on James Joyce's poetry, even one in a book devoted to nature, home, and landscape (which figures prominently in Joyce's poetry), still must answer the question: Why the poetry? For one thing, the implications of the prose have been discussed elsewhere.[1] Perhaps even more specifically, why the lyrics, which have always been viewed as slighter than the satires? I have argued elsewhere that it is the lyric moment, the epiphany, that proved as important if not more important to author and reader than the satirical voice. The simplicity of Joyce's best lyric poems is central to his aesthetic project as a whole. One may rightly criticize Joyce for being too slight, but one must remember that this is a self-conscious end, a style, that, when matched to a theme, proved justified.[2] Such a choice moved the Nobel Prize winner and hermetic Italian poet Eugenio Montale (1896–1981) to translate two of *Pomes Penyeach*, a collection of poetry that will be the main text of the subsequent discussion. Argument for the importance of Joyce's lyrics is part of what follows here, but this chapter particularly aims to examine the role of landscape and nature in Joyce's poetry—hence the later parallels with Montale, one of the great modernist poets of landscape and nature in the twentieth century.

Like Montale's, Joyce's poetry relies on landscape to give it meaning. Landscape is Joyce's chief concern, while nature tends to be more psychological and appears in Oedipal formations. Nature, often figured as Oedipal, and landscape are significant in Joyce's prose from *Dubliners* to *Finnegans Wake*—particularly in the latter, nature, landscape, and Oedipal structures are linguistically intertwined (with abundant critical coverage)—but voice, landscape, and nature (that foreign element, the uncanny other) may be said to be the primary players in his poems. Even the title "Pomes" plays on the connections between art, religion, and nature as it plays on "poems" and "*pommes*" (French for "apple"); the booklet was covered in a pale apple-green paper, which biographer Richard Ellmann reveals to be the same shade as Joyce's favorite apple, the Calville.[3] If nature as emblem of psychological wounds reminds Joyce of exile and suffering in the image from "Tilly" of the "torn bough," then in these poems landscape provides the common ground for love and escape. Anne Fogarty makes this incisive comment about the image of the torn bough and Joyce's general use of animals: "The conjoint rural and semi-urban landscape traced in this poem ["Tilly"] seems to provide succor for the cattle, but to be inhospitable to the humans who inhabit it and witness its destruction or violation. In fact, animal tropes are frequently used by Joyce to disturb hierarchies of the human and the non-human rather than to suggest continuities between them."[4]

With Joyce, darker inner truths of nature are revealed, truths that deeply complicate the pastoral or nostalgic as terms for literary interpretation and invite discussions of nature onto the scene in specifically religious and psychoanalytical terms. The present chapter traces reactions to Revivalist (mainly Protestant) celebrations of nature in the works of James Joyce's poetry, especially in *Pomes Penyeach* (written over a twenty-year period from 1904 to 1924 and published in 1927). It is a reaction that assiduously employs what Fred Davis calls "interpretive nostalgia."[5] Responding to the pastoral meditations of the Irish Renaissance, James Joyce gives us an urban pastoral not only to show how the pastoral myth excludes the city dweller, but also to illustrate how the land has often been a sign of exclusion for the Irish.

"Tilly," the first poem in *Pomes Penyeach*, written after the death of Joyce's mother in August 1903, was added to this collection as the thirteenth poem—hence the title ("Tilly" meaning baker's dozen). Joyce considered its tone out of harmony with the earlier volume *Chamber Music* (1907). Here, the family romance is finally given the more fitting setting of the Joyce family's descent into poverty and distress, a distress and poverty signified in the poem by the Dublin neighborhood of Cabra, where the impoverished family was forced to reside. That Cabra has its roots in the Latin for "goat" cannot have been lost on the linguist Joyce, nor its horns that reference sexuality and Oedipal crisis. The poem is separated, albeit in a somewhat sublimated fashion, between the prelapsarian feminine interior of home and the fallen masculine exterior world, through which the cowherd must journey.[6] The herdsman is symbolically following the same flowering branch he uses to lead the cows. This feminine symbol of Eden also carries the pain of separation, associated in the poem with the river one must cross (but cannot) to reach the promised land of home:

> Boor, bond of the herd,
> Tonight stretch full by the fire!
> I bleed by the black stream
> For my torn bough!

In this poem of 1904 there is none of the "heavy end stopping of the lines or candid rhymes" that Heaney dislikes in Joyce's poetry, but there is much of the "raw distress" noted by Grennan as a harbinger of Kinsella's experiments.[7] The formal elements of the language are highly controlled.

Chester Anderson carefully observes: "Perhaps it would not be worthwhile to suggest that the repeated sounds have any intrinsic meanings, that is, for example, the c's and r's in stanza 1 tend to evoke the notion of cold or the m's in stanza 2 the notion of warmth, or the plosive b's in stanza 3 and throughout, the notion of violence, discord, activity." Anderson concludes that "like the disjunctive imagery, the paired sounds . . . suggest the principal conflict (betrayal) and support the main comparison and contrasts (cold and heat, servility and dominion, animalism and spirit, will and intellect, health and disease, material contentment and spiritual pain). The alliteration helps [to] stitch the poem into a unity of some splendour."[8] In other words, though sounds do not contain intrinsic meaning, they do acquire contextual significance if appropriately linked to sense. This link is also evident in the simple but deep poem "Ecce Puer." Through sound and sense, this poem captures much of what Freud outlines as the pain of necessary separation from family in the justly legendary first line of his essay "Family Romances." Freud employs similarly simple and deep expression as Joyce: "The liberation of an individual, as he grows up, from the authority of his parents is one of the most necessary though one of the most painful results brought about by the course of his development."[9]

Richard Ellmann sees the pain of "Tilly" as a result of the death of Joyce's mother, while Anderson believes it concerns Joyce's complicated relationship with J. F. Byrne (Cranly of the *Portrait*). This interpretive disparity leads us from Joyce's preoccupation with the familial self to the larger web of social interactions. If the speaker suffers over his separation from his mother's or lover's home, it is not only because of distance but also because of betrayal. The "boor," the uncouth herdsman, the bond (or slave) of the herd, acts as interloper. If the poem is an allegorical account of Byrne's betrayal, or of the characters from *Portrait* who wounded Parnell, or any other similar betrayer, it is also by extension concerned with family, nation, and church. For Joyce to present any of them in the guise of a herd of cattle is true to form. Like the old woman who comes with milk in the first episode of *Ulysses*, representing ignorant pastoral Ireland and the Shan Van Vocht, the poem's movement toward home, with its overtones of death and estrangement, also makes it a brief allegory of Ireland. The smoke rising from the forehead of the beasts of burden is redolent of the smoke of sacrifice, which we see in Stephen's villanelle in *Portrait*. Here, it is a sacrifice made to reinvigorate the nation, but made ignorantly by the herdsman, who is one of the farrows eaten by the old sow of Ireland. The "torn bough," as Robert Scholes has pointed out, is borrowed from the tradition of Ovid, Virgil, Dante, and Spenser, among others, and is tied to spirits, captured in the tree, which when the bough is severed bleed and speak of their betrayal, of being forced to commit their sins, and of their banishment from paradise.[10] The torn bough takes on larger significance when used to represent Joyce, the loathed exile from Ireland, rejected for many years to come, even by his own university. If Joyce is a scandal, a blasphemer, he offers himself Christlike to redeem the nation with his blasphemy. As he writes in "The Holy Office," "That they may dream their dreamy dreams / I carry off their filthy streams."[11]

James Frazer, author of *The Golden Bough*, has suggested that the worship of trees usually includes the belief that trees are sensate. Trees that bleed and scream in pain or indignation when they are cut belong to mythology. According to Frazer, trees are symbols of fertility, and their dismemberment represents the death of the old year and the promise of the new. In *The Waste Land* Eliot borrows from Frazer the motif of the kingfisher whose impotence has led to his country's sterility. This motif is used by Yeats and Pound as well.[12] The blood of the torn bough in Joyce's poem is potentially replenishing because it bleeds for a land that shows signs neither of its injury nor even of realizing it is injured. Here Joyce's pastoral ideology is used as a point of resistance as well as a refuge, as nature in Irish literature is often both. For a similar example, in the poem "The Dedication to a Book of Stories Selected from the Irish Novelists," Yeats tears a "green branch" from the "barren boughs of Eire" in order to replicate the pastoral idyll of the land.[13] Here we see an attempt to explain why a vision of the beautiful has been so difficult to achieve in Ireland and why the Irish have so often sought escapist forms of beauty (as Yeats does in this poem itself). The exiles in Yeats's poem find a homeward eternal meaning to their sorrows in a fashion that is reminiscent of Wilde's comment that "what captivity was to the Jews exile has been to the Irish."[14]

Beneath the novelists' sentimental escapist vision of Ireland lies the harsh reality of nineteenth-century Irish experience, an experience that eluded most of the novelists. Like Thoreau, Yeats wants to represent the nation with the Walden-like enclosure as a counterpoint to industrial England (as in "The Lake Isle of Innisfree"), responding to the pastoral dreams of the Irish Renaissance. Joyce, on the other hand, does not. Yet "Tilly" is not a mere anti-idyll, no more than Yeats's poem is merely a form of "willed amnesia."[15] The phrase "willed amnesia" is from Lawrence Buell's *The Environmental Imagination* and is meant to suggest that the colonial classes often used landscape as a way of identifying themselves with the land of the colony without representing its history.[16] In this light, any effort to humanize the landscape becomes a political act. Yeats sometimes falls into that category as well for all of the political purposes of his poetry, while Joyce, like Kavanagh, Montague, and McGahern after him, does not. For the latter, landscape is most often a palimpsest of conquest, whether personal or national or both. Bleeding by "the black stream," Joyce's version of landscape is stained by the "torn bough" symbolizing the narcissistic wound of consciousness and separation from Mother Nature. Yet, as for Yeats, nature remains a luminous ideal, "a flowering branch," for Joyce. Nature is double-sided: a blessing and a curse, a sign of sin and a pathway to redemption. Through the redemptive side of nature, the pastoral retains the capacity to assume oppositional forms, a form that is recurrent in Irish literature. Whether in prose or in poetry, the best of Joyce's work records both the necessity and the pain of liberation, in personal and in national terms.

There are other perhaps more conventional images in Joyce's poetry that serve to highlight its larger aims and place him firmly in the tradition of the urban pastoral. In "Nightpiece," for example, we see an image of the fallen world; it is a poem that is noteworthy for the communal image of the damned it presents during Mass at Notre Dame in Paris on Good Friday. This third-person description of the "waste of souls" stands in contrast to the typical first-person voice (I/you relationship) of Joyce's other poems. The poem is also noteworthy for its language, reminiscent of Dedalus's from *Portrait* and *Ulysses*, with its use of the composite adjective "sindark nave"; this phrase is also repeated in *Giacomo Joyce*.[17] It is interesting to note that this scene has connections both with Emma Clery, virginal muse of Stephen Dedalus, and with the death of Joyce's mother, again making Christ and Mary a vision of salvation and mode of sublimation in the family romance.[18] Joyce the novelist and Joyce the poet have different responses to this predicament and mode of redemption, though the dynamic is quite similar.

A Nobel Prize winner like Montale, Seamus Heaney thinks that Joyce the poet has little to do with Joyce the novelist, though he has shown real appreciation for some of his poems.[19] Heaney asks if we can square the poems with the author whose motto was "silence, cunning, exile."[20] Perhaps we might do well to find another triumvirate in order to characterize Joyce's poems. Eugenio Montale's own poetic motto of *paesaggio, amore, evasione* (landscape, love, evasion)[21] sheds more light on Joyce's poetry than does his own novelistic motto—especially upon *Pomes Penyeach.* The landscape setting often establishes the tone of the poems (be they stormy or sunlit), while love is the subject of almost all of them, and evasion, or escape, is their chief tactic. Why Montale? Most of *Pomes Penyeach* were written in Trieste (some in Dublin and Zurich), many of the poems have an Italian touch, and some are set in Italy or use Italian phrases, or both. Most important, Montale has translated two of Joyce's poems, "Watching the Needle-boats at San Sabba" and "A Flower Given to My Daughter" (translated as "Guardando i canottieri di San Sabba" [Watching the Oarsmen of San Sabba] and "Per un fiore dato all mia bambina"),[22] which suggests that the exceptionally subtle Italian poet felt some affinity for Joyce's delicate poems. Perhaps Montale saw in Joyce's poetry a kindred poetic spirit. Though the Italian poet's work is more difficult, more ambitious, more modernist, like Joyce's prose, in fact, his poetic themes are closer to Joyce's poetry, as Montale's motto suggests. His translations of Joyce's poems provide other insights.

In Montale's translation of "Watching the Needleboats at San Sabba," the Italian poet achieves a couple of ends. First, if we accept Ellmann's contention that the poem's refrain ("Return no more," "non torna, non torna più")[23] is from Puccini's "La fanciulla del West," and that the scullers, or oarsmen, are singing it, then Montale draws the operatic reference closer to the poem by making the singing oarsmen (*canottieri*) part of the title. (A needleboat is a skiff-like boat, a "racing-shell," as Ellmann notes,[24] and is rendered *canotto* in Italian.) On the other hand, Montale translates "prairie," clearly a subtle reference to the American plains, as meadows (*prati*), which moves the poem away from the opera. The opera is important; it concerns the Wild West and was first performed in 1910 in New York City with Enrico Caruso.[25] Like other "exotic" foreign places in Joyce's work (from South America to the Orient), the Wild West serves as an alternative landscape, offering hope to the oppressed while emphasizing the comparative drabness of existence in Ireland.

In *The Years of Bloom*, John McCourt's detailed and careful account of Joyce's time in Trieste, it is clear how important the play between Ireland and elsewhere is for Joyce: "The first poem in the sequence, a little gem called 'Watching the Needleboats at San Sabba,' was written in 1913 as Joyce watched Stanislaus take part in a sculling race at San Sabba, then a country village overlooking the sea near Trieste, now an industrial suburb. Watching the Italian boats, Joyce is reminded of the Galway of his wife Nora and its 'needleboats,' and the melancholic 'No more, return no more' refrain suggests his now permanent exile from his native land." McCourt continues, "The poem is also a forceful expression of Joyce's coming to terms with the passing of time and of his own youth."[26] Perhaps Ellmann's highlighting of Joyce's amorous ambitions to be unfaithful to his wife, Nora, with the heady whiff of consequent betrayal, and McCourt's emphasis on the national significance of these poems together place Joyce within the tradition of Irish landscape writing in which original sin, colonization, and nature are inextricable, a tradition that dates back to Lady Morgan's *The Wild Irish Girl* (1806). Joyce's sense of exile reflects his feelings of having betrayed and been betrayed by his country. The landscape (culture and nature combined) reflects his mood, while the confrontation with disruptive nature (contra culture) unveils his sense of sin. As in Joyce's play *Exiles* (1917), sexual and spiritual experiments in freedom are what turns him and his characters into exiles (whether exiles at home or abroad), people afflicted by restlessness and doubt. In both Montale's translation and Joyce's original, the landscape is sympathetic to this restless doubt, "sighing" in the sea winds.

Like Joyce, Montale likes to blur the boundaries between nature and culture. In Montale's translation of "A Flower Given to My Daughter,"[27] Montale seems taken by how wave, flower, and girl blend together, how steeped in nature being is, and why nature's beauty ("the flowering branch" as implicitly opposed to its brutality, "the torn branch") is highlighted by the delicacy of the little girl. Joyce has an almost Georgian finesse here, or what Heaney criticizes as a "conventional touch."[28] If anything, Montale furthers the inextricable relationship between girl, flower, and sea, which is an even more fragile and strange marvel ("*ancora / più fragile la strana meraviglia*") for the Italian. The use of *azzurro* may also be said to emphasize the sea's coloring in this flowerlike child. Landscape is subtly implicated in her very being.[29]

Montale's comments on the place of landscape are germane. "Curious to think," Montale would write of Monterosso in 1943, "how each of us has a *paese* like this . . . which must remain *his very own landscape*, forever immutable. Curious how the physical order is so slow to filter into us and then so impossible to cancel." Joyce has a complicated relationship with how landscape and politics interconnect in Ireland, as we see in "The Dead" when Gabriel does not want to go to the West of Ireland, to authentic romantic Ireland of bog and windswept barren hills, but would rather travel through continental Europe. Nevertheless, the landscape and cityscape of Ireland, with its mythical and political resonance, were almost an obsessive focus of his writing too, particularly of *Finnegans Wake.* Joyce has his own "*paese* . . . which must remain *his very own landscape*, forever immutable." What has been said of Montale might equally be said of Joyce: "Not only is it not friable or porous or an emanation of spirit like Ungaretti's, not only is it [the landscape] not simply an historically experienced sensation or 'view' like Sbarbaro's, but it has its own massive life which impinges upon and threatens to engulf the poet's."[30] Both cityscape and landscape threaten to engulf Joyce and his characters. Gabriel's predicament at the end of "The Dead" when the image of the whole of Ireland, both its mutiny and its hospitality, threatens to undo him is indicative of Joyce's response.

Challenged by nature, all must in turn challenge nature and, with it, Ireland's history as well. Gabriel must be able to find a way to transcend the frustration of the evening, which has come from his confrontation with desire and death and the specter of politics at the end of the colonial period. The poem "She Weeps over Rahoon" repeats the same themes and situations as does "The Dead," recalling Nora's, Joyce's wife's, relationship to Michael Bodkin.[31] Though it may be said that this poem is spoken by the figure of "Greta," it is nevertheless a poetic evocation of Gabriel's mood before the sense of forgiveness falls upon him at the end of the story. Again, the "dark rain" of nature mirrors the human mood, a pathetic fallacy coming to claim its melancholy victim.

Pomes Penyeach moves through a selection of poems like the above in which nature "whines," "moans," "lashes" (as the title of one poem notes, "Tutto è sciolto" [All is lost]); the only hope is found in an image of love, that is, until we come to the last poem, "A Prayer," the title of which is clearly an appeal for grace. The blessedness that Gabriel feels at the end of "The Dead," oppressed by the weight of Ireland, nature, lives past and present, comes only through suffering and a struggling sense of place. Tim Robinson's comments on the compass rose in a map as emblem of the self are pertinent: "The compass rose represents the self in these potential relationships; it is usually discreetly located in some unoccupied corner [of a map], but is conceptually transplantable to any point of the map sheet. Its meager petals are a conventional selection of the transfinity of directions radiating from the self to the terrain. It is a skeletal flower, befitting our starved spatial consciousness. . . . It comes from a god unrecognized, a ghost denied, a lost friend, a self to whom you had died. . . . For I do not know that I understand what I have written. No; I am writing blind, as a pilot has to fly blind in fog or cloud, sustained by faith in a compass course rather than by vision of a destination. But this much is clear: the recommended situation for the cultivation of the compass rose is on the very edge of the cliff."[32] In all of Joyce's poems, the self is lost on nature's edge, on the "edge of the cliff," and the speakers are haunted by "a ghost denied, a lost friend, a self to whom you had died," with only the slightest suggestion of a course or direction to be taken.

Take the first stanza of "Tutto è sciolto":

> A birdless heaven, seadusk one lone star
> Piercing the west,
> As thou fond heard, love's time, so faint, so far,
> Rememberest.

Or compare the last two stanzas of "On the Beach at Fontana":

> From whining wind and colder
> Grey sea I wrap him warm
> And touch his trembling fineboned shoulder
> And boyish arm.
>
> Around us fear, descending
> Darkness of fear above
> And in my heart how deep unending
> Ache of love!

In both, there is a sense that human relationships have precarious meaning, even if there is distrust, amid a meaningless and vaguely cruel nature, that they provide a compass to navigate through the fog of existence. McCourt notes that the themes of national and amorous betrayal unite in the desolate world and mood of the poem: "'Tutto è sciolto' takes its title from Elvin's moving lament in Bellini's opera *La sonnambula*, which was produced in the Teatro Politeama Rossetti in the autumn of 1914, the probable time of the poem's composition. All was lost in many senses: Ireland was no longer home to Joyce, while shortly it would no longer be possible for him to remain in Trieste, because war had just broken out in Europe. More particularly the poem seems to centre on Joyce's distress over Prezioso's courting of Nora, hence the desolate emptiness of the opening stanza."[33] Interestingly, in the aria "Tutto è sciolto" of *La Sonnambula* (1831), Elvino soliloquizes on his misery because he has discovered his betrothed in a rival's room (she was sleepwalking, as the title suggests),[34] which further supports the theme of romantic indiscretion that accompanies the scenery of the poem.

There is some hope in "Simples," less so in the next two poems after it, as love, human feeling, is more specifically tied to shame over the experience of desire. In previous poems the shame is more implicit and biographical. We return to the "torn bough" of "Tilly" and being forced to face one's sin. Joyce is reimagining the reclamation of the wild that was central to the place of nature and the primitive in the Irish literary revival. The central paradigm of original sin and redemption through love and sexuality, be they personal or historical or both, is repeated in Joyce; however, he must imagine a way out of this exhausted model of the nature/culture dialectic. It is not enough to be in nature, to have only an immediate, unthinking, sensory, or aesthetic responsiveness to it. As must be clear by now, Joyce is not merely critiquing the immanent nonreflective relations to nature of an idealized "peasantry"; rather, he is reimagining it. Self-conscious awareness of the Fall and the need for redemption, coupled with an awareness of the difficulties of our relationship to nature, is essential. Once this awareness is achieved, we are in a position to realize (most often through aesthetic and/or religious reflection) the promise of authentic relations to being, with all of the personal, political, and ethical relevance of the idea of authenticity.[35]

In "Simples," we have already a sense of what that reflection might be. Innocence and prelapsarian relations to nature abound, but danger lies in its beauty. Nature provides the medicine in the very purity of its elements, yet risks a great deal in the gathering:

> Of cool sweet dew and radiance mild
> The moon a web of silence weaves
> In the still garden where a child
> Gathers the simple salad leaves.
>
> A moondew stars her hanging hair
> And moonlight kisses her young brow
> And, gathering, she sings an air:
> *Fair as the wave is, fair art thou!*
>
> Be mine, I pray, a waxen ear
> To shield me from her childish croon
> And mine a shielded heart for her
> Who gathers simples of the moon.[36]

What is a simple? It is an archaic word: "a medicine or medicament composed or concocted of only one constituent, especially of one herb or plant (obsolete); hence a plant or herb employed for medical purposes" (*The Oxford English Dictionary*, 2nd edition, 1989). The simple salad leaves become the medicines gathered from the moon. If this poem is to Joyce's troubled daughter, Lucia,[37] then the moon reflects her mental instability. Taken at face value, regardless of who it refers to, it still has an eerie quality. The speaker (and listener) is wary of the poison and antidote that the child represents. She is nature's child and, like nature, has an untamable genius. There is hope because there is medicine, but the medicine comes from elsewhere, from the lunar world of the imagination, not from earth; this sense of elsewhere gives the poem a sickly even sinful pallor from which the poet seeks protection.

"Alone" also has a sickly quality, only with a more decadent feel. Flowers of evil ("sly reeds whisper") become the delight of a "swoon of shame," reminding one of the scene from *A Portrait of the Artist as a Young Man* in which Stephen first visits the prostitutes. "A Memory of the Players in a Mirror at Midnight" has a similar tone ("nude greed of the flesh"). The latter poem ends with a type of Satanic mass: "Pluck forth your heart, saltblood, a fruit of tears. / Pluck and devour." When one is truly lost, only such gestures are left. In "Bahnohfstrasse," the "trysting and twining star" between lovers is now a mocking sign of pain. Reflecting this penitential gloom, nature in "Flood" is without hope, and love itself is as promising as the fruit of the vine, but just as uncertain and wild in its genesis and fate:

> Uplift and sway, O golden vine,
> Your clustered fruits to love's full flood,
> Lambent and vast and ruthless as is thine
> Incertitude!

At the heart of Joyce's version of nature is the forever frustrated and projected Oedipal desire. The "swoon of shame" transgresses the incest taboo. The hope invested in nineteenth-century marriages (from Lady Morgan's novel *The Wild Irish Girl* [1806] to William Allingham's epic poem *Laurence Bloomfield in Ireland* [1864]) to redeem nature and history has been winnowed down to this act of perversity, trapped between nature and culture, in the early twentieth century. The incest taboo may be said to both escape and ground the difference between nature and culture; a paradox, the incestual theme forms the basis of Joyce's meditation on a thin but real line.[38] It is as thin and as real a line as sometimes exists between nature and landscape and as difficult to draw and traverse. The torn bough of Joyce as loathed exile takes on larger significance.

In one of Joyce's most important poems, "Ecce Puer," the shifting relationship through the four generations of Joyce's family (as well as among the Holy Family that is implicit in the poem) forms the basis for the moment in which the poet, confronted, on the one hand, with the estrangement of death and, on the other, with the familiarizing homogeneity of birth, must face his deep yearning for reconciliation. The poem ends in a transport of feeling, in that upward longing that results from a fall from grace, from the nonknowledge, the despair of God, the *via negativa* that Saint John of the Cross believed we must pursue in order to imitate Christ. The speaker feels that he has deserted his father, and, being moved by the image of infancy and of the maternal world, he craves his father's forgiveness. His effort to rejoin the family, then, is a transcendent act of sympathy, one that he extends from his vision of maternal love and mercy.

If Joyce is a scandal, a blasphemer, he offers himself Christlike to redeem himself with his blasphemy. And he can redeem himself only through the intercession of the wronged mother, or parent, which is what he does in "A Prayer," the closing poem of *Pomes Penyeach*. The gender of the "you" in the poem is, for the most part, unspecified, except for the confusing phrase "Gentling her awe," where the object and subject are difficult to distinguish, but the mood seems one of lover/mother. The taboo returns in "dark nearness" with an implicit image of Mother Nature and Virgin conflated with the long-sought, but harsh, maternal judgment. The maternal body becomes like a landscape (that "lay[s] on earth"); that is, it is mediator between nature and culture. Nature is at once opposed to culture and God and indistinguishable from them, for surely nature and God in the primordial maternal darkness are one and the same, yet they work in opposition. Their opposition is historical, lapsarian, and Joyce, as ever, wants to be released from history. The inhuman he prays for help from is foreign to him: she is an "enemy" of his "will" and has a "cold touch" that he dreads. The "love" that has given the collection of poems its direction and hope has now become linked to "doom," to fate. There is a type of liberation into consciousness here that has personal as well as national implications.

In Joyce's poetry, which is a protest against himself, as he told Nora,[39] he is facing his own uncanny ghosts through landscape, love, and evasion, much as Bowen, O'Faoláin, and others would do in the decades to come. In his strange evocation of *la pietà* (one wonders whether it is Satan lying alive, "Proud by [his] downfall," Christlike in his mother's arms?), Joyce prays that the larger force bending her "threatening head" over him, and "pitying / Him who is, him who was," may "spare" him in the end. Joyce's dark complexity, full of unresolved tensions between the Oedipal/Satanic and the Christian, between nature and culture, remains influential for all writers who follow, Irish and otherwise.

7

Like Splintered Darkness

Nature, Home, Landscape, and Rebellion in Elizabeth Bowen's *The Last September* (1929)

Hermione Lee notes that "the novel is dominated above all by a sense of place."[1] With this dominant sense of place in mind, one can see that palimpsests of conquest, in nature, home, and landscape, are so interwoven in *The Last September* (1929) as at times to be inextricable. Their interrelationship, however, provides a key to understanding the text. The landscape of the novel is as much an inner landscape, to use Bowen's term,[2] as it is an outer one. The landscape seems to have its own consciousness and its own subconscious, that is, the force of rebellious nature forever threatening to erupt. Paul Stasis writes eloquently of these inner/outer aspects of landscape in *The Last September*: "Bowen here works at the boundary of the subject-object relationship, for it is never clear if this reading of the landscape is a subjective projection of the observer or a function of the land itself. And this indeterminacy is not only formal but is also the very content of the sentences themselves, whose dusk moves from land to eyes to mind without being definitively located in any of these positions."[3]

The threats of nature are apparent throughout on psychological as well as political levels, particularly in a colonial landscape. Susan Osborn writes similarly: "There is an unfamiliar and unruly quality to this novel, something that oscillates between the formed and the perceived." For Osborn, there is "exquisite tension between the rational modern world and a sense of long-forgotten forces acting within it." Though her essay is concerned with how Bowen's style manifests this tension, Osborn recognizes that much of the description on which her analysis relies centers on nature. And though she elides the difference between "nature" and "landscape," which in the present reading underlies this colonial narrative of wilderness threatening civilization, she highlights the "monstrous" aspect of nature in which "laurels breathe, leaves are like tongues, light claws like hands" that bears a "shocking taint of primitivism, of pressures exerted by energies more typically repressed, that provokes unease and anxiety and suggests a freedom of association that borders on anarchy."[4] In the present reading, the difference between nature and landscape is fundamental to understanding the significance of the "unease" that "borders on anarchy."

Most critics acknowledge in some way or another how the colonial landscape evokes class consciousness, isolation, dispossession, and national identity, and how landscape and nature can be read as illustrations of the characters' beliefs, values, and political as well as personal predicaments in *The Last September*.[5] Vera Kreilkamp writes that "such distances between the gentry home and the village . . . suggest both the social isolation and defensive self-sufficiency of Anglo-Irish life and the spatial barriers that the Big House had erected against Catholic Ireland by the early twentieth century." Yena Wang concludes that "place and time in those novels are not just the setting of backdrops for human behavior, but problematic, personified and metaphorized between lines and beyond lines."[6] Bowen's comments on Edmund Spenser's experience in Ireland and the burning of his residence Castle Kilcolman contains the threats of nature erupting in the landscape, which have been outlined so far: "Kilcolman keep, a torn-open ruin, still stands; winds race round it at every time of year. The view is of Ireland at its most intimidating—the marsh, the heartless mountains with their occasional black frown. The landscape fulfilled, for Spenser, its conveyed threat; the castle was burnt by the Irish in his absence, and one of his sons, an infant died in the fire."[7] This chapter will show how the descriptions of landscape, the threats of nature, and the political and personal ramifications thereof unfold throughout the narrative, until by the last section of the novel, the dark forces of nature and the "wild Irish" will rebel and coincidentally ensure that there is no chance of Lois marrying the English soldier Gerald Lesworth, particularly after her desire for him has dissipated in the winds of change and circumstance.

Bowen insists that we remember the ways in which the English wanted to guarantee that the Anglo-Irish, like their Norman predecessors, separated themselves from the Irish. She writes: "It was in the English interest to separate the Anglo-Irish from the Irish—the menacing solidarity of 1782, the armed hope and flourishing patriotism of the Volunteers, the sense, in fact of their Irishness in the upper classes must not occur again."[8] Bowen writes that the English viewed the Irish as "subhuman," and so the Anglo-Irish were encouraged to separate themselves from such an image. What comes between them is what separates nature from culture, animal from human. In the novel the cultivation of the aesthetic sense is another way the Anglo-Irish separate themselves from the mere Irish, but this difference is a subtle one. Much more brutal ones are made manifest and drive the country toward rebellion. Nature and the "wild Irish" are on the verge of eruption, and Gerald out on the roads, and the house at Danielstown will stand helplessly where the eruptions in the novel take place.

Seán O'Faoláin notes that what is striking about Bowen's prose, with the first paragraph of the novel being a prime example, is the "diminishment of human agency." Maud Ellmann observes how this first paragraph "floats free of human consciousness. The emphasis upon the moment intimates its brevity: forces are gathering within this landscape to erase such moments, just as the syntax conspires to erase the human will."[9] Those natural as well as political forces (sometimes one and the same) continue to gather. By the second page we hear that the wind has felled three trees. Similarly, Lois trips on "the jaws"[10] of a tiger-skin rug in an act that links nature and colonialism (the tiger was ostensibly brought back with ebony elephants from India) and intimates how this combination troubles Lois's every move. Some references to nature are subtle. The emphasis on clothes is a way of masking nature (of hiding nakedness) that goes beyond the mere haute couture of the upper classes. Lois is horrified at the idea that nails on one's fingers continually grow, that nature is a force we must constantly prune. Sometimes she seems to repress or be ignorant of our animal nature. She seems unacquainted with the body; her sexuality is virginal throughout the narrative, and she wonders how married people lying in bed don't talk all night long.[11] The implication is that the virginal Anglo-Irish talk but don't act (as the epigraph to the novel laments).

By chapter 3, we come across our first vision of the house named Danielstown as a locus for the political implications of the onslaught of nature into culture. The passage combines scenes straight out of the literature of the beautiful and the sublime, which is in fact the axis of landscape and nature. We move from the landscape of the beautiful, "lawns, banks and terraces," to the "splintered darkness" of the sublime forest.[12] The trees, symbols of nature, press upon the demesne of the Anglo-Irish like an invasion, one that will be directly connected to the rebel Irish, much as the Ribbonmen were called "vagrant seeds" (book 12, line 313) in *Laurence Bloomfield in Ireland* and threatened Bloomfield's husbandry. Finally, the darkness of the forest is offset by the lightness of the room into which Lois turns after viewing the struggle outside between the forces of light and dark, between culture and nature.

Immediately after this scene, we are told that because of the rumblings of rebellion, which the Naylors seem not to register, Cork is dangerous. The visiting Montmorencys seem more attuned to this threat. Laurence, a somewhat itinerant cousin to Lois, positively looks forward to the coming rebellion, without seeming to know what it entails. He wants some "crude intrusion of the actual." The looming eruption of nature is there to remind them all of what that thought actually means, though only Marda seems finally to grasp it. Sir Richard is perhaps the most glaring example of the obliviousness of the Anglo-Irish to their predicament. This notion is particularly true in terms of the present discussion, as he does not want to be "distracted . . . by introspection . . . or the *observation of nature*." The house, symbol of the cultural dominance of the colonial class, has become a symbol of their precarious if dominant position: "Night now held the trees with a toneless finality. The sky shone, whiter than glass, fainting down to the fretted leaf line, but was being steadily drained by the dark below, to which the grey of the lawns, like smoke, as steadily mounted. The house was highest of all with toppling imminence, like a cliff." Sitting outside, they hear the army patrols in the distance, and in their apprehension nature and war become one: "The sound paused, for a moment a pale light showed up the sky in darkness. Then behind the screen of trees at the skyline demesne boundary, the sound moved shakily, stoopingly, like someone running and crouching behind a hedge." The sound is like a rebellious intruder. The effect on the group gathered there is palpable and underscores how intricate is the relationship between nature, culture, and rebellion. "The jarring echoed down the spines of the listeners. They heard with a sense of complexity."[13] The very idea of rebellion is an obdurate truth that makes them feel awkward, an awkwardness that is reflected in the strange but clearly intentional use of the phrasing "shakily, stoopingly" to describe a sound.[14]

Lois then walks down the dark avenue alone and has a confrontation with an actual rebel on their demesne (rather than merely a sound that moves like an intruder, as in the above description). What she fears is not only the potential violence he represents, the political turmoil of the era, but also a much deeper irrational force of nature itself, a type of original sin associated with her life in the womb of her deceased mother, Laura: "A shrubbery path was solid with darkness, she pressed down it. Laurels breathed coldly and close on her bare arms, the tips of the leaves were timid and dank, like tongues of dead animals. Her fear of the shrubberies tugged at its chain, fear behind reason, fear before her birth, fear like the earliest germ of her life that had stirred in Laura. She went forward eagerly, daring a snap of the chain, singing, with a hand to the thump of her heart dramatic with terror." Lois seems ill-prepared for this event, we are told, having experienced little to strengthen the "muscle" of courage. More important, she has great difficulty understanding Ireland; "she could not conceive of her country emotionally," and doesn't know what to say to the man as he surreptitiously passes. The countryside seems no more than an "abstract of several countrysides, or an oblique, frayed island moored at the north but with an air of being detached and drawn out west from the British coast."[15] She understands only its relationship to Britain, and British civilization, moored as Ireland is by the Protestant stronghold in Northern Ireland. Gerald Lesworth, the British soldier who courts her throughout the text and is fated to be killed in an ambush, will remind her that they are there for the defense of civilization. But the natives have their own consciousness of the land, as the English and Anglo-Irish shall discover in their several ways.

What makes the situation more complicated is that in Ireland politics is a "matter of family feeling," much as, we shall see, Louis MacNeice points out in *Autumn Journal.* This sentiment is why the Naylors cannot conceive of the Irish as a malevolent force in their lives or the rebellion as a threat to their home. It is also something that Gerald doesn't understand. He is "horrified" when he learns that some of the rebels may be "friends" of Laurence (how much more horrified would Gerald be if he knew that Laurence in his cynical naïveté wishes he himself were a gunman?). But family feeling is a powerful matrix from which dark forces may erupt. The family members of the British soldiers are keenly aware of how the countryside, and nature in Ireland, is linked to the rebellion. They feel that the countryside may be "picturesque," but it is perilous as well. In an image straight out of Carleton's "Wildgoose Lodge," we hear that two members of the Royal Irish Constabulary were burned inside their barracks while defending it. The threats are real, even as the Anglo-Irish continue their game of tennis. Finding this incongruous, Lois asks, "How is it that in this country that ought to be full of such violent realness there seems nothing for me but clothes and what people say? I might as well be in some kind of cocoon."[16]

If this novel is a portrait of the artist as a young woman, we see why Lois finds particular difficulty flying by the nets of nationality, language, and religion. Women either represent the repressed nation, as they do in the *aisling* tradition, or are the image of what needs to be protected from the dark forces of rebellion, the eruptions of nature, as is also suggested in *The Last September.* We also understand why some critics believe that the rebels and women of the upper class are somehow in league together in this gender-conscious novel.[17] Gerald represents that protection, but Lois finds herself disoriented from his attention and what he represents. She also feels strangely cast into the sphere of Irish rebellion, as when she meets the rebel intruder or in the mill scene later in the novel. Gerald represents a vision of the imperial past and not the freedom of the future, whatever it proves to be, as Lois shall discover soon enough.

This confrontation for Lois not only is figurative of the Irish, English, Anglo-Irish triangulation (the Anglo-Irish look down on their English protectors much as they patronize their Irish neighbors), but also figures something deeper, more internal, a struggle of mind, body, and world. The perceptions of nature, home, landscape, and the political ramifications thereof are framed as an internal contest in a long passage at the end of the first part of the novel, titled "Mr. & Mrs. Montmorency." It is a key passage for the present discussion that needs to be quoted at length:

> The house seemed to be pressing down low in apprehension, hiding its face, as though it had her vision of where it was. It seemed to huddle its trees close in fright and amazement at the wide light lovely unloving country, the unwilling bosom whereon it was set. . . . The cabins lifting their pointed white ends, the pink and yellow farms were but half opaque, cast doubtfully on their fields the shadow of living. Square cattle moved in the fields like saints, with a mindless certainty. Single trees, on a rath, at the turn of a road, drew up light at their roots. Only the massed trees—spread like a rug to dull some keenness, break some contact between self and senses perilous to the routine of living—only the trees of the demesne were dark and exhaled darkness.[18]

That the house seems like a "rug" emphasizes its foreignness in the natural surroundings and its attempt to unify the outside and inside, to domesticate nature. It is not so easily done, however; the space is on the verge of being "blotted out" by the forest. Lois wonders how they are not afraid, as the description notes how they seem apprehensive in the paradoxical face of a "lovely unloving country, the unwilling bosom whereon it was set." The trees left superstitiously on the "rath," or fairy fort (which farmers would not plow over for fearing of angering the fairy folk), the spirits of the land are gone underground; the kitchen smoke, the lives of those individuals in the cabins cast a doubtful glance on the place of the Anglo-Irish and the colonial order in which they find themselves oppressed. The dark of twilight, the dusk, is infused throughout until it seems that the very fountain of perception is one of darkness, is a force of nature within the self, a form of subconsciousness that threatens all and sets the stage for the inner struggle of Lois, for the doomed affair between her and Gerald, for the house itself that will be in flames by the end of the novel.

The "rath," with all of the sexual significance pointed out by Angela Bourke in the first chapter of this book, is a particularly fitting symbol of the subconscious nature of perception. When Lois and Gerald cannot communicate, it is the sign of a much deeper malaise between all forms of identity (Protestants and Catholics, the Anglo-Irish and the Irish, the Anglo-Irish and the English, the Irish and the English, men and women), but also reflects the novel-long personal struggle of Lois. The cattle present a contrast to this tangle. In their saintliness, like the cattle in the Christmas crèche, they counter the malevolence of nature much as the picturesque beauty of the land belies the political dangers of Ireland. For the loveliness of the unloving country is bound to confuse the beholder. When Marda, Miss Norton, arrives in the next section, Lois will find herself caught in the historical web of psychological, political, and social significance, which will further confuse Lois and rattle the self-confident Miss Norton.

To Lois, the sexually inexperienced nineteen-year-old Marda is a revelation of sorts. Marda is a modishly androgynous figure of modernity who brings a psychological as well as historical charge that changes the makeup of the house. In fact, the importance of landscape and nature, which so marked the first part of the narrative, diminishes with the entrance of Miss Norton. The few times landscape appears, it is as though it can symbolize only ruin and disorientation: "The green strip, measureless on ahead but narrow, slanted on their left to the open meadows, on their right was bounded by a broken wall. Below the wall an unseen swift stream flowed, tinkling and knocking. The path hesitated ahead of them, faint on the turf. Here the few beeches stood unrelated, lovely, desultory between their trunks." It is as if the old paradigms of nature and culture, male and female, even Englishness and Irishness, are knocked out of their normal positions—at least for a while. In her inability to register the social constitution of Irish society, Marda, as Sir Richard notes, seems to have "come from America."[19]

She upsets the social goings-on at the house, from the Naylors to Hugo (who falls in love with yet often disapproves of her) to the friends of the house who don't know what to make of her. Marda's influence is summed up nicely in this passage: "Standing vaguely she had still that quality of directedness—from which they all swerved off in their different ways. A hardy unawareness of self in her heightened one's own consciousness. Her lightest look watched, her casual listening assessed, her speech was a lightning attack on one's integrity out of the stronghold of her indifference."[20] For Lois, however, her presence becomes a type of molting in which she figuratively steps out of herself as she literally steps out of her wet mackintosh.[21] Marda's importance is that she represents the possibilities of modernity to these people who are trapped in a dynamic of an earlier colonial, patriarchal age, even if she shies away from that modern world in the end.

Like Marda's suggestion of shifting gender roles, the Black and Tans show the effects of World War I and suggest the demise of English rule by figuring the corruption of its values. The forces of the Black and Tans are seen as a lawless if not criminal troop of British soldiers. They, like many of the soldiers, but particularly Daventry, who will be the one who informs Lois of Gerald's death, have become jaded if not cynical members of an army weary from the brutalities of trench warfare and thrust into the ambushes of a colonial rebellion for which they are likewise ill-prepared. While Marda embodies a presentiment of the modern world outside of this colonial intrigue, the cultures of the barracks and demesne seem unable to move beyond colonial and gender stereotypes. In her disorientation and yearning for a life beyond these shores, Lois represents Anglo-Irish identity caught forever on the Irish Sea between Kingstown, Ireland (present-day Dún Laoghaire), and Holyhead in Wales.

In the midst of a conversation with Gerald, who in the scene represents another intrusion of the actual, Lois "was lonely, and saw there was no future. She shut her eyes and tried—as sometimes when she was seasick, locked in misery between Holyhead and Kingstown—to be enclosed in nonentity, in some ideal no-place perfect and clear as a bubble." Yet the melodramatic scene between Gerald and Lois continues unabated until Gerald declares he would die for her. Instead of being moved by the melodrama, Lois has a strange and unconscious premonition of his death: "She thought of death and glanced at his body, quick, lovely, present and yet destructible. Something passed sensation and touched her consciousness with a kind of weight and warmth, she glimpsed a quiet beyond experience, as though for many nights he had been sleeping beside her." Their romance has an air of death about it from then on, and the sexuality erupting between them contains the motion of an "attack."[22] Laurence, both sexually and socially queered in a more substantial way than is Lois, remains aware of how differently he and Gerald understand the idea of civilization and the mission of empire. Shortly after the meetings between Gerald and Lois and then between Gerald and Laurence, Marda and Lois discuss Lois's artistic pretensions and her desire for a world away from politics and religion; in this discussion her taste for an urban sublime, rather than a natural one, is revealed. This taste for the modern will combine with the nexus of nature, home, and landscape in the climax of the section in which the mill and Mount Isabel appear.

In the last third of the section titled "The Visit of Miss Norton," landscape, nature, and rebellion return to the main focus. The Anglo-Irish group, Lois and her friends, visits the Careys at Mount Isabel. We are given a vision of both the beauty of these homes and the threats that come from the servants within. "Over the roof of Mount Isabel a mountain sheathed in pink air looked gentle and distant. Light slid over the heavy burnished trees; the cream facade of the house was like cardboard, highland confident in the sun—a house without weight, an appearance, less actual than the begonias' scarlet and wax-pink flesh. Begonias, burning in an impatience of colour, crowded over the edge of heart-shaped beds. As the four came up from the court there was silence over the sheen of grass. Then a maid leaned out from the dark through the drawing-room window sounding the brass tea-gong: a minor note." The servants have been ominously disappearing from the homes of the upper class. The upper class wonders if they have gone over to the other side. The abiding issue is whether the servants remain loyal. Laurence, rather more aware of the politics of the moment than most in this tale, understands how vulnerable his class is to history and political violence at this place and time: "A sense of exposure, of being offered without resistance to some ironic uncuriosity, made Laurence look up at the mountain over the roof of the house. In some gaze—of a man's up there hiding, watching among the clefts and ridges—they seemed held, included and to have their only being. The sense of a watcher, reserve of energy and intention, abashed Laurence, who turned from the mountain."[23] The Anglo-Irish are not entirely conscious of how they are passively defined and haunted by the Irish and the Irish countryside. Again, the personification of nature and the intentionally jagged grammar are indicative of their unstable political and psychological condition.

The stage has been set for Marda to quite literally push Lois into the future. Yet it is a future set in Gothic landscape terms that have political and sexual resonance. The only key difference from the novel's previous evocations of the Gothic is that it takes place in an abandoned mill. The chapter begins with Hugo remembering a quarrel with Laura, Lois's mother, with whom Hugo had once been enamored. The quarrel had taken place in a Norman keep, the original palimpsest of conquest, and the quarrel had grown so heated that Laura "had wished aloud it would fall on them." The sense of imminent collapse remains dominant throughout the chapter. As Marda, Hugo, and Lois approach the mill, Hugo reflects on how industry was "strangled" by "English law,"[24] though Lois runs ahead in order not to hear the end of Hugo's sentence (much as she had avoided overhearing Lady Naylor's discussion of her). It is the ruin of the industrial or modern future that never was, the industry the Anglo-Irish never promoted and that Lois will have to escape Ireland to realize.[25] For now, however, she must confront the very real specter of the "roofless" Irish themselves, who have their own future to grasp. Bowen's soft jab at "the democracy of ghostliness, [which] equalled broken palaces in futility and sadness," doesn't detract from her sense that the future is an Irish and not an Anglo-Irish one. The mill is a symbol both of nature taking over culture and of the Irish reclaiming the land that is rightfully theirs. Lois and Hugo are afraid to enter—for which Marda accuses Hugo of being a coward.

In contrast, Marda pushes Lois into the mill in a type of sexual initiation that summons the fall of Eve, the fall of the House of Usher, and the end of Anglo-Irish rule: "Marda put an arm round her waist, and in an ecstasy at this compulsion Lois entered the mill. Fear heightened her gratification; she welcomed its inrush, letting her look climb the scabby and livid walls to the frightful stare of the sky. Cracks ran down, she expected, with detachment, to see them widen, to see the walls peel back from a cleft—like the House of Usher." Once inside the mill they come across a sleeping Irish rebel. He is presented in simian stereotypes of the wild Irish. His gun looks oddly phallic, and we are not certain but it seems he fires it. Marda is injured in this sexual and political confrontation in which the rebel warns them not to be out walking and to stay in their "house" while they still "have it." This foray into the colonial ruins frightens Marda and curbs her liberating influence in the novel. She will go on to think that her fluid Irish nature will be fixed by the English nature of Leslie, her fiancé, in "a clipped and traditional garden, in Kentish light."[26] Lois, in her turn, wants to rush to Gerald and get married, but her conniving aunt, the dark forces of nature, and the wild Irish will combine to make certain there is no chance of that.

The title of part 3, "The Departure of Gerald," is purposefully misleading. One thinks he is going to leave, rather than be killed. The implication, however, is that inevitably Gerald and the Royal Army will have to depart in many manners of speaking. There is not much of a choice. From the beginning of this part, the novel becomes a type of elegy, as are many modernist novels. The decline can be measured in a number of ways: the sense of self depends on a sense of place, and the latter has been harshly questioned, leaving the self on uneven ground. There are various intertwined landscapes in this part. There is the landscape of desire and of self among the most obvious. In the end, landscape mirrors all that the English and the Anglo-Irish do not understand about Ireland and about themselves. This unfamiliar landscape verging on savage nature underlies both the conflagration that consumes the house at Danielstown and the ambush that kills Gerald. What threatens the landscape most is wilderness, is nature in its wild state, untouched by civilization. This wilderness literally burns down the house. It has been threatening the house throughout the elegiac novel, and only Lois and Laurence seem to pay heed.

The dance that begins this part of the novel is set against the social gatherings earlier in the novel because we notice how wildly despairing is the mood when compared with other earlier gatherings. The two types of dance remind us of the happy versus the dangerously bacchanalian and rebellious one in *Laurence Bloomfield in Ireland*. The coming of the dance at the Raltes is attended by fears that the roads may be too dangerous. The Raltes themselves are "cast as wild young Irish," for which "they rather liked themselves." The shell-shocked soldier Mr. Daventry is described as "a shade satanic," making this description a marker for the coming collapse of the colonial system. He is beginning to "hate Ireland." And in his wry anger, he grabs his dancing partner's ankles "harshly, as though it had been a man's. She kicked, and a high-heeled slipper went rocketing through the air. A forest of hands went up."[27] Bowen is subtly signaling with the phrase "forest of hands" that the eruption of nature, the march of the forest into the houses of the ruling class, is imminent.

Lois still intends to marry Gerald and has written to her friend Viola to tell her, but it is only a gesture at this point. The marriage is as doomed as the house, as well as Anglo-Irish and English rule (at least in the South of Ireland). The women seem not to understand the soldiers' increasingly desperate plight, which contributes to the air of unease. When the dancing finally begins in earnest, it is clear what moves the dancers: "The evening 'went' with a rush, with a kind of high impetuousness out of everybody's control. Everyone looked and spoke and danced close up with a kind of exalted helplessness, intimacy tightened the very air." The situation in Ireland is clearly spinning out of control. It is a dance of despair. The intimacy is one of governed appetite, grown desperate and afraid. Lois remembers Gerald's kiss as being "administered," not "exchanged." The ruling metaphor of marriage between Ireland and England has been revealed for what it is—a colonial administration: "Under the wall a sentry inhumanly paced like a pendulum. The country bore in its strong menace."[28]

In this atmosphere, Lois and Gerald struggle to understand one another: "The soft sound of her dress in the wind became, by some connection of mood, painfully inexplicable to her—the pain was its own, from not being understood." A more general conversation ensues on the dance floor as to whether the Raltes are loyal to the Irish or the English. Meanwhile, Daventry is drawn to Lois, but he is so deeply wounded as to have seemingly lost his humanity. As Lois thinks, "She saw there was not a man here, hardly even a person." The dance goes on and on until it seems that the "cracks of the walls that had been straight a minute ago like bars now seemed to bulge out visibly." Again, the House of Usher seems about to fall. Lois is still thinking of the kiss, but "one kiss in the wind, in the dark, was no longer particularized: she could not remember herself, or remember him." Desire, political and sexual, has become amorphous and vague. Gerald cannot sharpen it, though in a letter he later tries; Lois knows only that she craves specific weight, clarity, and density. The autumnal quality of the novel, for Lois, possesses the "sweet shocks of goodbye, transition." Clearly, for her, as for Ireland, change is impending. Discussing Marda's possible happiness with Hugo, she thinks, "Even now, shall we never be natural?" This reference to the natural is not a casual one, as it is what people on all sides crave. They crave an unfettered, un-self-conscious nature but discover the violence of nature instead. Nature, like Ireland, has two sides: its redemptive beauty and its ferocity. For Lois, what she discovers is what she is missing: "She and these home surroundings still further penetrated each other mutually in the discovery of a lack."[29]

For the rest of the novel she will attempt to fill that lack, with her drawing, with the idea of marriage, with notions of travel and the fulfillment of elsewhere. Even as she appreciates the beauty of where she is and how she loved the "sense of being located, warmed her surroundings," she quickly imagines her life "constructed" in "China." Hugo perhaps understands best how landscape can mirror desire and human encounters as well as how "perishable" the sense of being located is if the inner state is as "barren" as his, "until finally, by even the same conjunction of mountains and light and trees, it would not be evoked again."[30] In many ways, he is alter ego to Lois. He is haunted by his love for Lois's mother, Laura, much as Lois is. Hugo then becomes an object of a muted Electra complex for Lois.

Soon after this scene, Lois has a type of negative epiphany in which she realizes again what is missing and the ways in which she has betrayed herself. The relation of the landscape of plantation, the wilderness of nature, and the narcissism of self helps her to understand:

> For to have followed the stream to this loneliest reach, beyond the plantation wall where the meadow's hedge showered unknown blackberries over the water, was not to have walked, to have strolled even, but to have betrayed oneself in an emotional kind of straying. Further down, stepping-stones had been displaced by last winter's flood, there was a ruined cottage, nobody came here. Even Lois had given up, since her eighteenth birthday, coming to lie on her stomach along the bank, weep out a bottomless despair at nothing and look at herself in the stream. And this wildness within the demesne boundaries, within sound of the farmyard bell, had a particular desolation.[31]

Still thinking she will marry Gerald, Lois is denied the vision of place and self she so desires. Instead, she is left with the "desolation" of "wildness" within the demesne. To have indulged herself in the walk to its narcissistic end would have been an act of self-betrayal at this stage of her maturation (which has by now developed into romantic disillusionment). This awareness is a sort of coming of age in her eighteenth and nineteenth years.

Lady Naylor, who is very much like Wilde's Lady Bracknell (just as Laurence is Wilde-like), intervenes and essentially dismantles the relationship between Lois and Gerald. Yet neither Lois nor Gerald understands it is finished. When they meet again, the stage has been set for the dissolution of their engagement. The brutality of nature and of political violence contributes to the breakup. Laurence steps on a snail, thinking it is just a shell, and Lois is horrified. She later tells Gerald that he is killing her like a snail, which of course confounds the straightforward Englishman. It also highlights Lois's confusion as she herself wants to be compelled by Gerald, who resists this wish, much as she was compelled by Marda to enter the mill. Laurence, on the other hand, meets three armed men on a "boreen" and is robbed of his shoes (to ensure his inability to report the encounter) and his watch. It happens shortly after his stepping on a snail. The denial of agency to either snail or man or woman underscores the colonial horror that haunts this September tale. As a result, the wood becomes "incredible" to the now "numbed" Gerald, while the "glare of summer" becomes "incomprehensible" to Lois.[32] The reticulation of nature, home, and landscape has become a web of all those aspects of self that no one understands about themselves or their situations.

The news of Gerald's death exposes this uncertain aspect of the novel in no uncertain terms: "The shocking news reached Clonmore about eight o'clock. It crashed upon the unknowingness of the town like a wave that for two hours, since the event, had been standing and toppling, imminent. The news crept down streets from door to door like a dull wind, fingering the nerves, pausing. In the hotel bars heads went this way and that way, quick with suspicion." The people are like Adam and Eve after the Fall—guilty, angry, and divided: "They all felt naked and were ashamed of each other, as though they had been wrecked. From the hut floor—where they had danced—the wicker furniture seems to rise and waver." They have been cast out of Eden and face their expulsion to the wasteland. No art school for Lois, merely travel. The Montmorencys—Hugo and his wife, Francie—have left, having given up the idea of building a bungalow. In *Bowen's Court* (1942), written more than a decade after *The Last September*,

Bowen notes that Spenser kept a vision of Ireland's beauty alive in *The Faerie Queene*, one untouched by the flames that took down Kilcolman, yet we may note that in his other writing he was also haunted by the terror and famine hidden in the woods. Similarly, the landscape of Ireland, though beautiful to Daventry, has become "unfamiliar" as he arrives to inform Lois and the family of Gerald's death. Truisms are passed around about the nobility of Gerald's death and the English cause, but they count as futile reminders of the implacability of this historical moment and its independence from the colonial design. Sir Richard is the most fitting emblem of the Anglo-Irish. He suffers knowing that his neighbors and acquaintances the Connors are aware of who did what, but he "was an old man, really, outside all this, and did not know what to do."[33] Autumn is moving toward winter, toward the final eruption of wilderness and wild Irishness into this emptied landscape and barren culture.

There has been a harsh intrusion of the actual, as Laurence portended. Autumn will not be seen again in the same light by Lady Naylor or Sir Richard. Only nature will record the season in the changing leaves:

> The two did not, however, again see Danielstown at such a moment, such a particular happy point of decline in the short curve of the day, the long curve of the season. Here, there were no more autumns, except for the trees. By next year light had possessed itself of the vacancy, still with surprise. Next year, the chestnuts and acorns pattered unheard on the avenues, that, filmed over with green already, should have been dull to the footsteps—but there were no footsteps. Leaves, fluttering down the slope with the wind's hesitation, banked formless, frightened, against the too clear form of the ruin.[34]

The question remains: What can survive? What will grow from this wilderness? There is a certain amount of ambivalence about Irish independence. As Patricia Craig writes of Bowen, "She thought that however dubiously her ancestors and others had obtained their Irish holdings, they'd sufficiently enriched the life of the country to mitigate the initial injustice."[35] That awareness of the "initial injustice" is perhaps why there is a sense in the final description that the burning of the Big Houses in the immediate area is in fact a natural return to native ground and ownership. *The Last September* is a typical colonial/postcolonial text in that its conscious design is often tellingly complicated by contrary allegiances. As Bowen observes of the Anglo-Irish in general in her preface to *The Last September*, "Inherited loyalty (or at least adherence) to Britain . . . pulled them one way, their own temperamental Irishness the other."[36] Regardless, the loss of the Anglo-Irish will be a loss of culture, almost a loss of those with the capacity to appreciate the beauty of autumn as Lady Naylor perceives it. Who will be there to admire the scenery? No one will hear the acorns pattering on the ground. Yet autumn has an air of "homecoming," like the leaves spinning down from the gate, as though nature and the Irish were reclaiming their rightful place. The decline has become too extreme. The long curve of the season has reached its end.

Danielstown will not be the only victim, but one of many that died with the day itself, as the country was on fire, cabin and Big House alike in a state of despair. In fact, nature itself seems part of the panic and despair. The strange juxtaposition of "order and panic" emphasizes the inevitability and ambiguity of this eruption, as if it were in the order of things, but of what it is difficult to say:

> For in February, before those leaves had visibly budded, the death—the execution, rather—of the three houses, Danielstown, Castle Trent, Mount Isabel, occurred in the same night. A fearful scarlet ate up the hard spring darkness; indeed, it seemed that an extra day, unreckoned, had come to abortive birth that these things might happen. It seemed, looking from east to west at the sky tall with scarlet, that the country itself was burning, while to the north the neck of mountain before Mount Isabel was frightfully outlined. The roads in unnatural dusk ran dark with movement, secretive or terrified; not a tree, brushed pale by wind from the flames, not a cabin pressed in despair to the bosom of night, not a gate too starkly visible but had its place in the design of order and panic.[37]

The play on execution, as Ellmann has shown, points both to death and to legality, like the execution of a will. The houses have become personalities,[38] and this final act is part of the execution of a will, as if, against their intentions, the Anglo-Irish were bequeathing Ireland to the Irish. Yet will the latter group be up to the task of taking over? Is the day coming to an "abortive birth," a sign of what's to come or rather not to come? This personification is meant to highlight the human aspect of the landscapes created by the Anglo-Irish that nature and the wild Irish consistently threatened. There is the pale (whether around Dublin or Cork) and then what lies beyond it. "At Danielstown, half way up the avenue under the beeches, the thin iron gate twanged (missed its latch, remained swinging aghast) as the last unlit car slid out with the executioners bland from accomplished duty. The sound of the last car widened, gave itself to the open and empty country and was demolished. Then the first wave of a silence that was to be ultimate flowed back confidently to the steps. The door stood open hospitably upon a furnace." The entrance of what lies beyond the pale leaves the house "aghast."

Oddly enough, the entrance of the wild Irish is aided by the modern, by the car that carries the incendiaries in and hurries them out, but this combination of modern and pagan is often made. It is techno-paganism of a sort that destroys the old sanctities of tradition, as Marda promised to do before her acquiescence. The incursion also interferes with intimate human encounters. The last lines of the novel make this clear: "Sir Richard and Lady Naylor, not saying anything, did not look at each other, for in the light from the sky they saw too distinctly."[39] What they see distinctly remains for us indistinct and perhaps in the end for them as well, which is why Bowen leaves what they see unnamed and merely implicit. For what do they see, but the turning of the gyres, the coming of a new era, to which they and their world are no longer central? The eruption of nature has finally made them irrelevant, but, as with any social upheaval, one is not sure what the lie of the land will be in the not-so-distant future.

8

Through Tightly Closed Eyes

History, Guilt, and the Aesthetic in Seán O'Faoláin

❧ In a number of well-known early short stories ("Fugue," "Midsummer Night Madness," "A Broken World," and "Admiring the Scenery"), Seán O'Faoláin describes how the dialectic of landscape and nature reiterates the original sin of decolonization during the revolutionary action and reaction taking place in the Ireland of that time. The first two stories reflect specifically on Ireland's revolutionary struggle, but all the stories consider communal and individual consciousness within the larger frame of Irish history. The relationship of nature and landscape reflects how community is in tension with loneliness and solitude, while simultaneously recording history and marking the need for the aesthetic perspective that landscape and wilderness (nature) provide. Such perspective points the way toward reconciliation, however partial and deferred, however imbued with longing and suffering. Nature is both darkly foreboding and potentially redemptive.

The shortest and most impressionistic story, "Fugue," begins with a powerful rendering that captures, first, how a flooded landscape mirrors the curse of history; second, how nature, particularly mountain scenery, provides an avenue for escape; and last, how human habitations, particularly the culture of home, cannot escape the influence of the negative aspect of nature even though they provide shelter from it. Landscape is the bridge that carries us to and away from nature itself, and to and away from culture as well. Importantly, the feminine bears the brunt of the curse of nature and history, while the two men at the heart of the story (Rory and the narrator) are preparing for an onslaught by the Black and Tans. The latter notorious military group, often if mistakenly described as recently released prisoners,[1] is indicative of the lawless nature of the scene. This scene is followed by a memory of retreating on the previous night through a sublime setting: "We were retreating from Inchigeela by the back-roads and we two had lost ourselves in the barren and rocky place they call the Rough, a difficult place by day and almost impassable by night."[2] The deserted quality of the Rough, its very name, the barking of dogs, the physical exhaustion of "trudging" for such a long time, felt more keenly by the narrator and less by the country boy Rory, all combine in the fear of getting a "bullet in the head before the dawn."

The men proceed through what is described as "a boggy hollow" (a phrase for female genitalia used more recently by John McGahern in *That They May Face the Setting Sun*), where they find a woman "used to this sort of thing [men on the run one presumes] and pitying [them]." She comes down "barefooted, her black hair around her, a black cloak on her shoulders, not altogether drawn over her pale breast, a candle blown madly by the wind slanting in her hand." Though this refuge proves short-lived, there is communication between the narrator and the woman: "Thrice that morning I longed for an end to this vagabond life, longed for I dared not think what; but there was in it the scent and light of flowers and the scent of woman and her soft caresses. She had looked at me as if we had between us some secret love: not one woman in ten thousand will look so at one man in as many thousand, perhaps not one in all his life, never more than one would I have said a day ago and now one such had looked at my eyes." This shared perspective, sudden familiarity with a stranger, makes the narrator envision the mystery of his native city inundated by the twilight, which turns the city into a version of the previous mountain scene: "I thought at once of the evening glow of the city streets when the sun has gone behind the tallest houses, when the end of the day is near, and the canyon-alleys are suffused with dusk and slow-moving lights." The transformation reveals the deep solitude at evening like that exposed in the epic flight of these two men from the death that trails them. It is a type of awakening, a return to nature: "When men waken from the sleep of day and returning in upon themselves think of love, and the darkness where love is, and wander out from the city to the dark fields seeking a secret loneliness for the pain."[3]

Later the men come across farmers threshing wheat, separating the seed from the chaff, in a biblical mirror of their predicament, not knowing whether in this war of independence they are doing the will of the Lord or the work of Satan (when it is probably both). To feel the heavy weight of this condition, it helps to first compare the parable of the Tares to the ending of the short story and its images of the Deluge, and then to the earlier description of the threshing (which is best seen in light of the story's close):

> The kingdom of heaven is likened unto a man which sowed good seed in his field: But while men slept, his enemy came and sowed tares among the wheat, and went his way. . . . The servants said unto him [the householder], Wilt thou then that we go and gather them up? But he said, Nay; lest while ye gather up the tares, ye root up also the wheat with them. Let both grow together until the harvest: and in the time of harvest I will say to the reapers, Gather ye together first the tares, and bind them in bundles to burn them: but gather the wheat into my barn. (Matt. 13:24–30)

The parable shows the way to heaven through ethical behavior, but also acknowledges that evil is inevitably sown and reaped with the good. The narrator, alone now at the conclusion of the story, with Rory, his partner, dead, reflects: "I might have been the last human creature to crawl to the last summit of the world waiting until the Deluge and the fortieth night of rain would strain him upwards on his toes while the water licked his stretched neck. Yet everywhere they slept sound abed, my dark woman curling her warm body beneath the bed-clothes, the warmer for the wet fall without, thinking if she turned and heard the dripping eaves—that winter was at last come. . . . Down below me in the valley I heard an early cart; the morning wind, light and bitter, sang occasionally in the key of the flooded streams. The dawn moved along the rim of the mountains and as I went down the hill felt life begin once more its ancient, ceaseless gyre."[4] In this

Yeatsian allusion (to "gyre"), there is a parallel to the threshing of the parable, that good and evil shall be sorted in the apocalypse or revelation of the next historical phase.

Seen in light of the end of the story and the biblical parable, the description of the threshing in the mountains earlier in the story takes on powerful allegorical significance. It does so particularly because it comes in the middle of what is a pitched battle between Irish nationalists on the run and the Black and Tans chasing them:

> The chaff was always driving away before the wind, and now and again someone would look up and around at the sky and say to the man whose stack was being threshed in this communal fashion of the mountains:
>
> "Maybe, it will hold dry."
>
> The other would look up and around and say:
>
> "Maybe it will. It might then, it's a strong wind."
>
> Then they would set to work again, piking and tossing the broken sheaves and we moved down at last to the road.[5]

The mystery of this story rises from the combination of sex, landscape, history, and guilt. In the allusion to the separation of seed from chaff, like the reference to the Deluge, there is a sense that the original sin remains to be cleansed, the Oedipus or Electra complex to be resolved. The narrator seems as much a passive vessel for the feelings associated with this motif as he is conscious of what they mean. There is little reflection on the events; it is more of a catalog of merely sensual and descriptive observations. The erotic encounters are both imagined and real, and they function as both a blessing and a curse, full, as they are, of the sense of sin and the hope of escape from his historical predicament. In many ways, he is no less innocent in these encounters than that child he finds himself next to in the cart as he makes his retreat, only more aware of his power and prideful of it. For both there is a need for closeness and familiarity amid the darkness and fear:

> My eyes were beginning to close with the rough swaying of the cart when suddenly the child clasping my hand said:

> "Are you afraid of the pookas? I am!"
>
> And fell upon my breast and laid her head by mine and I put an arm around her and we lay so, jolting along under the stars and the driving fleeces overhead. But as suddenly, when about a mile had passed she pressed nearer and swiftly kissed me. Then she rolled away from me to the other side of the cart, though still grasping my coat-sleeve in terror of the black night all around.[6]

The most openly erotic encounter is with the "woman from the morning," and it takes place just after the scene with the child. The juxtaposition highlights the line between nature and culture in the taboo that reigns between adult and child. In this scene, which is about to fall into lovemaking (though not with the child), the body becomes almost like the landscape the two men have been hurrying through and mirrors the wounds of war that underlie the scene. The breast is like a "casque," or helmet. The woman looks on the encounter as would a sick woman to a doctor.[7]

Like the pooka, one of the solitary fairies, the scenario can bring either good or bad fortune. For the narrator, it is the calm before the storm. The imminent lovemaking is interrupted. He is forced to flee and finds himself in the most desolate landscapes, then in a ruin, before he faces the Deluge, with memories of the woman haunting him and a strong sense of the turning of the gyres. The Deluge and the "dark woman" follow, and both are colored by the image of threshing and the parable of the Tares. There is a dramatic reordering of history taking place. A long Irish folk song, which O'Faoláin had himself collected, intervenes before the conclusion of the story, and it promises some future change left undescribed. The song is one of nature flooded and helter-skelter. "Each lake is a great tidal sea." The "wolves" cannot "rest," the birds cannot find shelter, the snow has "crushed" the wood, the "ancient bird of Glenn Rye / Is grieved by the cold wind." The opening question of the song—"Cold till doom?"—is simply answered "cold till doom." In the depths of such a mood, of nature gone astray, the narrator walks into dawn with a sense of a "new day." It is as if the palimpsests of history have been erased by the Deluge, the war, the human encounters (taboo threatening and otherwise), and the experience of death and change in the turning of the "ancient, ceaseless gyre."[8]

Another early short story that binds the sexual, the historical, and nature/landscape is "Midsummer Night Madness," in which a rebel on the run tries to take refuge in a Big House, where he thinks no one—the Black and Tans being the prime worry—will think to look for him. His first exit out of the city where he has been hiding finds him taking solace in the pastoral like "one long in city pent," which is how Milton describes Satan as he enters Paradise.[9] "Then I turned to the open fields and drew in a long draught of their sweetness, the May-month sweetness as only a man could who had been cooped up for months past under one of those tiny roofs, seeing the life of men and women only through a peep-hole in a window-blind, seeing those green fields only in the far distance from an attic skylight."[10] On his way to the crumbling Anglo-Irish demesne, he reflects on the aristocrat of the eponymous Henn house. The Miltonic reference turns sour, much as Satan's momentary hesitation at the beauty of Eve before bringing about the Fall lapses quickly into the sin of covetousness. Henn is notorious for his lechery; the narrator recalls a story his mother told him of when, as a young girl, she and all her friends decided to take off their new shoes and stockings to bathe in the river. There they find Henn himself bathing naked (in his "pelt"). The ensuing Ovidian encounter in which animal and human imagery metamorphoses tells a mythic tale, mixing Christian and pagan themes:

> My mother often told us how as she and a crowd of school girl friends were returning from their first Communion one cold autumn afternoon they entered his fields to take a short way by the river to their homes, removing their new shoes and stockings as they always did when they left the high road, and they came on Henn—and he was a grown man then—standing in his pelt by the river, ready for a swim. She used shudder as she told how he chased them, and they ran from him, screaming with fear, throwing away the new shoes and stockings as they ran, their legs all torn on the withered rushes

> of the bog and the furzed hedge-tops, not daring to look back to see if the naked "madman" were catching up with them, until, as she said, they had left his fields "forty miles behind" and panting and exhausted they ran into their homes.[11]

This memory of postcommunion relapse into the Fall leads to the narrator recalling the fear, common among the populace, that Henn would "salt" any girl he could catch and how on the night of a wedding he would in fact invoke *le droit de seigneur.* The original sin of conquest is indelibly a part of this brutally sexualized relationship between the conquered and the conquerors.

The early celebration of nature is doomed as the narrator heads into the grips of a nature long fallen into the sins of history. The "sweetness" now is mixed with something much more Satanic and fearful, combining the chaos of nature with the soft temptations of the feminine, tinged with the darkness of death: "Everything here too seeming to send up its sweetness into the soft wet air, even the weeds bursting through the gravel, and when I came to the front of the house the great dark cypresses might in the wet failing light have been plumes of billowy smoke that rose against the sky. . . . I almost expected to see the old libertine come floating up like a spectre or a long-legged ogre through the hills." Landscape here is a palimpsest of conquest in which the niceties of pronunciation and manners veil the violence and Oedipal nightmare of the house's colonial roots: "The home [is] one of the 'garrison' people, one of those thousand unofficial blockhouses of the English on Irish soil." Henn then appears with "the face of a bird, mottled and bead-eyed, and his hair, tawny in streaks with the glister of oil . . . with one lock at the back that stood out like a cock's comb."[12] Not only does he blur nature and culture, but his vision is fading so that all of the seasons of the year look like "a foggy autumn." This image is at the end of his last September, and he is still obsessed by the "backwardness" of the Irish.[13] Henn, however, has inverted the usual animal/man dialectic between Anglo-Irish and Irish. He is now animallike.

Inside the mansion, the narrator encounters a battalion commander, Stevey, a tinker woman who is called Gypsy, as well as Henn.

It is an odd triangle, a sort of malevolent Trinity in which it is difficult and perhaps useless to tell who is sleeping with whom, but the woman is pregnant, and Stevey, the rebel friend, is abusive to both of them. Stevey has not been doing his national military duty. The narrator had been sent to check on him and find out why. Yet he is ambivalent at first because Stevey had been in prison with him. His ambivalence vanishes by the end of the story. There is one moment when at night the rebel narrator, who is an insomniac, comes upon the tinker girl and Henn in a deserted Lodge, a foreboding image of their later union and what it tells us of the future of Ireland: "For somehow country and freedom seemed a small thing under this austere darkness with that pair, heavy with one another's sorrow, down in the weather-streaked decaying cottage; and with the memory of those drooping mother's breasts and that large mother's belly on the young girl, and the look of pity on the old libertine's face, I find myself walking aimlessly on and on."[14]

In the denouement, Stevey and his battalion of men have burned another Anglo-Irish family (the Blakes) out of their home. The Blake family consists of two old maids, both of whom stand in stark contrast to the lecherous Henn and their captain father. It is as though the gentry was either rapacious or aloof. Stevey insists that Henn marry the girl or his house will be burned as well. Henn finally agrees, and the marriage of sad young pregnant girl and dirty old man seems a sorry image of the future of Ireland rising amid the Oedipal morass of its history. The original sin is repeated in this misshapen *aisling*, which in the end the narrator is left to consider. We are left with this discomforting image of their exile in Paris: "But I find it too painful to think of him, there in Paris, with his scraps of governess-French, guiding his tinker wife through the boulevards, the cafés, the theatres—seeing once more the lovely women and the men gay in their hour. Life is too pitiful in this recapturing of the *temps perdu*, these brief intervals of reality." The story of Ireland itself then is reduced to such a Proustian interval, the mind reflecting on its own processes, retracing the harsh history that has been written in the Irish countryside, and is now left for the Irish to read.

One of the most subtle renderings of the Catholic, or peasant Irish, attitude toward nature is found in O'Faoláin's short story "Admiring the Scenery" (1938), in which several men wait for and then ride a train through the Irish countryside. "Admiring the Scenery," like the other stories, places the individual against the historical backdrop that the landscape provides in order to paint a picture of individual as well as communal suffering and need. The story consists of three characters, and a number of remembered ones. There is Mr. Governey, referred to at times as the "small dark man"; there is the priest; and there's finally Mr. Hanafan. The remembered ones consist of what seems to be the beloved of Hanafan, a memory that haunts and surrounds him, much as does the mnemonic device of the landscape itself. Then there is Boyhan, a stationmaster Hanafan had met and whose family had either left him or died. Boyhan in his loneliness is driven to sing in the immensity of the landscape around him. His figure will provide the underlying motif of the story and answer the question of what constitutes admiration of the scenery. He provides the story within the story and, with it, the emotional color of the deepest springs of aesthetic understanding. As recalled by Hanafan, his daughter is a nun, his son is gone, and his wife has died. Though he is not a good singer, he has hope that his talent will be discovered by someone passing through the station. The sense of being steeped in the night (Boyhan's singing is of "the whole night," as Hanafan states), of being constellated in the night sky, stays with Hanafan until the end of the story, at which point we discover him weeping at the thought of the admiration of scenery and the lives of those individuals living amid it. General grief and people's recurrent needs upset Hanafan, altering his perception of himself.

Whether Hanafan is disillusioned or transcends his predicament through the aesthetic reflection of the artist, which many readers feel that he represents, is a matter of critical debate. Butler thinks that "Hanafan attempts to find some consolation in the beauty of the evening and in the possibility of a subtle communication between human beings and nature, but he is an unhappy and frustrated man, and his sensitivity to memories and impressions forms an ironic contrast with the bleakness of his inner life. The only possible solution to the predicament of life in Ireland, O'Faoláin seems to suggest, is that of the priest: 'a good-humored fatalism that inures one against hope.'"[15] Harmon, on the other hand, believes that "Hanafan in 'Admiring the Scenery' [is] the most rational and sensitive of the three (characters) with the most balanced response to life. . . . [He] suffers from the knowledge that his environment cannot satisfy his imaginative needs. External marks of frustration prevail but the artist himself is not defeated. Out of the negative factors that appeal to him, and despite the general feeling of hopelessness, he continues to create ordered and disciplined work."[16] The present discussion tends toward the belief that the beauty of the lonely landscape retains its significance even in the face of perhaps irremediable suffering and disappointment. In short, he is able to achieve perspective on his own condition, which may be a sufficient end in itself—for what, one may ask, is transcendence, but the ability at times to stand apart and understand one's own position?

From the opening sentence of "Admiring the Scenery," it is clear how much human perspective defines the landscape: "From between the little platforms the railway shot two shining arrows off into the vast bogland where they vanished over a rise that might have been imperceptible without them." Denis Sampson in his essay on this short story observes of this sentence:

> A central paradox of the story is also introduced: the curve of the terrain "might have been imperceptible" without the human intervention, and this epistemological ambiguity is intensified later in the first paragraph in such phrases as "seemed to be" and "might have been." "Eyes" assume a significance throughout as a motif related to the human engagement through the senses with nature, but already an area of concern is delimited for the reader: the separation of human consciousness from, and desire for integration with, the earth on which the process of living occurs, and which is perhaps a symbol of universal harmony and coherence.[17]

The question of whether the common people admire the scenery is asked by Hanafan, whose own life will provide an extraordinary answer: "I wonder . . . do the common people ever admire scenery?" There is an interchange in which the priest insists they do admire the scenery while the others debate the issue. They also debate what such admiration requires. Governey insists one must be conscious of one's admiration for it to be true appreciation:

> "I know what you mean," interrupted the small man, and he wagged his finger into the priest's face [with whom he agreed]. "I know. I met men like that. Our gardener at home, for example, I'd say to him—he was an awful old drunkard—he'd be lying of a hot summer's afternoon under an apple-tree—a lazy old ruffian. "Grand day, Murphy," I'd say. "Oh, a grand day, God bless it," he'd say, "and isn't it good to be alive?"
>
> "But that's not admiring the scenery," went on the small man. "It's not being conscious of it. It isn't, if you understand me, projecting the idea of the beauty of the scene, the idea, into one's own consciousness. Is it now, Hanafan? And that's what you mean by admiring the scenery."[18]

Hanafan replies that he is not sure what he meant, but assures them that one can admire the scenery without being conscious of one's admiration. The notion that the mind should be aware of its own processes is a crucial part of the romantic (Kantian) idea of nature from Wordsworth to the contemporary period. The story asks if this self-consciousness is what is missing from Irish attitudes, even Irish romantic ones. Perhaps it may be because Irish attitudes toward nature were projected onto folklore and myth and have as much in common with Greek ideas of nature's universal animus (certainly Yeats's do) as with Enlightenment ones.[19] O'Faoláin gives us another reason, however. Landscapes are a series of personal secrets waiting to be unlocked.[20]

The men begin to reminisce, thinking of Gray, Moore, melancholy poets of sensibility and romanticism. The songs of the poets, like the songs of the birds, are of different value, whether elegiac or visionary. Gray's evocation in the "Elegy" of the plowman "homeward plodding his weary way" and his unquoted scrutiny of how a poet might never come into existence in the neglected rural world mirror the predicament of Boyhan, the stationmaster, who is badly singing his broken heart out. Governey insists that admiration consists of some form of "intellectual concept."[21] As stated earlier, we learn that Hanafan is moved by a memory of some secret grief, perhaps the loss of the beloved linked to the image of Boyhan, which the scenery seems to reveal to him. In the last paragraph of the story there is an almost subconscious sympathy between the landscape outside the train and the weeping Hanafan within. This sympathy has little to do with the conscious awareness of the landscape that the conversation had presumed was necessary for admiration of the scenery, relying instead on another much deeper awareness of the relationship between humanity and nature:

> As they rolled on through the bog the small man kept looking around him restlessly, and at last he shifted over to the three countrymen, determined to find out if the common people really do admire the scenery. He started a conversation about turf-cutting, but before he could lead up to the question the train halted at a small station and the strangers got out. Then the three friends were left alone in the cold, damp carriage, listening to the battering rain. Tired and sleepy, nobody noticed that, in his corner, Hanafan was weeping to himself, the drops creeping through his tightly closed eyes.[22]

The rain outside and the weeping Hanafan, within the train, remind us of the mutual sympathy of the medieval Irish writers, of some unconscious connection between nature and mind that is not self-conscious. As Hanafan says of another man who had no "intellectual concept" of his admiration, but was immersed in the depths of perception, "I'd say that the man was enjoying the scenery even though he might not know he was doing so at all." Where history is so psychologically invasive, so radical in *nature*, barren or fertile landscapes mirror the complexities of experience in unconscious ways, yet the land has not become a conscious part of the scenery. In Synge's *The Aran Islands*, there is an episode in part 3 where another such moment is imagined, where nature and self are indistinguishable and landscape has not yet appeared: "At one moment she is a simple peasant, at another she seems to be looking out at the world with a sense of prehistoric disillusion and to sum up in the expression of her grey-blue eyes the whole external despondency of the clouds and sea."[23]

In *Landscape and Memory*, after Simon Schama has discussed how the movement from nature to landscape occurs, he continues, "But it should also be acknowledged that once a certain idea of landscape, a myth, a vision, establishes itself in an actual place, it has a peculiar way of muddling categories, of making metaphors more real than their referents; of becoming, in fact, part of the scenery."[24] By nature we must mean something different from landscape or culture and something that, regardless of Schama's ordering, precedes them both—something we feel we are a part of, without being aware of how. This primitive feeling appealed to Synge, as it appealed to many modernists. We may say that often it is nature, like the long-lost primeval Irish forest, with its depths of origins, its dream of the unconscious, that tells us as much about Irish experience as does landscape, especially in the ways that violence historically erupts, for the latter too often paints the Irish caught between the metaphor and the real, trying to redefine the conventions that have been imposed upon them, trying, like Hanafan in "Admiring the Scenery," to find some absolution in nature. To find absolution in nature, however, one must enlarge the question of self to enclose the question of community, of family, and of home.

O'Faoláin's story "A Broken World" presents an image of community that harks back to *The Deserted Village*, Goldsmith's eighteenth-century pastoral celebration and lamentation over a lost way of life. In "A Broken World," a priest despairs over the world of parishes like his, believing that "where there is no moral unity there is no life . . . that life is a moral unity with a common thought. The compositum of one's being, emerging from the Divine Essence, which is harmony itself, cannot, unless it abdicates its own intelligence and lives in chaos, that is to say, in sin, a disunity with itself. Since society, however, is an entity composed of many members, life becomes a moral unity with a common thought." Lacking moral unity, common thought, and harmony, he concludes, you are left with "a broken world."[25] The priest and the narrator discuss the social conditions that have created this predicament. The ascendancy class has abandoned the land to the former tenants who in turn don't want it, preferring instead to "live in the towns and cities and work for wages." Loneliness, isolation, and land that is hardly arable seem to be the root causes of this desolation. The narrator's closing meditation is on the need for some sort of redemptive power to flow from the land: "What image of life that would fire and fuse us all, what music bursting like the spring, what triumph, what engendering love, so that those breasting mountains that now looked cold should appear brilliant and gay, the white land that seemed to sleep should appear to smile, and these people who huddled over the embers of their lives should become like the peasants who held the hand of Faust with their singing one Easter morning?"[26] This condition, the landscape that represents it, and this desire for redemption from the Faustian bargain are a common theme in early O'Faoláin, especially its sense of loneliness and desolation answered by the feminized "breasting" landscape. It is also important to Patrick Kavanagh, as shall be shown.

There is a moment in "Admiring the Scenery" when Hanafan remembers addressing Boyhan with a quote from Sir Thomas Browne's *The Garden of Cyrus* after Boyhan has shown him "photographs of his daughter, the nun, and of his son, Timsy, with, as he said, a lawn-tennis in his hand. He had no wife. She was dead." Hanafan seems to be trying to soothe this man living "alone in the station, three miles from the village and his only two children in the world away in exile."[27] He wants to offer him restoration through references to dreams. In the missing part of the quotation, the substantial lack that haunts Hanafan, is a reference to the great Cleopatra. Such a reference might reconfigure the family and, with it, it is implied, the nation; however, he leaves out the "conjecture" at the conclusion of Browne's meditation that after death, "all shall wake again." The quote, even in the truncated version in the story, provides an elegant rejoinder to the suffering and loss. It is very like O'Faoláin's lyrical evocation above from "A Broken World." Sampson writes of the literary allusions in "Admiring the Scenery," "The quotations from Browne and

Gray . . . introduce into the visionary and elegiac aspects of the story two perspectives on man's relation to nature."[28] As quoted in the story, Browne's passage runs "the quincunx of heaven runs low, and 'tis time to close the five ports of knowledge. . . . The huntsmen are up in America, and they are already past their first sleep in Persia. But who can be drowsy at that hour which freed us from everlasting sleep or have slumbering thoughts at that time, when sleep itself must end."

Importantly for this story, the passage in full resists sleep even more emphatically, highlighting the power of sensual perception, the five ports of knowledge, as forceful reminders of life in the face of sleep or death: "Nor will the sweetest delight of gardens afford much comfort in sleep; wherein the dulness of that sense shakes hands with delectable odours; and though in the bed of Cleopatra, can hardly with any delight raise up the ghost of a rose." The reader is left to observe with Hanafan at the end of the story or to observe the man whom Hanafan imagines saying, "I do be sometimes sitting here . . . enjoying the cool of the evening," that one needn't "project the idea of the beauty of the scene, the idea, into [his] own consciousness," to be truly admiring the scenery. Admiring the scenery depends less on consciousness than it does, in Browne's words, on the "mystical mathematicks of the city of heaven." In Hanafan's sympathetic imagination, the aesthetic and religious categories, always parallel, converge. It is Christ's mystical answer to Oedipus; rather than the contagion of the scapegoat, it is the sacrifice that means to end it. That concept of landscape is why O'Faoláin, like Yeats, finds succor in the Irish landscape and escape from the bitterness of history. Even as the landscape bears the marks of historical incidence, something of the beauty of "Munster grass and Connemara skies" remains untouched and continues to provide relief in the Pentecostal wilderness.[29]

9

Solving Ambiguities

Family Feeling in Louis MacNeice

In a letter to T. S. Eliot, Louis MacNeice described *Autumn Journal* as both "a panorama and a confession of faith," acknowledging that personal and public themes are intertwined in this long poem on the outbreak of World War II. Throughout the various meditations on love, violence, philosophy, the classics, and the urban and rural landscape, similarities are drawn from the confines of self-reflection on the relationship of body and soul, or from the intimacy of the bedroom, out to the governing halls of power. We see how issues that lead to his divorce are like the ones that lead to war, how the philosophical divide between the spirit and the flesh is played out in the violence on the street, how the forces that determine the condition of family life become the chief archetypes and even architects of the political world. The last point becomes especially apparent in the section on Ireland, a country small enough to still be "thought of with family feeling," as MacNeice writes in *Autumn Journal*, where the politics of family has local and national resonance.[1]

One of the central tenets of this book is that from the eighteenth to the twentieth centuries, the idea of family remained a ruling aesthetic and political concept in Irish writing. With this concept in mind, MacNeice's projection of the family romance onto the landscape in his lyric poems will appear alongside *Autumn Journal* as evidence of national consciousness. The aim is to illustrate family feeling as the solving ambiguity between the poem's panorama of a society preparing for war and the particular landscape of his confession of faith after the collapse of his marriage.

In many of MacNeice's poems, the poet's father and mother seem to fuse with natural forces of the landscape. His father, a minister in the Church of Ireland who believed in Home Rule, exudes something "solitary and wild" ("The Strand"), while his mother, dying early in his life, becomes "the pre-natal mountain" ("Carrick Revisited").[2] At times, while reading MacNeice, such projection of the family onto the landscape seems aligned to, if not the same as, the historical Anglo-Irish desire to separate cultural and political allegiances, as, for example, the nineteenth-century political unionist and cultural nationalist Samuel Ferguson had endeavored to do.[3] Is the ideal of beauty, "nature untainted by humanity,"[4] a drive to place the colonizer within a hostile landscape but with no record of the conquest, no record of guilt? Is the pathology of literary unionism witnessed in the land? Is it comparable to what Richard Murphy believes was an inculcated amnesia among the Anglo-Irish gentry regarding the Great Famine?[5]

MacNeice asks many of these questions and also makes an effort toward humanization; he consequently provides a variety of answers that are politically distanced from both nationalist and unionist aspirations, but are at once cognizant of the dangers contained within nature's alterity, aware of the political significance of its dark side, and romanced by the aesthetic beauty of the landscape. The landscape, if not exactly neutral in MacNeice, nevertheless provides a potentially transcendent place to counter the darkness that nature unleashes. Such an aesthetic response to landscape (rather than to nature) has been ascribed to many Anglo-American writers within the North American landscape tradition (Thoreau, Emerson), as well as to Anglo-Irish authors within the Irish one (Goldsmith, Edgeworth); it is also part of Wordsworth's postrevolutionary retreat from nature's bloody eruptions, and the political parallels, toward a more closely guarded aesthetic of self and family. For Northern Irish Protestant writers like MacNeice, or Derek Mahon, for that matter, landscape reflects a cultural condition of distance from the nation, a further evidence of partition but also of redemption. Yet such aestheticizing for MacNeice, as for Michael Longley and Mahon, has deep implications that have taken on ecological significance in recent years.

From his earliest writings, Louis MacNeice is aware of how history is inscribed in the land around him, and most often he is reminded of his inherited position as colonizer. The opening two stanzas from "Carrickfergus" amply illustrate the connection between history and landscape, while also emphasizing the poet's uneasy relationship with his native region, the North of Ireland:

> I was born in Belfast between the mountain and the gantries
> To the hooting of lost sirens and the clang of trams:
> Thence to Smoky Carrick in County Antrim
> Where the bottle-neck harbour collects the mud which jams
>
> The little boats beneath the Norman castle,
> The pier shining with lumps of crystal salt:
> The Scotch Quarter was a line of residential houses,
> But the Irish Quarter was a slum for the blind and halt.

Evident in these lines are the divisions that mark the Northern Irish countryside: the Norman castle, the differing Irish and Scots homes and streets, the Anglican order of the gentry, the hawthorn hedges, symbols of folk tradition,[6] and the memories of war attached to rivers and fields. MacNeice places himself tellingly between the land ("the mountains") and the symbols of Protestant industry ("the gantries") to visualize his status as reader of natural and cultural signs.

As his poem "The Strand" shows, MacNeice inherited a love for western Irish landscape from his father, the Anglican rector, which would prove formative. One of the most interesting aspects of a comparison between the western and northern landscapes in MacNeice's work is that the landscapes of the West are sparsely populated at best and full of redemptive promise ("no tree's green / Fulfilled him like these contours"), whereas the northern home tends to be peopled almost exclusively by the poet's immediate family (who yearn for the West) and is marred by signs of sectarianism. He writes of his family forced from their home in the West of Ireland: "We did not belong to the North of Ireland. We were a West of Ireland family exiled from our homeland."[7] The split between northern and western homes, with all of the political resonance those places bring to mind in Ireland, is what draws MacNeice to what he calls his "island truancies," to islands in the West, or places on the edge of the ocean, which are the counterparts to a family origin islanded in history. MacNeice's version of Ireland in "Western Landscape" considers many of these questions in extended fashion.

Early in the poem, MacNeice proposes a transcendental, escapist version of the landscape that is very familiar to readers of his work:

> So the kiss of the past is narcotic, the ocean
> . . . .
> For the western climate is Lethe
> The smoky taste of cooking on turf is lotus.

He proceeds to illustrate how even the escape that the landscape provides nevertheless reflects the fearful terms of departure from history. Such terms always accompany, indeed precede, the introduction of the pastoral mode, as the lotus still carries the scent of turf and the ideal the smell of the real. In the end, the landscape reflects our desires, our predicaments, and, in the poem's repetition of "from," our origins. The signs of affirmation ("amber water") and abnegation ("broken bog") within the landscape make it a riddle of erotic perception and sacred knowledge. The meaning may somewhat tragically be as unhealthy as the donkey or as melancholy and entranced as the heron. The landscape is both a body "barely grip[ping] the sea" of its passions and a holy vessel ("mitred mountain") coming to terms with its suffering ("weeping shale"). MacNeice hopes it will remain unaffected by the historical catastrophe it bears and endeavors to transcend: "O grail of emerald passing light // Webs that will last and will not." This hope recalls Yeats's declaration that the "bitterness" of Irish history has left no traces on "Munster grass and Connemara skies."[8] For Yeats, the untouched land can be pagan mockery of human despair. What effects such a grail may have, for MacNeice, are temporary at best and ultimately just as removed from his immediate social vision as was the romantic idea of "nature" from the world of famine and the Land League in the nineteenth century.

The grail is an ideal untainted by history. The effects are too distant from life for any tangible practical good. Even though the ideal is removed, it continues to inform the journey, as the unreachable grail informs the search for it. We move toward a realization of our desires, reflected back to us in the green contours of the land, uniting the inner with the outer world. We may then find compensation in the beautiful landscape, even if the ageless inhuman world around us, the "permanence" of "cloud and rock"[9] we wish to share, challenges our mortality. By placing the transcendent world in opposition to reality, MacNeice is invoking the Platonism whose oppositions, though fascinating for the poet, continue to plague his personal philosophy. Interestingly, here natural forms rather than ideational ones possess the relevant permanence to which we aspire. Already MacNeice seeks some resolution between the physical and spiritual worlds. This version of nature, however, proves to be like an inhuman, mocking lover, and history seems barely to intrude upon nature's seductive illustration of temporary and permanent forms.

The intrusion comes in a way that is very reminiscent of eighteenth-century styles of encoding history:

> The flock of mountain sheep belong
> To tumbled screes, to tumbling seas
> The ribboned wrack, and moor to mist.

Like Swift, MacNeice upsets perspective and emphasizes the dishevelment of land and sky in order to hint at the terms of Irish history. Beneath such interlinking of land and history are more universal questions of our relationship to nature, for the physical world is loving though faithless, leaving us only the ears and, by implication, the husks of our harvest:

> But we who savour longingly
> This plenitude of solitude
> Have lost the right to residence,
> . . . .

> The soft rain kisses and forgets,
> Silken mesh on skin and mind.

Nature's beauty is reduced to a siren song and the pastoral reduced to an elixir that helps us to forget our disgrace at nature's hands, which came "welcoming, abandoning." Platonic transcendence is the only other alternative to embracing nature in all its disruptive faithlessness. Yet those terms of transcendence are what MacNeice in *Autumn Journal* must reject if he is to be reconciled with the physical memories of lost love that continually beset him. As he suffers over his recent divorce, he links its private terms with the public demonstrations of war. In "Western Landscape," written later, he wonders if transcendence might be best, and thus he models himself on an ascetic, medieval traveler from the *immram* tradition.

The world of Saint Brandan in "Western Landscape" is adrift. His material rootlessness and spiritual transcendence are mirrored by the ever-changing sea. He is where "sea met sky" and "turf-smoke and mountain" are left behind; the saint, then, is beyond landscape. He, in fact, achieves a sense of place that is placeless ("knot[ted] to the horizon"), a sense of home that seems strange ("unhoming"), and a duration that is timeless ("undo / Time in quintessential West"). All of it is experienced through the flux of the sea and the expressive lightness of the curragh. The sea and sky become symbols of the changing grounds of the journey. They become symbols of God, especially if we remember that the hierarchy of the four elements is reflected in fire, air, water, earth. MacNeice never forgets that the beyond may be no more than simply beyond us. The vision of the beyond threatens to exceed, and thereby undermine, the rendering of it, unless it gives shape to the experience of the here and now, the promontory on which we stand.

The West of Ireland, in MacNeice's vision, is like art, dance, or poetry, the creative spirit blending body and spirit together, being "brute and ghost at once." This reconciliation proves important in much of MacNeice's poetry, as it is based on one of his primary antagonisms. Caught in the dialectic of body and spirit, flesh and word, earth and sky, we are stuck with the eruptions of an "arbitrary" but "necessary Nature," which universally seduces and rejects us with alternating plenitude and poverty, leaving us unsatisfied with either the body or the spirit. As a promontory, "Reluctant to be land," such a reconciliation presents its own inherent dangers of falling. From these larger ruminations on Platonic forms versus the shadow world of nature, MacNeice moves to a more specific and personal vision of the same argument regarding what finally constitutes home: the land that rejects him, or the spirit that sets him, like Brandan, free.

MacNeice is aware of his partial sense of home in Ireland ("not being a rooted peasant") and of his need for a fuller sense of home there, however elusive. He ends the poem with a confession of the familial roots of his relationship with the land, one in which the intellect is fostered by the world around it, mother to child:

> Let me at least in token that my mother
> Earth was a rocky earth with breast uncovered
> To suckle solitary intellects
> And limber instincts, let me, if a bastard
> Out of the West by urban civilization
> (Which unwished father claims me—so I must take
> What I can before I go) let me who am neither Brandan
> Free of all roots nor yet a rooted peasant
> Here add one stone to the indifferent cairn
> With a stone on the cairn, with a word on the wind, with a
> prayer in the flesh let me honour this country.

The gesture of honoring his country with "a word on the wind," with "a prayer in the flesh," is MacNeice's final gesture toward home. It is linked to the maternal body and made atop a cairn (a fairy fort and passage tomb). It is the liminal place of transcendence that paradoxically roots him.

Such a place of transcendence paradoxically binding him to earth, solving the contradictions of the spirit and the flesh, acknowledging the family romance, aligning the desires and frustrations of the public and private worlds, forms the nexus of MacNeice's solving ambiguities throughout the meditation of *Autumn Journal.* From the beginning of this long multipart poem, the chief philosophical, personal, and political concerns are laid out. Wars as ancient and contemporary as the Peloponnesian and Spanish Civil Wars are used as guides for the reader and writer, while Europe prepares for another great conflict (World War II), wondering what arrogance should be avoided, what fights are worth the resulting violence, what moral lessons are in store for democracies and empires. There are long reminiscences on the relative values of MacNeice's education, specifically his training in Greek culture and philosophy, and on his relationship with his estranged wife, as well as reflections over the effects of martial preparation upon English society. The whole is linked by a concern with some type of reconciliation between the desires of the body and the imperatives of the spirit, between Plato's forms and the seductions of appearance. We see it in "Western Landscape," where "Earth was a rocky earth with breast uncovered / To suckle solitary intellects." Yet it is section 16 of *Autumn Journal*, on Ireland, that exposes the fault lines in his philosophy. Here we finally see the "jumble of opposites" that informs the poem as a whole. There is a fear of war, a fear of men who "never / See the victim's face become their own / Or find his motive sabotage their motives," coupled with an effort to unveil the sources of our antagonisms.

If the landscape of the West reflects both promise and its frustration, the industrial badlands of the North are symbolized by the linen mills and "the ragged hawthorn," the tree of enchantment, the fairy thorn, which is diminished by the industrial and skeptical world surrounding it. The "voodoo of the Orange bands" is matched by the "shawled woman [the Shan Van Vocht] weeping at the garish altar." Both sects are driven by the same blind tribal instinct that drives Europe toward war and distorts the face of the other. Why does MacNeice, the urbane poet, "educated and domiciled in English," continue to "like being Irish"? It is because Ireland continues to represent all the possibilities of native place, and the Irish are "members of a world that never was, / Baptized with fairy water." Also, and as importantly, it is "because Ireland is small enough / To be still thought of with a family feeling." This linking of transcendental concepts of the land with ideas of family and nation, in this section of *Autumn Journal*, returns us to the themes of "Western Landscape," to the liminal place binding the poet to earth.

The well-known close of the section is telling: Ireland, as MacNeice writes earlier in the poem, is like "Mother or sweetheart." She is like his estranged wife or his long-lost mother, whose death brought on his "black dreams" ("Autobiography"). Ireland is a grand sublimation of MacNeice's family romance, in which only the landscape is not besmirched:

> Why should I want to go back
>   To you, Ireland, my Ireland?
> The blots on the page are so black
>   That they cannot be covered with shamrock.
> I hate your grandiose airs,
>   Your sob-stuff, your laugh and your swagger,
> Your assumption that everyone cares
>   Who is king of your castle.
> Castles are out of date.

This passage, his most disdainful approach to Ireland, unsalvageable by any political allegiance, reaches its climax in a Latin tag from Catullus: *Odi atque amo.* The whole quotation translates as "I hate you and I love you, why I do so, I do not know, but I feel it and I am in torment." It is a lover's reproach. If he hates and loves Ireland, he hates and loves his former wife who left many days "intolerable or perplexed / But so many more so happy" (section 4). Angry at his wife who left him for another man, angry at his mother for leaving him when young, the poet turns on Ireland for betraying his childhood dreams. As he observes about Ireland, "The tide flows round the children's sandy fancy." Yet this feeling of hatred and love is so strong, he wonders if the landscape of Ireland should also bear the marks of the country's suffering:

> Shall we cut this name on trees with a rusty dagger?
> Her mountains are still blue, her rivers flow
> Bubbling over the boulders.

After allowing the land its lofty permanence once more, its "inhuman effluence," MacNeice considers his earlier question, "Why must a country, like a ship or a car, be always female, / Mother or sweetheart?" Although it is a valid critique of the dangers of gendering a nation, it proves to be no more than idealistic rhetoric. The gendering of Ireland now seems inevitable. MacNeice has done it himself. At the close of this section, Ireland is "both a bore and a bitch," for which he can only say: "Better close the horizon / Send her no more fantasy." The land, streaming forth its promise of transcendence, finally offers only a "faggot of useless memories," a bundle of sticks to be offered up on the pyre of spiritual renunciation.

Spiritual renunciation, however, is not to MacNeice's liking, no matter how much his experience suggests its uses. The next section of the poem (section 17) states that Plato's world of "capital initials, of transcendent / Ideas is too bleak." Agreeing with Aristotle, MacNeice would rather "stress the function" than the form. Yet he knows that he must suffer the strife between the functional world of desire and the transcendent one of form, if only because his wife inhabits every corner of the world he would like to transcend. Her very "word would tumble over each and pelt from pure excitement," as he writes in section 4. She made the air "shot silk," the "streets . . . music." MacNeice recognizes that he must "evolve at length / An equal thrust and pattern" between the body and spirit. He must re-create the sexual ecstasy that he has lost. In the philosophical section 17, following the attack on Ireland, MacNeice, like Joyce's character Leopold Bloom, is lying in a bath contemplating the body and its transgressions. We watch as the poet finally and reluctantly admits that "Plato was right to define the bodily pleasures / As the pouring [of] water into a hungry sieve." Ireland, like his wife, has reminded him that the physical world sometimes offers only paltry rewards, that it can be faithless. This admission is only partial, however, for MacNeice insists that Plato was wrong to "ignore the rhythm which the intercrossing / Coloured waters permanently give." This chiasmic structure, like Catullus's well-known lines about love and hate, is the equal thrust and pattern that MacNeice is seeking throughout the poem. He hopes in the last lines for balance.

It all depends on how one perceives the world outside, how one interacts emotionally with what and whom one meets. In MacNeice's rendering, when confronting the landscape, the city streets, the face of the other, one commits various sexual, familial, and national sins of perception, the imagined killing of the parents chief among them, which must then be sacrificially redeemed, purified, just as the suffering or sinning body hopefully becomes Eucharistic:

> Virtue going out of us always; the eyes grow weary
> With vision but it is vision builds the eye;
> And in a sense the children kill their parents
> But do the parents die?
> And the beloved destroys like fire or water
> But water scours and sculpts and fire refines
> And if you are going to read the testaments of cynics,
> You must read between the lines.
> A point here and a point there: the current
> Jumps the gaps, the ego cannot live
> Without becoming other for the Other
> Has got yourself to give.
> And even the sense of taste provides communion
> With God as plant or beast;
> The sea in fish, the field in a salad of endive,
> A sacramental feast.

As the culmination of the passage reveals, the soul or spirit longs for flesh as flesh for soul or spirit, although they threaten each other's reign, much as lover desires and threatens lover or child desires and threatens parent. Both sets of desires are visionary wishes in both senses of the word "vision."

There is the wish to see the sensual splendor of the world, in micro- and macrocosm, and the wish to have the truth revealed at any cost, including the sacrifice of the senses:

> The soul's long searchlight hankers for a body
> The single body hungers for its kind,
> The eye demands the light at risk of blindness
> And the mind that did not doubt would not be mind.

As MacNeice writes, "discontent is eternal" within us, desiring the present moment, while risking its violation; at the close of section 17, such discontent, rooted in the soul's desire for the body, becomes the cause of the coming war:

> Open the world wide, open the senses
> Let the soul stretch its blind enormous arms,
> There is vision in the fingers only needing waking
> Ready for light's alarms.
> O light, terror of light, hoofs and ruthless
> Wheels of steel and brass
> Dragging behind our lacerated captives.

Here is one of the great lessons poetry teaches. It is what poetry has to tell us about politics. The soul dreams of Tír-na-nÓg and South Sea Islands, of *houri* (willing nymphs of the Muslim paradise who await the martyrs of the faith), of gathering Christian crusaders, and it does so at deep moral peril to us all. If not given the terms of its transcendence, the soul threatens the altar itself: we will end raping "the angels off the golden reredos / Before we're done."[10]

This agonized realization leaves MacNeice in the last section of the poem appealing forlornly to his own ironical, loving poetic of the "drunkenness of things being various" ("Snow"). In that poem, he wants to solve the strife between body and soul, by providing a place that both exhilarates and binds him to earth. In *Autumn Journal*, such a solution seems to be as dry and distant as the "distant snow and dried roses" in which he bids his sins to sleep. He waits until the soul's long searchlight finds its transfigured body and calms the desires and frustrations of the public and private worlds, which have left both him and Europe bereft. The image of personal and public reconciliation underlies the last stanza of "In Carrowdore Churchyard," Derek Mahon's eulogy to MacNeice. In this poem, Mahon is able to capture the larger scope of MacNeice's poetic, of how aesthetic perception might compensate for the suffering of the poet and the terrors of war, how the yearly renovation of nature parallels the possibilities of renovation for humankind.[11]

For MacNeice, as we have seen, the landscape has distinctly familial hues. If aesthetic renderings of place offer hope for individual renewal, then these hues carry hopes for familial redemption as well. Finally, if the family is the local figure for the nation, then political problems, seen as family altercations, may be redeemed in turn. These relationships are ambiguous, difficult to prove, unwieldy to maintain, yet unrelentingly felt; the solutions are also ambiguous. We will have to pass through the war before the solving ambiguity might be found:

> On the banks of Rubicon—the die is cast;
> There will be time to audit
> The accounts later, there will be sunlight later
> And the equation will come out at last.

The image of "sunlight later" in the last lines of the poem links the language of landscape aesthetics, the emotions surrounding MacNeice's divorce, the struggle between self and soul, and the sense of coming war in an attempt to achieve reconciliation or at least some type of balance.

Just as earlier in *Autumn Journal* MacNeice had called the reader's attention to the roses from "Snow," here the sunlight brings the attentive mind back to his poem "The Sunlight on the Garden." It is a reconciliatory meditation on the aesthetic appreciation of nature, the inability to capture transitory beauty, the pressures of war, the unforgiving sorrows of love, and the growing threats of history:

> The sunlight on the garden
> Hardens and grows cold,

We cannot cage the minute
Within its nets of gold,
When all is told
We cannot beg for pardon.

The fertility that the sunlight represents when it is warm is dependent on the seasons and changes with them. The ethereal aspect of the sky depends on its being clear of threatening planes. The beautiful phrase "the earth compels" both haunts the poem and delivers it from darkness, as its compulsion is both fateful and hopeful, bringing winter and spring. "We are dying, Egypt, dying" is a paraphrase of a line from Shakespeare's *Antony and Cleopatra*, which is reminiscent of the bonds between the various landscapes and personages in that play. Antony is Rome and Hercules, while Cleopatra is Egypt and Isis. Passion and personality as emanations of the land are quietly reinforced in MacNeice's poem through this echo of Shakespeare. Similarly, we remember that when Antony says to Cleopatra, "I am dying, Egypt, dying," the characters are slowly shifting from history to myth.[12]

In MacNeice's lyric, the historical characters of MacNeice and his wife together (hence the "we") have become like mythological figures of sky and earth or, better still, like the figures of Adam and Eve after the Fall, waiting for sunlight to grace the garden, so that they can sadly recall the treasures of their lost Eden. The allusion to "The Sunlight on the Garden" at the close of *Autumn Journal* emphasizes the intent of the latter long love/war poem to unveil the subconscious mythic forces at work in personal and public history. Family feeling takes on a political dimension, but it has far deeper roots. The various meditations on the classics and philosophy, on the urban and rural landscape, politics and divorce, sexual love and war have plumbed their origins in the mythical contest between body and spirit. Such a mythical battle is at the core of the Oedipus complex and begs the questions, who will be sacrificed, and who will be redeemed? We sleep on the banks of the Rubicon,[13] a small stream on the east coast of northern Italy, the crossing of which by Caesar marked the beginning of the internecine war with Pompey and the subsequent consolidation of Caesar's power. In MacNeice's poem the river divides the conscious and subconscious, soul and body, self and society, nature and culture. Tonight we sleep knowing that something fateful will occur when we awake, turning the "Wheels of steel and brass, / Dragging behind our lacerated captives" from our private nightmares and through our public streets. We can only hope "the equation will come out at last."

10

The Rising Sap

Oedipal Burdens and Christian/Pagan Ecstasy in Patrick Kavanagh

❦ Premodern sympathies between nature and the Celtic world have become a New Age mantra in some quarters, while in others (including Seamus Heaney, Patrick Kavanagh, Frank O'Connor) they have provided a literary, often saintly, conceit that balances pagan and Christian attitudes and provides muted answers to the disturbing questions of Irish history. It is the disjunctions, however, the downright antipathy between man and nature, as it existed in the Great Famine that are, perhaps, more justly known. They are certainly more indicative of Irish history. In this light, colonization, and alongside it the potato blight, may be termed an ecological as well as political disaster.[1] Between the medieval saints and a postwar writer such as Patrick Kavanagh, the changing Irish views of nature, and with them the acculturated version of nature that we call landscape, have altered many times, and the changes have reflected violent shifts in the history of the country.

There is a twofold aspect of landscape: revelations or discoveries of the relationship of place and identity within the process of remembering have consistently demonstrated that remembrances and cures for the ills of social relationships are situated in specific and meaningful landscapes. For Patrick Kavanagh, and others, nature and the Irish landscape have remained not only a sometimes satirical reflection of Irish troubles whatever their scope but also, like aesthetic experience, a force for cultural renewal and reflection. If Kavanagh's pastoral is burdened by Oedipal nightmares, it is also driven by Christian and pagan dreams of redemption and nature worship that particularly characterize his later period. As for many Irish writers, the synthesis or reconciliation of pagan and Christian visions is one of Kavanagh's lifelong aims.

Kavanagh's career moves from the "purity of inspiration of his early Monaghan lyrics"[2] to the satirical antipastoral or realism of "The Great Hunger" (1942) and then to the mystical ideals of his later years.[3] Places and place-names from his native region, as well as from Dublin, feature prominently in his writings. They move through various transformations, starting from the rural town lands of his youth to the bitter "apocalypse of clay" of his maturity and on to the "leafy banks" of Dublin city canals, where he had his last pastoral rebirth. The lyrical blend of idealist dreaming and the natural world reveals a great deal of what is at work in the Irish imagination: the need for familiarity that, after repeated frustration, becomes a desire for the transcendent. Such sympathy resurfaces and submerges many times in Irish literature, though perhaps nowhere more obviously than in the poetry of Patrick Kavanagh. Kavanagh's career, moving as it does between the pastoral and antipastoral modes, mirrors the history of the landscape aesthetic in Ireland; one might say it is ontogeny recapitulating phylogeny, or the life of the individual recapitulating the development of the nation.

The last stage of rebirth combines the effects of his satirical and pastoral stages. Antoinette Quinn believes that there was always "a quarrel in his own psyche between love and satire," between his need to snatch out of time the passionate moment and the need simply to attack. Eamon Grennan eloquently describes Kavanagh's progression in his essay "From Simplicity to Simplicity: Pastoral Design in Patrick Kavanagh": "In this final pastoral state, *being itself* becomes the poet's unselfconscious prayer." The "unselfconscious" and "literate" relation to nature expressed in Kavanagh's poems was important to Seamus Heaney and helped him prepare a critical paradigm for understanding its uses. Heaney writes: "I think there are two ways in which place is known and cherished, two ways which may be complementary but which are just as likely to be antipathetic. One is lived, illiterate and unconscious, the other learned, literate and conscious." Heaney says that the "quarrel" for Kavanagh "was the quarrel between the illiterate self that was tied to the little hills and earthed in stony grey soil, and the literate that pined for the 'city of Kings / Where art, music and letters were the real things.'" Kavanagh's gifts were "vigorous speech," an antiheroic posture toward ordinary experience, and an instinctual relation to nature.[4] The last precedes and informs Kavanagh's and Heaney's ambivalent relationship to the pastoral, which both resists and acknowledges the importance of this literary genre.

Like Heaney, Kavanagh "has kept up a more or less constant thematic resistance to the pastoral as a genre that discloses the merely literary nature of the rural poem's relationship to agricultural life."[5] Kavanagh's poem "The Great Hunger" sets out to explore and comment on a relation between man and nature that strikes neither the elegiac note of the British pastoral nor the social protest of the Irish one. Rather, it marks out a painful and achieved connection between private suffering and the complex references of local faith, sexual anguish as a great hunger equal in many ways to famine. The original sin of Irish history, of consciousness, and of nature itself is at the core of "The Great Hunger." The cause and cure are sexual, religious, and historical, as they have always been.

From the beginning of the poem the physical body of the scriptural reading is made manifest: "Clay is the word and clay is the flesh."[6] Kavanagh mourns for those who are "lost" in a "passion that never needs a wife." Early in the poem the Oedipal quality of the sin is made apparent. Equally apparent, however, is the Christian dream of redemption rising from the guarded tomb or in the green leaves of the tree:

> Yet sometimes when the sun comes through a gap
> These men know God the Father in a tree:
> The Holy Spirit is the rising sap,
> And Christ will be the green leaves that will come
> At Easter from the sealed and guarded tomb.

Original sin and the redemptive impulse have familial and political as well as aesthetic implications. Whether the forces of redemption and sin can be reconciled is the question; they stand in stark juxtaposition in the poem.

In Kavanagh, the forever frustrated and projected Oedipal desire (plowing is Maguire's only expression of sexuality beyond masturbation) is symbolic of the state of the nation. Kavanagh's verdict is often harsh: "for the strangled impulse there is no redemption." Such harshness is not entirely representative of the sympathy that Kavanagh generally has for victims. For one thing, there is the sympathetically portrayed "sin" of Maguire's masturbation over the hearth. If we take the hearth as a feminine, or maternal, symbol of the consciousness of the house, as Synge suggests in the eviction scene of *The Aran Islands*, then the act of self-fulfillment has perverse potential for redemption, or at least for sublimation.[7] It also implies without enacting the transgression of the incest taboo that underlies much of the frustration of "The Great Hunger."

In nineteenth-century Irish literature, the hope of marriages (from *The Wild Irish Girl* to *Laurence Bloomfield in Ireland*) is meant to redeem nature and history. By the mid-twentieth century, however, such a hope has been winnowed down to an act of perversity in order to illustrate how trapped between pagan nature and Christian culture the peasantry had become in postcolonial Ireland. For Claude Lévi-Strauss, the incest taboo establishes the transition from disruptive nature to culture and is what distinguishes us from other animals.[8] Kavanagh's peasantry is not exactly aware of this transition, which makes them all the more pitiable:

> But the peasant in his little acres is tied
> To a mother's womb by the wind-toughened navel-cord
> Like a goat tethered to the stump of a tree—
> He circles around and around wondering why it should be.

The peasant's inability to understand the scandal of his situation, plowing mother earth while tied to his own mother, is a powerful indictment of the culture.[9] The incest taboo may be said both to escape and to ground this difference; a paradox, the theme of incest forms the basis of Kavanagh's meditation on the real line between culture and nature in "The Great Hunger." The peasant's "weak, washy tragedy" is his un-self-consciousness, but it is also his strength, for, even in his frustration, he lives in the instinctual world.

Kavanagh is not simply condemning the peasantry; he is specific about the need to be sympathetic to the peasant's plight. Even more important, he insists on the need for a connection between humankind and nature, for although nature is the seed of sinfulness, it is also the source of ecstasy and redemption. That belief is why he has always been in many ways also a pagan poet, like the blackbird he extols in the poem "To a Blackbird":

> O pagan poet, you
> And I are one
> In this—we lose our god
> At set of sun.
> And we are kindred when
> The hill wind shakes
> Sweet song like blossoms on
> The calm green lakes.

Being close to its supersensible rhythms (to borrow a phrase from Yeats)[10] is vital to the shepherd's and the peasant's worldview:

> There is the source from which all cultures rise,
> And all religions,
> There is the pool in which the poet dips
> And the musician.
> Without the peasant base civilization must die.

Kavanagh is reimagining the reclamation of the primitive that was central to the Irish literary revival. The central paradigm of original sin (personal or historical), with its redemption through love and sexuality, features repeatedly in Kavanagh, though he wishes to imagine a way out of this exhausted model of the nature/culture dialectic. It is not enough to be in nature, to have only an immediate, unthinking, sensory, or aesthetic responsiveness to it. For Kavanagh, as for Joyce, self-conscious awareness of both the Fall and the troubling inauthenticity of our relationship to nature is essential.

The image of resurrection, the "rising sap," and Easter are at the heart of his mystical vision that endeavors to unite pagan and Christian visions of the land—visions that were often conflicting in the dramatic action but reconciled in the imaginative vision of Yeats and Synge.[11] This union is, and has always been, an uneasy one. For Kavanagh, too, it is troubled: "The Great Hunger" ends with an image of apocalypse, with Maguire standing

> . . . in the doorway of his house
> A ragged sculpture of the wind,
> October creaks the rotted mattress,
> The bedposts fall. No hope. No lust.
> The hungry fiend
> Screams the apocalypse of clay
> In every corner of this land.

And "To a Blackbird" ends with this acknowledgment of the split in Kavanagh's consciousness as it seeks a natural synthesis of pagan and Christian beliefs:

> We dream while Earth's sad children
> Go slowly by
> Pleading for our conversion
> With the Most High.

The only harbinger of Kavanagh's late solution in the poetic of the urban pastoral is the artifice of the "ragged sculpture." Similar to Yeats's artifice of eternity, the apocalyptic image of the sculpture stands on the threshold of the house, as well as of time and space. The month of October rocks the bed that the people should be rocking in sensual fulfillment.

Like the penitents of "Lough Derg (1942–1944)," Maguire must renounce "the World, the Flesh, the Devil," but with this repudiation also comes a renunciation of the eruptions of nature, however qualified it may be by its insistence on the resurrection and purification of the body. Kavanagh captures this complexity at the end of the long poem "Lough Derg," when he is ready to leave the site of pilgrimage and reflects:

> Morning from the hostel windows was like the morning
> In some village street after a dance carouse,
> Debauchees of Venus and Bacchus
> Half-alive stumbling wearily out of a bleary house.
> So these pilgrims stumbled below in the sun
> Out of God's public-house.

He makes a comparison between the Bacchanalian celebrations of Irish culture and the Apollonian transfigurations imagined by Catholicism, but such a comparison is unsteady and dealing in contradiction exalts the boundary between culture and nature. He therefore concludes that the germ in the grain for the Christian moralist sprouts somewhere else, not here. What sprouts here is connected with pride and "burning emotion." Nature, in its eruptive manifestations, has an agonistic relationship with culture, planted there by God to lead to our disillusionment here on earth. The germ then sprouts at the end of the poem, but not as the moralist envisions. It is a pagan vision of "God's delight in disillusionment." In many ways, this vision of God acts as a prelude to Kavanagh's mystical vision of delight in the passionate transitory of being.

Pagan delight is the flip side of pagan despair. Nature then is a lover who, as in the poem "Innocence," knows nothing of the Fall and accepts her adherents back into the fold, regardless:

> Ashamed of what I loved
> I flung her from me and called her a ditch
> . . . .
> But now I am back in her briary arms.

Once back with nature, Kavanagh finds transcendence in the image of man in nature: "I cannot die / Unless I walk outside these whitethorn hedges." Nature forms the boundaries of our existence; this pastoral vision is of landscape, an intersection of culture and nature, like the hedges themselves. Many of Kavanagh's poems consider this boundary as enclosing fields of innocence. They are full of folk imagination and rustic realism. One in particular, one of his earliest, "Address to an Old Wooden Gate" (1929), shows how that intersection specifically reflects the human condition.

Here nature, original sin, history, and sexuality converge on the most quotidian of things, an old wooden gate. Although Kavanagh doesn't attempt a lyrical flight in this poem, and in fact assiduously eschews one, he also doesn't allow the subject to descend into the merely simple and banal. The gate is battered, all paint worn away, with rusty hinges. Its missing latch has been replaced by a "barbed wire clasp" with "evil charm." The "poplar tree" it hangs on has lost its beauty. Reflecting that the gate has become something to disdain, like his childhood self, Kavanagh reminisces on his youth when the gate was new:

> And many a time I've seen the laughing-eyed
> School-children, on your trusty back astride
> But time's long silver hand has touched our brows
> And I'm the scorn of women—you of cows.

He closes by considering how the modern iron fences of the wealthy lack such character and charm, indeed lack the folkloric potential of this gate, because the former seems more militaristic than pastoral. In this confrontation of modernity and tradition, Kavanagh continues to lean toward the traditional, which is not unusual in an Irish poet. His career would take him one step further in this equation.

Kavanagh's canal sonnets are examples of the reconciliation of culture and nature in a green urban space, one that would both challenge traditional conceptions of the nature poet and reinforce the importance of that role. Importantly, in this reconciliation, the sonnets also signal the exculpation of the historical implications of the original sin that underlies Irish literature. Of course, original sin in the larger biblical sense is not so easily resolved. In McGahern's *That They May Face the Rising Sun* (2002; published in the United States as *The Lake* in 2003), the former historical implications are presented in the figure of Bill Evans, the *Fear Gorta* (Man of Hunger), symbol of the Great Famine and nature's harshest treatment. His life takes a turn for the better by the end of the narrative; Irish history is relieved of the burden. But the modern society, and the young that have grown up in it, is strangely regarded by the more ritualistically minded older generation. Meanwhile, the biblical version of original sin is not so easily cleansed, but instead the ritual seems fated to be repeated in the novel's seasonal movement from Easter to Easter. The year encompasses the slaughter of livestock, the death of animals at the hand of pets, the various deaths and births of the community, with all the symbolic resonance of sacrifice and resurrection that it implies.

Kavanagh similarly seems to express a certain ritualistic need concerning any hopes for redemption. In "Canal Bank Walk" (1960), the historical but not religious implications of original sin, one of the central themes of "The Great Hunger," are not so much overcome as unmentioned, as if the questions of history are no longer relevant. Kavanagh begins with redemption and moves through the simple aesthetic qualities offered by the organic, natural world to "the gaping need of my senses," the original sin locked in the very instruments of perception: "For this soul needs to be honoured with a new dress woven / From green and blue things and arguments that cannot be proven." Like the "Holy Spirit" in "the rising sap" of "The Great Hunger," the bird who builds its nest for the "Word" is a combination of Christian and pagan or scientific views of nature. Whether Kavanagh attempts reconciliation is difficult to say. At times, he seems like a Celtic monk composing a book of hours that pays homage to God through a recognition of his creation. At other times, his almost pagan need to celebrate the senses seems a self-sufficient end in itself.

If we compare C. S. Lewis's to Rachel Carson's view of nature, we gain insight into Kavanagh's vision. In "The Weight of Glory," Lewis believes that attempts to find happiness and beauty in nature, even in books and music, inevitably fail because the good we desire is not there but, rather, only comes through them. "These things—the beauty, the memory of our own past—," he writes, "are good images of what we really desire; but if they are mistaken for the thing itself they turn into dumb idols, breaking the hearts of their worshippers; they are only the scent of a flower we have not found, the echo of a tune we have not heard, news from a country we have never yet visited."[12] The question of whether Lewis is being antimaterialistic begs the following question: Is nature in itself a godlike source and vehicle, or are God and nature separate if not opposed? Not an easy question to answer, but this religious view of nature is different from the scientific view. Rachel Carson's imagination, poetic as well as scientific, allows nature its full role in the drama of perception. She is not strictly utilitarian by any means, but she also does not emphasize God as much as what she calls "material immortality."[13] She writes, "There is symbolic as well as actual beauty in the migration of birds, the ebb and flow of the tides, the folded bud ready for the spring."[14] For Carson, it is a matter of appreciation, weighted so beautifully between her scientific objectivity toward the actual and her poetic sense of the symbol. Kavanagh also seems to make the idea of nature both actual and symbolic. Yet while acknowledging the place of observation, he insists on the need to move beyond merely scientific analysis. He combines Lewis's and Carson's views in this way. In the tension between idealist and material monisms, according to Peter Godfrey-Smith, there is what is called a "neutral monism." He explains: "Rather than explaining the mental in physical terms or explaining the physical in mental terms, we explain both the physical and mental in terms of something else. That 'something else' tends to remain rather mysterious."[15] This third neutral monism seems an apt description of the poet's way. Kavanagh's mysticism cures the mind of the curse of self-consciousness and redresses the body. Yet he asserts that this cure happens only in the "habitual" and "banal."

This emphasis on the quotidian is also part of a larger antiheroic strategy. In "Lines Written on a Seat on the Grand Canal, Dublin, Erected to the Memory of Mrs. Dermot O'Brien" (1960), Kavanagh makes clear that his poetic, though lyrical, and frequently cognizant of the epic quality of parochial life, is not heroic in the Yeatsian manner. At this stage, such a stance has become synonymous with his work. For the present purposes, what is important is how he uses the aesthetics of landscape to make his claims. Water has spiritual significance for Kavanagh, and though he insists that there is nothing "hero-courageous" about his stance, and gently employs archaisms such as "stilly" and "greeny," there is something in the poem that believes nature is sublime. The lock "Niagarously" roars, the silence "tremendous." As in his poem "Epic," in which the great martial themes are found in a "local row," Kavanagh believes that nature's universal themes are found among its most unprepossessing particulars. The canal bank is Parnassus, and the canal-bank seat is the seat of poetic reverie: the source of inspiration and the beacon of aesthetic reflection. Like Wordsworth, Kavanagh is suspicious of the trappings of poetry, but not of poetry itself. He, too, seeks poetry in an "impulse from the vernal wood."[16] It is not a rejection of culture for nature, but rather an effort to inhabit them both in the house that poetry provides.

If "Canal Bank Walk" is a celebration of nature as a "web of fabulous grass," "Lines Written on a Seat on the Grand Canal" ends seated on a symbol of culture, with Kavanagh looking at nature from the perspective that culture affords. This pastoral view of nature, one mediated by culture, is one even Thoreau acknowledged late in his life. It is the product of having experienced nature in all its manifold characteristics. In *What Is Nature?* Sally Roper outlines these characteristics with a concisely flighted gender analysis:

> Nature is both machine and organism, passive matter and vitalist agency. It is represented as both savage and noble, polluted and wholesome, lewd and innocent, carnal and pure, chaotic and ordered. Conceived as a feminine principle, nature is equally lover, mother and virago: a source of sensual delight, a nurturing bosom, a site of treacherous and vindictive forces bent on retribution for her human violation. Sublime and pastoral, indifferent to human purposes and willing servant of them, nature awes as she consoles, strikes terror as she pacifies, presents herself as both the best of friends and the worst of foes.[17]

Nearly all of these embodiments appear in Kavanagh's treatment of nature. In the end he chooses to inhabit the border between nature and culture. In order to remain on this border, his career is spent measuring benevolent against hostile nature.

These two sides of nature are most evident in Kavanagh's early to midcareer, before his later urban-pastoral quasi resolution of the crisis. On the one hand, there is his sense of nature as his foe in the early poem "Stony Grey Soil," in which nature is the force that thwarted his dreams and burdened his thoughts of poetic inspiration, until they were clumsy parodies:

> And I believed that my stumble
> Had the poise and stride of Apollo
> And his voice my thick tongued mumble.

Nature is like poetry, but it is not the same thing. It is connected to the lowest forms of animal life ("steaming dunghills," "weasel itch") that impede his ideals ("You flung a ditch on my vision") and hence, sometimes, is an inversion of poetry's transcendental. He knows, however, that it is the force he must tame in order to describe it. He must turn and face the place, record its names and the damage done:

> O can I still stroke the monster's back
> Or write with unpoisoned pen.
> His name in these lonely verses.

He doesn't come to terms with it, beyond merely recording its ill effects:

> Wherever I turn I see
> In the stony grey soil of Monaghan
> Dead loves that were born for me.

Kavanagh may be said to have realized what Mary Midgley has termed the "Beast Within," a realization that may be termed a means of self-exculpation.[18] We might say we have finally understood Kavanagh's view of nature in such a reckoning, except that there is another opposing friendlier perspective at work throughout his career.

Other poems of nature, such as "Tarry Flynn" (from the novel *Tarry Flynn*), view it as a friend, as a realm of un-self-conscious delight.[19] One must remember that Kavanagh's protagonist is about to leave the parish at this point in the novel. His positive image of the fields is the result of departure. He's happy because he is leaving. If the second of the late canal-bank sonnets shows that Kavanagh insists on the balance of culture and nature, there is another tale to tell: How does he view nature in light of poetic inspiration? In order to understand it, we must examine the series of ambivalences that attach to the mind-body dualism of the culture-nature distinction. Following Mikhail Bakhtin's vision of the grotesque body in his study of the carnivalesque, the below becomes the above, the derided body a site of celebration, the "backside" of humanity the source of revolutionary power. All that is "sacred and exalted is rethought on the level of the material bodily stratum or else combined and mixed with its images."[20] This carnivalesque reversal takes place in Kavanagh's poem "Kerr's Ass," in which, by the end of the poem, the ass, once released from the shackles of civilization (the "harness," the "collar," the "reins"), becomes a figure for poetic inspiration.

The "Mucker fog" is the blinding hindering landscape of Kavanagh's birthplace. The waking "God of imagination" relies on the landscape for its mystical visions. The three (man, animal, and God) engage each other until the force of the dialectic between mind and body, culture and nature, achieves synthesis. As in Yeats's rendering, God and nature are opposed and interpenetrating, just as are culture and nature, mind and body. This intersection is the complicated ground of our being. Or as Bakhtin writes:

> The starry sky, the gigantic material masses of the mountains, the sea, the cosmic upheavals, elementary catastrophes—these constitute the terror that pervades ancient mythologies, philosophies, the systems of images, and language itself with its semantics. . . . The struggle against cosmic terror in all its forms and manifestations did not rely on abstract hope or on eternal spirit, but on the material principle in man himself; he discovered them and became vividly conscious of them in his own body. He became aware of the cosmos within himself.[21]

This description contains most of the major themes in Kavanagh's view of nature: fear, folklore, landscape, religion, and self-mastery.

All that is missing is the place of the feminine as both disruptive and redemptive body, nature, and animal. Kavanagh's fear of women is much more difficult to accommodate. In this fear, he is unaccommodated man, for as he writes in the poem "Women":

> If any man says his view was limited to landscape
> Tell them they're fools.
> Above all, it was woman as the luxuriant
> Rotting of souls
> Coming down to ruin him
>
> . . . .
>
> God pity him for what he could look back at
> Last word in torture
> All to be present with each other at a deflowering
> O rapturous love, O holy whoring!

In the Ireland of the fifties, it is no surprise that he seemed to have trouble living up to this last apostrophe. As he wisely laments in "On Raglan Road": "That I had wooed not as I should a creature made of clay— / When the angel woos the clay he'd lose his wings at the dawn of day." This wooing was the original sin that infected the angels who fell in love with humans and humans who fell in love with the angels.[22] Angels lose their wings as they descend into the dross of the mortal world, while humans lose their hearts as they long for what they cannot reach. Kavanagh is a "creature made of clay," and in order to redeem himself he must obey the "rising sap" in "greeny" nature.

In the essay "The Placeless Heaven: Another Look at Kavanagh," Heaney concludes, "Where Kavanagh had once painted Monaghan like a Millet, with a thick and faithful pigment in which men rose from the puddled ground, all wattled in potato mould, he now paints like a Chagall, afloat above his native domain, airborne in the midst of his own dream place rather than earthbound in a literal field. Or perhaps it would be even truer to say that the later regenerated poet in Kavanagh does not paint at all, but draws." The idealist version of Kavanagh is masterfully outlined, but later in this essay Heaney allows that some of this floating was sublimation pure and simple: "Painting, after all, involves one in a more laboured relationship with a subject—or at least in a more conscious and immersed relationship with a medium—than drawing does. Drawing is closer to the pure moment of perception." For Heaney, this sublimation allows for the healthy play of instinct.

In the following sexualized description by Heaney, we see an example of Kavanagh's "rapturous love" and "holy whoring": "This then is truly creative writing. It does arise from the spontaneous overflow of powerful feeling, but the overflow is not a reaction to some stimulus in the world out there. Instead, it is a spurt of abundance from a source within and it spills over to irrigate the world beyond the self."[23] In this image idealist and realist are reconciled, profane and sacred united. The angel loses his wings but shapes the clay of his imagination with his newly bared hands—a body that the human must be fully ready to receive. Kavanagh captures this combination when he writes in "In Memory of My Mother": "Among your earthiest words the angels stray."

11

Beneath Tilth and Loam

Seamus Heaney's Journey to the Underworld

❦ The poetry of Seamus Heaney endeavors to recast the historical relationship with home and the Irish landscape in terms of present circumstances and future possibilities. The themes of the inhuman (the divine), the nonhuman (animal), the culture of family, the eruptions of nature and the unconscious, remain as central to the discussion as they have been hitherto. Within the cultural landscape, the locus of the family, the physical house called "home," takes prominent place. Beckett's idea of an "unspeakable home" from the short prose piece "Neither," written for the minimalist composer Morton Feldman (1962), functions as an urtext for contemporary Irish poetry. It underlies Derek Mahon's reflection in "Afterlives" of living "it bomb by bomb" and learning "what is meant by home," or Heaney's feeling "lost, / Unhappy and at home," as he writes in "Tollund Man."[1] Like Beckett's inner/outer landscapes[2] melding in a vision of "unspeakable home," Seamus Heaney's exploration of landscape, nature, home, and family is a conclusive focus of the Oedipal/Christian narrative of this book because it is so much a part of his vision of life and death, closing his career, as it does, in various confrontations with the ghost of his father, who becomes a standing metaphor for history, and for the folkloric Irish past, whose demise Heaney ritualized throughout his career.

Though the argument that the historical is more important than the aesthetic is often overstated, any study of landscape in Ireland is inseparable from history. In *Landscape and Power*, W. J. T. Mitchell in his essay "Imperial Landscapes" illustrates how the history of landscape is connected to the rise of imperialism and the claims of capitalism on the land. Because the history of writing in English in Ireland is coincident with the rise of the aesthetics of the pastoral, landscape is indispensably part of any discussion of its history; we must therefore keep in mind Mitchell's concluding lines: "We have known since Ruskin that the appreciation of landscape as an aesthetic object cannot be an occasion for complacency or untroubled contemplation; rather, it must be the focus of a historical, political, and yes aesthetic alertness to the violence and evil written on the land, projected there by the gazing eye."[3]

Derek Mahon's poem "The Hunt by Night" captures such a vision.[4] Like the painting by Paolo Uccello on which it is based, there is a destructive aspect of the hunt that threatens to consume both the hunter and the hunted. Mahon perceives how the eruptive violence of nature becomes part of culture itself. The ninth sonnet from Seamus Heaney's sequence "The Glanmore Sonnets" from *Field Work* (1979) likewise investigates the relationship between violence and the aesthetic. Heaney has often traced this tension back to the lines from Shakespeare: "How with this rage shall beauty hold a plea / Whose action is no stronger than a flower?"[5] This question interrogates the history of landscape from the modern and postmodern periods as they are delineated again by Mitchell: "The study of landscape has gone through two major shifts in this century: the first (associated with modernism) attempted to read the history of landscape primarily on the basis of a history of landscape painting and to narrativize that history as a progressive movement toward purification of the visual field [a movement Mitchell attributes to Ernst Gombrich and his popularizer Kenneth Clark]; the second (associated with postmodernism) tended to decenter the role of painting as pure formal visuality in favor of a semiotic and hermeneutic approach that treated landscape as an allegory of psychological or ideological themes."[6] Mahon and Heaney attest to the veracity of both impulses. Interestingly, so does Shakespeare purify and decenter the image for the sake of language in the above quote. One of the main arguments Mitchell also makes is to show how landscape mattered long before the eighteenth century, to which its rising importance is normally traced. This history remained relevant to Heaney's classical and medieval-minded attitudes toward landscape throughout his lifetime.

As noted in the chapter on Kavanagh, Heaney defines two outlooks toward the landscape: "I think there are two ways in which place is known and cherished, two ways which may be complementary but which are just as likely to be antipathetic. One is lived, illiterate and unconscious, the other learned, literate and conscious." He states that the "quarrel" for Kavanagh "was the quarrel between these views."[7] What Heaney learned from Montague is equally important: landscape as a record of conquest, a concept that *The Rough Field* (1972) outlines in detail. The violent origins of that rough field, both etymologically (Garvaghy is translated as rough field) and historically, stay with Heaney and inform his critique of Robert Praeger as a cultural tourist.

Landscape as a subject makes one consider sectarian connections to the land, as troubled as such reflections might be. Its history is often described along the dominant sectarian divide. One might say that Protestants withdraw into aesthetic or scientific reflections, or both, while Catholics historicize and personalize the landscape, but in the end no simple classification is satisfactory, as important exceptions abound. The poet Seán Lysaght has responded to Heaney's critique of Praeger. Lysaght's less politically and more scientific ecocritical view of nature is central to his own poetic project. He is author of *Robert Lloyd Praeger: The Life of a Naturalist* (1998), as well as of numerous essays on the subject of landscape and nature in Ireland. The two forms of interest, academic and poetic, intertwine. Praeger is the "you" of Lysaght's poetic sequence "The Clare Island Survey," an homage to Praeger's survey of the island off the coast of County Mayo. Lysaght follows creatively in Praeger's footsteps "with a booty of old words, and new echoes."[8] In Lysaght's case, what is particularly interesting about his indebtedness is that he is both acknowledging the beginnings of the naturalist movement and marking the beginning of a new stage.

In a comparative essay on Heaney and Praeger, Lysaght endeavors to defuse the tension between Catholic and Protestant ideas of landscape in Ireland. While Heaney sets himself in learned opposition to both Praeger and the Protestant poet John Hewitt, Lysaght looks assiduously for similarities. The direct and often necessary historical use of landscape is seen as the essentially and essentialist Catholic view of Montague, McGahern, and Heaney. Lysaght endeavors to do more than defend Praeger against what he feels are unfair characterizations. He seeks to discover that element of nature that transcends history. He writes that "as a geologist, Praeger is conscious of a dimension to landscape, nature and the universe which transcends the competing political claims of nationalist and unionist, native and Planter."[9] The scientific view of nature that Lysaght endeavors to uphold has traditionally been seen as a Protestant view of nature, and of culture, for that matter. It has allowed Protestants to be cultural nationalists and political unionists at the same time.

Lysaght's transhistorical view of nature and landscape has the real virtue of presenting a foundation for future understanding. He is not denying history, nor is he taking sides, as it may seem; instead, he is trying to let nature speak on its own terms. In this respect, Montague, Meehan, and even the late Heaney must at least partially share his vision. Lysaght is aware of the social and economic implications of nature and landscape and says so regarding Praeger's sense of privilege and Heaney's careful opposition to it. Though Montague inspired him, Heaney had been thinking of the relevance of history and the place of home and family in perceptions of landscape for his whole career.

As in many texts from Swift onward, where landscape is central, home, marriage, and union (sexual, political) are dominant themes. Poems by Seamus Heaney in which the actual word "landscape" appears make this particularly evident. They are from different periods in his life and reflect concerns of those years in his poetic career, but all circle around the potent themes listed above. In the early poem "Honeymoon Flight" from *Death of a Naturalist* (1966), the poet imagines himself and his wife in an airplane above the landscape endeavoring to piece the "patchwork" together from the bird's-eye view, while "the coastline slips away beneath the wing-tip." Like all of us in this era of speed, he has gained perspective but lost mooring. The roads both "bind and loose"; the "sure green world" has gone "topsy-turvy," and it is hard not to believe that the "casual marriage" between villages does not have a moral as well as a topographical sense. Thus, they leave the "familiar landscape" below: "familiar," here, playing on both family and custom, as well as the ethical centers of life. The second stanza's closing "look" of wife to poet confirms the challenge that lies ahead as they hang "miraculous, above the water," but remain "dependent on the invisible air" to stay "airborne." The "calm" voice on the loudspeaker speaks of the weather, yet the turbulence reminds the couple that their honeymoon flight is prophetic of the journey ahead, and they as "travellers, at this point, can only trust" in the miracle that keeps them hanging, that keeps them alive. This flight is not typical of Heaney's early landscape poems. Normally, he digs deep into the earth's landscape itself.

"Belderg," for example, is an excavated site from the Neolithic period in County Mayo, in the West of Ireland. Heaney uses his experience at this site to set up a conversation about cultural memory and its artifacts, which was part of the controversial project of *North* (1975). He begins by noting that even in this archaeological setting, the dialectic between the foreign and the natural is raised in conversation. The "quernstone" seemed like something from another country, yet something that has been that long in the ground must itself be the definition of its grounds, having inhabited them for so long. Heaney sees this stone as indicative of when Neolithic people plowed the land. With the discovery of the stones comes a sense that the earth itself is being exposed again to the plows of the Stone Age. The earth itself seems like a body harrowed and seeded many times over in some elaborate ritual from *The Golden Bough* or from the story of Deucalion and Pyrrha. The "landscape" itself, as Heaney writes, is "fossilized" with stone walls.

There is an implicit mirroring going on between the Neolithic period and the present age. The speaker then recalls what his interlocutor replied: that the ages since the stone was buried have cultural symbols that tell their own story; these are "growth rings / Of iron, flint and bronze." This thought makes Heaney consider the name of his homeland and ponder the political and social intersections between Norse, Irish, Planter, and Gael. It leads to a moment of vision in which he "passed through" the hole of the quernstone. Heaney can imagine the interconnectedness of peoples in the image of the world tree or Yggdrasil, an immense mythical tree that connects the nine worlds in Norse cosmology. The cryptic last line combines essences of body and land (tree and body blended in the crushed marrow). The effort seems to be part of a larger one in Irish poetry to find a representative "home" landscape, even as deep experiences of nature consistently elude representation. The aim is "a balance . . . between culture and the wild," what Robinson calls an "echosphere."[10] The idea of what eludes representation, what is visionary but seems illusory, becomes central to Heaney's middle and later poetry and often centers on marriage as a metaphor for home and the nuclear family. Elusive representation is also apparent in the space left behind after the death of his parents.

Probably nowhere does home become so inextricably part of nature as in "Homecomings," from the volume *Field Work* (1979). In this sequence, the poet becomes one with a bird on its flight for food and, on its return home, he notes how it is "gloved and kissed." Heaney's wish to become one with the bird is an attempt to view nature through nature's eyes, as Japanese American sculptor Isamu Noguchi aimed to do.[11] The homecoming is both the life of the sand martin under the "eaves" and the eye of the poet trying to integrate that property on the horizon that, as Emerson insists, no one can own. The paradoxical intent to listen to silence, to hide and simultaneously be a visible part, to be the oxymoronic "glottal stillness," points to an impossible homecoming, a grasping at presence that has eluded and will continue to elude his grasp. This attempt parallels the effort at the end of "Clearances" to picture the "bright nowhere," to capture the "soul ramifying . . . / Silent beyond the silence listened for."[12] Similarly, in "The Peninsula," the drive back home after a visit to a "land without marks" finds the addressee, the "you," of the poem, "still with nothing to say." The "uncod[ing]" of "all landscapes" defines the career of Heaney's poetry, as is most obvious perhaps in his poem "A Peacock's Feather" from *The Haw Lantern* (1987), which places the sense of home in more traditional aesthetic landscapes, where gentle, ordered lands signify the beautiful English countryside and rugged, mountainous ones signify the sublime Irish ones. Though published in 1987, the poem is dated 1972, which places it prominently at the beginning of the Troubles in the year of Bloody Sunday and makes its national and colonial significance particularly salient.

Heaney begins the poem with an appeal to the transcendental dimension (the christening) but also with an acknowledgment of the strength of the empiricist one (sleep and food). The idea of cleansing the child of original sin brings one to the root of the aesthetics of sublimity, because sublime feeling is associated with the sense of sin. The sublimity of birth is somehow cured by the beauty of baptism. Heaney hopes, or perhaps ironically suggests, that his English niece stands a better chance of being so cleansed because of her surroundings, that her fate is with the seemingly innocent though distinctly walled beautiful of the English countryside rather than with her mother's sublime "scraggy" Irish origins. The formal reality of the baptism is proved in the empirical reality of the surroundings. Such transcendence from the empirical paradoxically does not deny its claims. The boundaries of the beautiful in the above stanza are protected by the same violence that protects Edgar Linton's estate in *Wuthering Heights*. Daisy's mother, like Emily Brontë's father, comes from a landscape other than this "mellowness / Of topiary, lawn and brick."

In the next stanza, Heaney makes plain the sublime landscape of his and his sister's origin and explains why the choice of rhyming couplets is suitable for the neoclassical subject of the beautiful in England but not in Ireland. He begins with images out of paintings of the landscape sublime, and then, because the images are at odds with the chosen style, Heaney explains that his style is predicated by the garden tones of the beautiful, tones closer to Yeats's famous beginning of "Meditations in Time of Civil War" than those for which Heaney is known. Yet, as if to weave some irony into the style, Heaney has shortened the usual rich pentameter to a more chastened tetrameter. He is suspicious of the "rich man's flowering lawns" of Yeats's poem, because he knows them to be walled and nostalgic. The closure suggested by the rhyming couplets, echoing Goldsmith's and Allingham's uses, is belied by the instability of the lyric voice and lack of closure in the poem.

As Luke Gibbons has pointed out about Burke, eighteenth-century Ireland, and the birth of aesthetics, the terrors of the natural sublime in Ireland are the very real ones of roving Irish brigands and English militias; there is no aesthetic distance as there is in England, and Heaney, like Burke, is aware of this fact.[13] History has left the land "dishevelled." In an echo of the aspect of Yeats suggested by the "bare hills and stunted trees" of the poem "Hound Voice," a type of landscape in Yeats that remains unacknowledged in Heaney's poem, Heaney chooses as his home "scraggy farm and moss."

Heaney then proceeds to bear in upon the Yeatsian theme of social order when he parallels the close of Yeats's "A Prayer for My Daughter" and the Coole Park poems with something much less "accustomed and ceremonious" than what Yeats imagines. Yeats's marriages and alliances are very different from Heaney's. The latter has no "rich horn" and "spreading tree" to symbolize the erotic basis of the beautiful, of the subject-object mystery of aesthetic experience. Rather, his families ravel and "mesh," and, since the "future's not our own," they probably unravel and unmesh as well, especially as there is "trust but little intimacy" between the Irish and English branches of the family. There is only a legal labyrinth or an "in-law maze."

There is also Heaney's poetic billet-doux. Heaney, unlike Yeats in Coole Park, has difficulty imagining the reconciliation of the Anglo and the Irish traditions. Much of the poem centers on a destabilized sense of both home and the lyric *I*—a destabilization in Heaney that is often overlooked but nevertheless apparent in his poetry. Here he is "self-conscious in [the] gathering dark." Heaney has brought us to the difficult moment in which recognizing the humanity of the other challenges the self. If sublimity is Irishness and the beautiful is

Englishness, then any union should somehow reconcile their properties: the subjective, the objective, the masculine, the feminine—as well as their shared bloody history, which is precisely what Heaney imagines in the last stanza, but fears can be realized only in the future:

> So before I leave your ordered home,
> Let us pray. May tilth and loam,
> Darkened with Celts' and Saxons' blood,
> Breastfeed your love of house and wood
> Where I drop this for you, as I pass,
> Like the peacock's feather on the grass.

The tilled earth and wood that represent the natural Celts and the order and artifice of loam and house that represent the artificial English should be Daisy's soul food. As symbol of this possible union, Daisy, or day's eye, is appropriately named. She is the natural symbol of the movement toward some redemptive hybridity, of the reconciliation of the landscapes of the sublime and beautiful. Irish history moves from the beauty of its preconquest origins through its conquest and the processes of decolonization toward a reshaping. It is a reshaping here represented somewhat apocalyptically (figured as end and revelation) with a peacock's feather, a symbol that is again borrowed ironically from Yeats.

As so often with aesthetics, the dialectic of the beautiful and the sublime aims toward a synthesis in which the sublime returns from its negative manifestations to its more positive beginnings in a heightened form of the beautiful. In this scenario, there is a movement from the masculine terror of war to the maternal powers of the mother language. The tilled earth and the soil's building material of bricks, "darkened with Celts' and Saxons' blood," are meant rather mysteriously to be the matrix of the beautiful. This all takes us back to the eighteenth-century beginnings of the aesthetic, in which the sublime was seen as an extension of the beautiful and not as its opposite. Heaney has an incredulous attitude toward the exaltation of the terms of the beautiful. The poem is a symbol of apocalypse, like the feather, but it is not the revelation itself. It wasn't until the death of his parents that Heaney would address the idea of transcendence or revelation in the profound poems of *Seeing Things* (1991). The loss of his parents begins with the death of his mother.

The sonnet sequence "Clearances" from *The Haw Lantern* (1987) honors his mother after her death. The title can be traced to the land clearances in both Ireland and the Scottish highlands, making it a perfect vehicle for this poet of the Scots-Irish North of Ireland, who cherished and interrogated the region, its dialect, and its religion. This reference summarizes the sense of original sin and the historical guilt that was subsequent to those clearances and that reached a head in the Troubles that dominated so much of the poet's lifetime. Landscape functions almost purely by inference: the agricultural setting, the potatoes, the regional speech patterns, the allegorical hind, and the fallen tree of the last sonnet combine to paint a picture of the poet's complex feelings for his mother and his land. For Heaney, landscape is feminine; it is the bog goddess. His religion imagines the Virgin standing on top of the globe stamping on the serpent of the world. Those references provide the right form of elegiac expression for his mother.

What is also central to the poem is the domestic space, the inside of the family home. It is central because the home defines the Irish landscape, or any landscape, for that matter. Without habitation, it is nature or wilderness rather than landscape. Also, home is the scene of so many moving passages in Heaney's life. He is at its window, sharing in the perspective of his father "digging" in the poem of that name. He returns to it for the funeral of his brother in "Midterm Break." He is with his mother in probably one of his greatest poems ("Clearances"). Finally, the family, both nuclear and extended (the human race), is implicit in *Human Chain* (2010). Perhaps most significantly in the tenant history of Ireland, the family residence is predicated on an act of ownership that borders on some original sin, whether it be conquest, betrayal, or an unnamed sin. Vendler writes that this sequence "imagines all Oedipal longings fulfilled."[14] One might say instead that the Oedipal longings are not so much fulfilled as understood, or answered by the use of Christian myth.

"Clearances," as the title portends, begins with an act of violence. This act takes us back to the *Death of a Naturalist* (1966) and the analogy between a poet as gunman and the poet's laboring father. More specifically, it refers to "The Forge" of *Door into the Dark* (1969), Heaney's second volume, in which the blacksmith's volcanic arts are analogous to the art of poet. That his mother provides the example this time is telling within the domestic frame of these sonnets. Here family and nation converge in all their potent symbolism. His mother teaches him to "face the music" "between the hammer and the block." That home somehow reflects violence is made clear in part 2 of "Funeral Rites," in which the sectarian killings come home to roost, with Heaney preparing a poetic monument to honor the dead, one that would parallel the burial mounds of ancient Ireland. This gesture is meant to counter the experience of the Tollund man who "feel[s] lost / Unhappy and at home." The second sonnet in the sequence captures what Edmund Burke calls the "pedigrees of guilt."[15]

There is a turncoat, so like an informer; there is the convert, a term that burns in Irish memory, North and South, in Ireland and elsewhere. The "Exogamous Bride," someone who marries outside the "tribe," echoes throughout colonial history. Lundy is reviled in Ulster loyalism to this day as a traitor and is burned in effigy during the celebrations to mark the anniversary of the shutting of the gates of Derry in 1688. "Lundy" has also become a byword for traitor for unionists and loyalists. For our purposes, the most important line in the poem is the last: "The exonerating, exonerated stone." In its double quality, it is the pharmakon, the poison and antidote, the scapegoat, that which pronounces guilt, punishes guilt, and potentially releases it. The next or second sonnet reflects the attempt to teach culture in order to counter the idea of the intimate murder or scapegoating. It will take place only in the land of the dead when mother and grandfather sit down together.

This communion leads to the third sonnet, which, along with part 6, is the climax of the sequence, in which mother and son peel potatoes together. It is an act remembered in light of his mother's death. This act is the poet's answer to digging. The father digs the potatoes up, and the mother prepares them for supper. In the traditional role playing, Heaney, the son, again finds himself in the interior space of the house, the young scholar-poet helping out with the household chores. Silence again defines the scene in the sonnet, much as it dominates the entire sequence. The stoic silence of the taciturn culture of the North ("whatever you say, say nothing") combines with the underlying silence of shared knowledge in which nothing needs to be said. Such closeness borders on the silence that overwhelms lovers after lovemaking:

> When all the others were away at Mass
> I was all hers as we peeled potatoes.
> They broke the silence, let fall one by one
> Like solder weeping off the soldering iron:
> Cold comforts set between us, things to share
> Gleaming in a bucket of clean water.
> And again let fall. Little pleasant splashes
> From each other's work would bring us to our senses.
>
> So while the parish priest at her bedside
> Went hammer and tongs at the prayers for the dying
> And some were responding and some crying
> I remembered her head bent towards my head,
> Her breath in mine, our fluent dipping knives—
> Never closer the whole rest of our lives.

And so the potato peeling, the tension between educated son and less-educated mother ("In front of her, a genuinely well- / adjusted adequate betrayal / Of what I knew better. I'd naw and aye / And decently relapse into the wrong / Grammar which kept us allied and at bay"), and the erotic dance of the flour sacks ("Coming close again by holding back") lead to the admission of the incestual drive amid the angst and *la pietà* of Easter:

> In the first flush of the Easter holidays
> The ceremonies during Holy Week
> Were highpoints of our Sons and Lovers phase.

That the admission takes place during Easter week and at the altar acknowledges the power of the analogy between the family and the Trinity as well as the intention of Christianity to address the pessimism of the Oedipal myth. The erotic power of the first quotation from scripture ("As the hind longs for the streams, so my soul") and the pathos of the second ("Day and night my tears have been my bread") combine to express both the longing and the necessary sublimation of desire within the family as the foundation of religious and social life. The erotic power also implicitly addresses the historical guilt that begins the sequence: the exonerating and exonerated stone cast against the bride who marries outside the tribe.

The idea of marriage as the allegory of the union of Ireland and England has been referenced throughout Irish history, back to the Jacobite tradition. The breaking of the taboo haunts the family much as Irish history is haunted by the traces of conquest and everything the broken taboo entails. The mother's death recalls the clearances that first dispossessed the Irish. This recollection refers not only to the removal of the Gaelic Irish from their lands (admitting the complexity of the phrase "Gaelic Irish") but also to the deforestation of Ireland: "Clearances that suddenly stood open. / High cries were felled and a pure change happened." This realization becomes not only a kenosis for Heaney in terms of his mother, but also an emptying out of himself as he circles the wreckage of his own being, which is symbolized by the felling of a "coeval" chestnut tree. His own origins stretch back to what Montague calls the "dark permanence of ancient forms":[16]

> Through the shocked tips and wreckage of it all.
> Deep planted and long gone, my coeval
> Chestnut from a jam jar in a hole,
> Its heft and hush become a bright nowhere,
> A soul ramifying and forever
> Silent, beyond silence listened for.

We return to an impossible homecoming, a grasping of presence that has eluded and will continue to elude his grasp. The effort at the end of "Clearances" to picture the "bright nowhere," to capture the "soul ramifying" beyond the "silence listened for," is an effort to capture his own essence, his mother's, as well as the land from which his roots will eventually be torn. The moment circles around what Heaney describes as a "half-sacred and half-profaned" place.[17]

The "half-sacred and half-profaned" place is the space of the mother. What provides the tension for Heaney, as for many a male writer, is the identity of the father and his relation to the son. By taking individual poems—"Digging," "Follower," "A Call," "District and Circle," "The Stone Verdict," and finally Heaney's translation of book 6 of *The Aeneid*—a sequence can be constructed to link Heaney's musings on his father. In "Digging" the speaker watches his father digging potatoes from the vantage of the domestic space (the mother's space) of the house. While tracing the patrilineal line, he wonders about his place in it, because his scholarly bent situates him in an ambiguous place between father and mother. As Heaney in the early poem claims his pen as a weapon, it is important to note that both he and his mother have "fluent, dipping knives." Remembering bringing milk to his grandfather as a boy, the speaker/poet must reaffirm his role in the phallocentric order by making the pen both a weapon and a tool. This line of descent is both poetic and familial, but shared in ways with the mother that could be read as subversive.

The poem "Follower" builds on the theme of Heaney's admiration for his father. Here Heaney is both physically and figuratively following him on the farm. The poem begins with a close description of his father at work. Heaney writes about how his "shoulders globed like a full sail" and how his eyes "narrowed and angled at the ground." Not only does Heaney describe the physical aspects of his father working, but he also echoes the auditory aspects. The horses responded to his "clicking tongue." The description indicates that Heaney was near his father as he led the horses. Heaney is writing from his perspective as a child, whereas in "Digging" he was writing from an adult perspective, albeit a young adult. Heaney writes that as he followed his father, he "stumbled" and "fell," and "sometimes [his father] rode [him] on his back." Heaney admires him for being "an expert" at what he does. He writes that he "wanted to grow up and plough" like his father because all he "ever did was follow in [his father's] broad shadow round the farm." The last three lines of the poem return to the present in which Heaney's father is an older man. He is now the one who is "stumbling / Behind [Heaney], and will not go away." In old age, Heaney's father has become the "nuisance" that Heaney was as a child. Such is the Oedipal circle of life: from four appendages of a baby crawling, to two adult legs walking, to an old man walking with the third leg of a cane.

While not straying from the similar themes of the previous poems, "A Call" continues the action of what I am calling a sequence, as it reflects on a poignant moment before his father's death. At the beginning of "A Call," Heaney's mother is speaking to him over the phone and telling him that his father has gone outside "to do a bit of weeding." Even in his old age, Heaney's father persists in working the land. However, because his body is on the decline, he can weed only when "the weather here's so good." While waiting, Heaney envisions that moment of his father weeding. He sees his father "touching, inspecting, separating one / Stalk from the other." While this is a gentle remembrance of his father's lifework, it is also a bittersweet reminder of his father's imminent death. In this reverie, Heaney sees his father pulling up all the stalks that are "not tapered, frail and leafless" with a "rueful" vengeance. Heaney's father is angry that his life is coming to a close and that he is not as limber, like certain stalks, as he used to be. Transitioning from the reverie back into reality, Heaney listens to "the amplified grave ticking of hall clocks." His word choice of "grave" is twofold—the adjective, meaning "serious," that is used literally and then the noun, meaning where one is buried, that is alluded to. This diction demonstrates that Heaney is also aware of his father's death and is already feeling a proleptic sense of mourning. Further, the imagery of a loud ticking clock evokes the notion of a countdown, which in this case is the counting down of the minutes of his father's life.

Both images of "mirror glass" and "sunstruck pendulums" in the same stanza evoke the notion of time slowly passing and of facing one's own mortality. This scene that Heaney has created in his mind, in which his father can still be "down on his hands and knees beside the leek rig," is a calm one. Heaney wishes that "this is how Death would summon Everyman." With his father's death on the horizon, Heaney swells with emotion as his father comes to the phone. "Next thing he spoke and I nearly said I loved him," writes Heaney. This line is the most bold, clear, and exemplary on the theme of their father-son dynamic. In the previous poems of this sequence, when Heaney and his father were younger, their love for each other was subtler. It was shown when Heaney tagged alongside his father in "Follower" or when his father made the harvest bow for him in "The Harvest Bow." In this moment, although Heaney wants to tell his father that he loves him, he refrains, as speaking would disrupt the foundation of unspoken emotions of their younger years. "A Call" brings us closer to the death of the father. Mortality will be a common point of reflection in his later poems. A good example of his meditation on mortality is Heaney's evocation of his father's ghost in the poem "Seeing Things."

In the third section of "Seeing Things," Heaney confronts the ghost of his father, as he would in his posthumously published book 6 of *The Aeneid*, in which Aeneas's father, Anchises, describes his son's heralded destiny as maker of the Roman Empire. At the beginning of the poem, Heaney goes back to a time when his father was still alive, "undrowned." In this memory, which was "once upon a time," Heaney lists elements that were physically real during that time, such as "the horse-sprayer [that] / Was too big and new-fangled," "a bird on the shed roof," and "bluestone [that] might / Burn [him] in the eyes." Heaney lists items from the farm on which he matured, returning to the earlier themes of his father. There is little separation between the father and the land. Heaney even directly discusses his father's farmer life, writing that his "father had gone to spray / Potatoes in a field on the riverbank." However, Heaney's father "wouldn't bring [Heaney] with him." The fact that his father would not allow Heaney to accompany him engages the poem "Follower" in which Heaney, as a child, was a nuisance to his father. When Heaney's father returns, Heaney is "inside the house" and sees him arrive from "out the window." Again, he finds it difficult to locate himself in the landscape. This moment also engages his earlier poem "Digging," in which Heaney watched his father in the field from the window above his desk. This time, however, when he came back, his father was "scatter-eyed / And daunted, strange without his hat." Here is the image of Heaney's father in death, "his step unguided, his ghosthood immanent." There appears to be something strange and "off balance" about his father.

When Heaney saw his father "face to face," "there was nothing between us there / That might not still be happily ever after." In those last two lines, Heaney now places his father in the afterlife, as he would again in "District and Circle." His father and the land he represents enter a divine space, becoming godlike in association. In his interview with Denis O'Driscoll in *Stepping Stones*, Heaney states:

> The infinite spaces may be silent, but the human response is to say that this is not good enough, that there has to be more to it. . . . Admittedly we now know that the spaces are far from silent, that they are continuously alive and fluent in their own wordless language, but if you stand out in the country under a starry sky, you can still feel a primitive awe at the muteness of the vault.
>
> In "The Stone Verdict," I imagined this uncommunicativeness as a sort of divine corrective to human protestation. I was thinking of my father and his "old disdain of sweet talk and excuses": "He will expect more than words in the ultimate court / He relied on through a lifetime's speechlessness." So, to the extent that poetry is a pay-off for all the duplicities of language and disappointments of reality, it can also be said to be "a form of redemption."[18]

In a sense, Heaney's father becomes the judging sky-Father; from poetic precursor, he becomes a stoic voice in action if not in words of poetic redemption intimately connected with the starry landscape and the primitive world.

When in the "District and Circle" sonnet sequence Heaney sees his own image in the window of the underground train, behind the reflection he sees the image of his father. If "A Call" was the poem before the death of Heaney's father, "District and Circle" follows perfectly by becoming the poem of the underworld. "District and Circle" was written after the bombing attacks on the London Underground in 2005; to meditate on these attacks, Heaney begins a journey by entering the Underground (District and Circle is a line on the Underground). There, he finds a watcher, "his fingers perked, his two eyes eyeing me / In an unaccusing look I'd not avoid." This person is reminiscent of a gatekeeper, which one would find upon dying and accessing any sort of eternal life. With a "nod," they have an unspoken understanding about what Heaney is venturing into—a place of shadows. In the dark Underground, Heaney is reminded of the light of life. After describing the rumbling of the Underground, he writes, "I missed the light . . . / Parks at lunchtime where the sunners lay." By playing with these opposites of light and dark, Heaney invokes the opposites of death and life. On a train, Heaney continues "on [his] way, well girded, yet on edge." Traveling through the Underground, which stands in as metaphor for a gate-kept eternal life, Heaney feels both tranquil and anxious as he searches for some semblance of human recognition in that "jostling."[19]

In the last section of "District and Circle," Heaney looks into the window of the Underground train. He finds his "father's glazed face in [his] own waning." This moment embodies a passage in Virgil's *Aeneid*, of which Heaney translated a version of book 6, when Aeneas encounters his father in the underworld. The window in which Heaney saw his father is "mirror-backed."[20] Heaney sees himself as a reflection of his father. As Heaney rides the Underground, it is evident in this poem that he is placing himself in the image of eternal life, where his father would be. By doing so, Heaney moves past the culmination of his father's death and still allows himself to invoke previous themes in "District and Circle" by seeing his father in his windowed reflection.

Michael Parker in "Fallout from the Thunder: Poetry and Politics in Seamus Heaney's *District and Circle*," writes of the moment when Heaney sees himself in and as a reflection of his father: "However much he tries to blend in, to adjust to his surroundings, he cannot escape what Freud terms *das Unheimliche*, the uncanny. The most significant motif in the closing sonnet is that of the mirror, a surface which creates 'a doubling, dividing and interchanging of the self . . .

repetition of the same features.' Although it appears only fleetingly, it is the recognition of his father's 'glazed face' in his own which evidently haunts him, and which may lie behind those earlier references to disloyalty. The 'flail' simile on line 2 both connects and disconnects farmer-father and self-scourging poet-son." Parker later goes on to make a significant observation that ties this Oedipal motif back to the uncanny confrontations of *Gulliver's Travels*: "Throughout, the poem maintains an ambivalent stance towards its all-too human subject; it disapproves of his roughness and intolerance in the domestic sphere, yet seems to admire his drive, commitment, and unflinching belief in 'hammered iron.' . . . In comparing this 'ungullible' farmer with one of the canon's most famous and enduring sons, the narrator inscribes him within literature, and so confers a kind of immortality. Those familiar with the fourth book of *Gulliver's Travels*, will recall, however, how Gulliver's long stay in equine company, with the Houyhnhnms, leaves him incapable of re-integrating with his family."[21] These critical assertions precisely formulate much of what has been discussed in this book. Gulliver's inability to recognize his human lineage, compared to Heaney's ability to do so, recalls Don Pedro's recognition of Gulliver's humanity despite Gulliver's equine disdain. In Swift's pessimistically Christian tale, Don Pedro carries the cross; Gulliver figuratively steps on it. Heaney understands that redemption is possible in his alignment with his father. There is a mystical blending of Father and Son, so Christian in its meaning and so hopeful in how it answers, or indeed conquers, the Oedipal narrative, the founding murder, the original sin, the dark passages of nature's murderous and incestual drives.

There also is an emptying out of history in these late stages of Heaney's work. The world he knew was disappearing. Ireland was approaching its post-Ireland stage.[22] He often felt that his was a transitional age. He says as much to Denis O'Driscoll many times and in many different ways in *Stepping Stones*. The transition would include changing Irish views of landscape, nature, and the ecocritical. Palimpsests of conquest give way to deep ecologies, to accepting that there is an important aspect of landscape that is not a document of family, nation, and home, that something of nature does not merely raise the shadow of the Oedipus complex or yearn for Christian redemption. But in all transitions, the future was implied in the past. Perhaps Yeats foresaw the changes when he noted, "We and our bitterness have left no traces / On Munster grass and Connemara skies."[23]

12

In Defiance of Human Frontiers

From Landscape to Ecology in Eiléan Ní Chuilleanáin and Paula Meehan

A view of nature and landscape that moves beyond historical and geographical borders has the virtue of being able to present a global foundation for future understanding. One is conscious of the landscape's historical emblems, with all of the social and political implications, yet sure that "nature should be viewed as something greater than man, and, particularly, something greater than the domain of human political conflicts," as Lysaght writes of Praeger.[1] Derek Mahon understands that ecopoetry is different from the poetry of landscape: ". . . we consumed landscape / in the days before ecology came around."[2] More ecologically minded poets look through the eyes of a naturalist, which of course means that they are half scientist and half aesthetician; the history of the naturalist's view of nature has been divided between the scientist (for example, Darwin) and the literary man (Thoreau).

Most naturalist views, such as the worldviews of Rachel Carson or Loren Eiseley, combine the two perspectives. The poets discussed in this chapter tend to emphasize the mythological qualities of nature, while insisting that there is something in nature that escapes all mythologizing. In *Contemporary Irish Poetry and the Pastoral Tradition*, Donna Potts notes of Moya Cannon's work (and she speaks similarly of Paula Meehan): "Cannon leaves the reader little choice, but to value nature for its own sake."[3] For most recent poets, the rendering of nature as nature sometimes parallels and sometimes blends with the mythological rendering.

Any poet of landscape must confront the antagonism between nature and culture; it is at the roots of our consciousness. For Cannon, myth best expresses this tension. Often the pagan roots show through the religious culture (in the case of Ireland, Christian). "Holy Well" reveals the eel flashing through the waters as the source of Marian devotion. "Images of old fertilities . . . testify" to the "miracle" of water trapped in a normally dry valley.[4] The blessing associated with water existing, as it does in the "Burren," in a cursed rocky land is fundamental to understanding the dual aspects of experience. A mythic almost animistic consciousness allows us to understand how the twined blessing and curse transport us into being: the "thirst of the inscrutable fern" is like the "human thirst / that beats on a stone" ("Thirst in the Burren"). Many of the poets are also attempting to find in the pastoral landscape of Ireland traces of the wilderness. Like Paula Meehan, Lysaght, and Cannon, Caitríona O'Reilly understands the significance of the nonhuman for our imagination. Culture is cradled by nature. Nature is both transhistorical and embedded in our history; it is mythic, yet linked to the workings of the rational mind. Wanting to be free of history, we turn to nature, yet she is the ur-mother, the salt in our blood that stirs us back into history. O'Reilly and Cannon are trying to move beyond rational understanding, or else trying to find something that predates it.

In O'Reilly, the civilization that nature constitutes, instead of merely presenting the unfathomable and obscurely barbaric heart of darkness, actually holds the key to our deepest symbols. Consciousness and the natural world also redefine each other in forceful ways. Potts considers O'Reilly part of the "post-pastoral" movement in Ireland.[5] Potts's comments point to the poet's emphasis on nature over the pastoral. In the Swiftian tradition, the lines between the natural and human worlds are blurred. O'Reilly endeavors to think like a mountain, to think objectively, to listen to see through the falcon's eye, to watch the birds' flight, to see herself upon the patient's table, with the same passive wisdom as the land views the life that takes place upon it. Some of this perspective is the product of the political shifts in Ireland of the past two decades; we see it in John Montague, Derek

Mahon, and Seamus Heaney. This way of thinking may be traceable to the public attention paid to women poets such as Medbh McGuckian, Eiléan Ní Chuilleanáin, and Paula Meehan. For the purposes of concentration and consistency, the rest of this chapter will center on Ní Chuilleanáin and Meehan.[6] In these two poets, there are many strands of thinking: ecological and aesthetic, religious and scientific, political and personal, to mention but a few.

Landscape and nature are so central to Ní Chuilleanáin that they are almost invisible, or seem to function as a background. If we look at one of the earliest poems, "The Lady's Tower," we see how nature is personified and then reflected in the terms of perception itself. The tower "leans / Back to the cliff," while behind is the "shifting oblique veins / of the hill" and the "river fills / A spoonful of light on the cellar walls below."[7] Throughout her career, the poet has been intensely interested in the subtle intersections of nature and the sacred. In "Ardnaturais," swimming becomes a meditation on death, and the implied advent of some revelatory truth awaits the prophet's cry in the wilderness and his subsequent beheading. The bee and water seem to be searching for something, flower or outlet, while the poet floats in the water and various water plants become images of the beheading and the later crucifixion. The confluence of nature and culture is where the sacred is born from the confrontation with mortality. The birth of the sacred is certainly one of the poet's main concerns. As the ever-flowing, changing natural world seeks to become eternal, mortal being seeks permanence and meaning. That effort underlies all monuments, artistic and political. Yet there is something else; the structures of our response to nature are unveiled. In other words, in Darwinian terms we respond to nature in ways meant to ensure our survival. This understanding is the scientific version of our struggle for immortality. In religious or psychoanalytic terms, our response to nature is tied to larger principles of sin and redemption, disease and therapy.

In Ní Chuilleanáin's poem "The Real Thing," the Brazen Serpent is the reliquary of such meaning. It represents the pharmakon quality of the serpent, the poison that is the source of the antidote, the cure, as well as the divine relief in the wilderness.[8] Understanding the significance of the snake/serpent as image of the combination of nature and culture requires a preface. Darwinian scholar E. O. Wilson captures both the behavioral and the imaginative presence of the image, which characterizes the snake and the serpent respectively:

> The snake and the serpent, flesh-and-blood reptile and demonic dream-image, reveal the complexity of our relation to nature and the fascination and beauty inherent in all organisms. Even the deadliest and most repugnant creatures are endowed with magic in the human mind. Human beings have an innate fear of snakes; more precisely, they have an innate propensity to learn such fear quickly and easily past the age of five. The images they build out of his peculiar mental set are both powerful and ambivalent, ranging from terror-stricken flight to the experience of power and male sexuality. As a consequence the serpent has become an important part of cultures around the world.[9]

At the opening of the essay, Wilson makes clear that in this combination of meaning, the humanities and sciences interlink: "Sciences and the humanities, biology and culture, are bridged in a dramatic manner by the phenomenon of the serpent. Fabricated from symbols and bearing portents of magic, the snake's image enters the conscious and unconscious mind with ease during reverie and dreams. It appears without warning and departs abruptly, leaving behind not a specific memory of any real snake but the vague sense of a more powerful creature, the serpent, surrounded by a mist of fear and wonderment."[10]

In the end, the magic symbolism of the imaginative encounter means less to the scientist than what it tells us of our struggle for survival. He celebrates the eruptions of nature and the sublime, but again posits it in empirical terms of survival: "And a sweet sense of horror, the shivery fascination with monsters and creeping forms that so delights us today even in the sterile hearts of the cities, could keep you alive until the next morning." He privileges the functional experience that the snake/serpent offers, but he ultimately does not devalue the mythic, ritualistic, and symbolic associations of the image as a result. He allows breathing space for the language of the humanities in his scenario and acknowledges that it is the very nexus of biology and culture that makes the experience so vital: "Organisms are the natural stuff of metaphor and ritual. Although the evidence is far from all in, the brain appears to have kept its old capacities, its channeled quickness. We stay alert and alive in the vanished forests of the world."[11] If we look at the last stanza of "The Real Thing," we see that it is the mythic structures behind the serpent, linked as they are to freedom, transgression, magic, and power, that make the "thing" a symbolic entity so paradoxically "real."[12] History, functionalism, even biology in its Darwinian aspects of adaptation and survival matter less to Ní Chuilleanáin. Erase history and (contra Locke) we might begin again in primitive awareness of our deepest connections to nature, unveiling our a priori or innate sense of the "real thing," so that the snake and the serpent are one. The wells of knowledge are truly *locked* against our inspection in such circumstances unless we allow the sacred image, the junction of nature and culture, to lift the "lace edge of the veil," to erupt into experience.[13]

There is some malevolence in the serpent and in our reaction to it that must be addressed, for, as Mary Midgley notes:

> If . . . there is no lawless beast outside man, it seems very strange to conclude that there is one inside him. It would be more natural to say that the beast within us gives us partial order; the task of conceptual thought will only be to complete it. But the opposite, *a priori* reasoning has prevailed. If the Beast Within was capable of every iniquity, people reasoned, then beasts without probably were too. This notion made man anxious to exaggerate his difference from all other species, and to ground all activities he valued in capacities unshared by animals, whether the evidence warranted it or not. In a way this evasion does the species credit, because it reflects our horror at the things we do. Man fears his own guilt and insists on fixing it on something evidently alien and external. Beasts Within solve the problem of evil.[14]

Here science (knowledge, history, truth) faces religion (imagination, myth, fiction), and what do we make of it? Wilson understands that the two are interconnected. Jung expands on this interconnection: "All science (*Wissenschaft*) however is a function of the soul, in which all knowledge is rooted. The soul is the greatest of all cosmic miracles; it is the *conditio sine qua non* of the world as an object. It is exceedingly astonishing that the Western world (apart from very rare exceptions) seems to have so little appreciation of this being so. The flood of external objects of cognizance has made the subject of all cognizance withdraw to the background, often to apparent nonexistence."[15] History thus is "a blank sheet," and "the real thing"[16] is the discovery of how mind (which is startled by the serpent) and object (the serpent) transcend time. If we replace the words "mathematical" and "fairy" with "religious" and "saint" in the following sentence by Erwin Schrödinger, we come close to the experience that Ní Chuilleanáin is describing in her depiction of the sacred relic and its importance to human experience: "A mathematical [religious] truth is timeless; it does not come into being when we discover it. Yet its discovery is a very real event, it may be an emotion like a great gift from a fairy [saint]."[17] The brazen serpent is such a gift.

Writing of Medbh McGuckian and Eiléan Ní Chuilleanáin, Eamon Grennan notes that both "insist upon the feminine dimension of the world." Quoting Donna Haraway's point that "feminist objectivity is about limited location and situated knowledge, not about transcendence and splitting of subject and object," he believes that such a perspective is necessary for an understanding of Eiléan Ní Chuilleanáin's feminism.[18] This shift is partially a reaction to the dominance of the Oedipal narrative of previous decades, particularly but not only in male discourse (the Oedipus and Electra complexes are central to both Morgan and Edgeworth). In this sense, it coincides with the idea of the anti-Oedipal, however complexly political the theory is, if only because it challenges the Oedipal patterning of desire in a way that encompasses "both sides of the nature/culture split."[19] This impasse provides its own relief when we examine the roles of landscape and nature in Ní Chuilleanáin's poetry, for they too are so rich in meaning, but so ambiguous in their depositions before the court of critical reckoning. They are centered on location and situated knowledge, what Lucy Collins calls "spaces of memory" in Ní Chuilleanáin's poetry, but are so resistant to any easy rational splitting (like that practical one between subject and object, culture and nature) that, in the end, landscape and the sacred carry much of the weight of her poems. Collins notes this fact when she says that in Ní Chuilleanáin's rendering, the "voice of nature itself" sometimes unites with the "spiritual contemplation of the monastic life."[20]

The poet does so by following the mythical (Ovidian) method of not locating the production of desire solely in the anthropocentric. As Peter Sirr writes of "Pygmalion's Image": "The poem can be read as a new myth, which, bypassing Pygmalion's exploitative and essentially misogynistic vision, posits instead a vision of creation as a collusion between nature and the created woman."[21] Much like the marriage of the girl and the reindeer, this collusion challenges the typical Oedipal resolution by moving toward nature rather than away from it. The title poem of its volume, "The Girl Who Married the Reindeer," imagines a union between a girl and a reindeer, between culture and nature, beginning with a seduction scene in which the girl herself prepares a meal for the reindeer from the fruits of nature, in the form of the sloe (the fruit of the blackthorn, *Prunus spinosa*). This seduction scene is a preparation for a *hieros gamos*, a sacred marriage between culture and nature. The offspring, a son, will be taken from the mother/culture figure because of a social fear of the natural, of the reindeer, that "strange beast." Yet these truths are interpenetrating: the girl herself, as woman, is not a simple version of culture. Perhaps Ní Chuilleanáin is playing on the assumption that being female, she is so close to nature that she is an enchanter. Likewise, it is the bridegroom's mother, the "old queen," who thinks that the girl should not live with her son, the reindeer.[22] In typical fashion, this folkloric world is notable for its blurring of the lines of nature and culture, the real and fantastic.[23]

Ní Chuilleanáin's political poems also challenge the Oedipal interpretation. Her translation of the Jacobite poem "Kilcash" (from the Irish original *Caoine Cill Chais*) places the mistreatment of Mother Nature as political and social testament at the heart of this ecocritical version of the well-known poem. If elsewhere the social and political had been oblique references, here they become central. The felling of the trees is symbolic of the decline of an aristocratic Catholic family, a branch of the Butlers.[24] As with Sweeney and the Children of Lir, the landscape reflects back the terms of the Butlers' exile. Quite realistically, the anonymous Jacobite poet knows that political help must come from abroad (France and Spain), but the poem matches that acknowledgment with hope for help from the transcendent (from Mary and Jesus).[25] One could say that this poem is an attempt at recuperation of this loss of sovereignty, containing all the sexual drama, the natural and political history, the sacred tension of the scene, but it is woman at the center of the drama, and not merely as the vehicle for its denouement. As in the poem "Hunger," we hope that through the "love of Christ and the law of nature," the sacred may labor toward a fulfilling harvest and that implicitly the girl who married the reindeer may reenvision her long-lost child.

A reconciliation between the "love of Christ and the law of nature" is possible if the imagination does its work. In Eiléan Ní Chuilleanáin's *The Sun-fish* (2010) and *The Boys of Bluehill* (2015), there are familiar themes of nature, landscape, and home. A phrase, "stenciled in shadows," from the title poem of the first volume could well be an *ars poetica* for the poet. It points to both the deep significance of these secret-but-never-secretive lines while capturing the exacting qualities of observations they contain. These elements combine to "make the verse hang right," as Ní Chuilleanáin states in "Curtain." As in her previous volumes, Eiléan Ní Chuilleanáin's *The Sun-fish* amply displays the poet's gift for parable ("A Bridge between Two Countries") and allegory ("The Polio Epidemic"), but always with a sense of the here and now, of lived experience, and with an acknowledgment of the everyday ("Ascribed").[26]

From the dedicatory epithalamium to the concluding poem of the volume ("The Copious Dark"), Ní Chuilleanáin's enigmatic poems often exude deep but unpretentious wisdom or ask simple questions that demand sufficient answers. In poems on nature, writing, women's lives, folklore, religion, love, grief, and family life, of many homes in different places, we are taught to "see who is there / In the whirling dance" so that we may trace the line between illusion and reality and grasp "The moment thinning the curtain, / Real, like the tricks of light." "The Copious Dark" is a poem of travel, landscape, and home, displaced and retrieved. It records how the journey itself, the sense of movement, awakens an awareness of the roots of home, even if the lighted window is someone else's.

The comment below by the poet explains the genesis of this poem and highlights the sense of home, dislocated, misplaced, as well as the mythical relationship between men and women, and the feeling that the links between landscape ("suburb"), nature ("forest"), and culture ("industry") define us in an elusive way:

> This poem was a long time in gestation. It started from a journey I took on a Greyhound bus. It was 1977, my first time touching the edges of the Western hemisphere. I had had serious doubts about the existence of land across the Atlantic and they had not really been allayed by the plane's long slow descent over, it seemed *into*, the sea that ended by skimming the tops of waves and then pretending to land on solid ground. I took a train to Baltimore and was somewhat reassured, though bothered by the amount of wilderness on show, and how it alternated with the human settlement: forest, then suburb and then forest and then industry.

The American wilderness unsettles the European poet. Nature to her must be framed by either religion or human habitation.

In the pastoral landscape of Virginia, among farms, fields, and battlefields, she recognizes the home-landscape and warring history of Ireland: "Next day I got on a series of buses, and when the first one headed out into Maryland and afterwards down the Shenandoah Valley, I saw fields with cows and horses, houses in the countryside with long verandas on which ancient men cuddled their shotguns, towns with the names of battles where people sat in the sun on the steps of the county jail. This was undoubtedly a real place."[27] Perhaps landscape for the poet is nature and culture reconciled. She proceeds to describe how she crossed into North Carolina and saw "Orpheus and Eurydice meeting in the underworld." This "high point" of her journey continues to take on mythic significance, linking "solitude and their coupleness," "light" and "darkness," and what they tell us of "interiors and desolate outsides." The concept of modern travel (automobiles for Joyce, cars and airplanes for Heaney, a bus here for Ní Chuilleanáin, trains for O'Faoláin and MacNeice, trams for Elizabeth Bowen) describes how technological speed often leads us to cover as much time in memory as the vehicle covers physical distance. It also leads to commensurately expanding thoughts of the social, religious, and political dimensions of landscape and nature as trains, automobiles, and planes cross greater expanses.[28]

Many of the poems of Eiléan Ní Chuilleanáin's *The Boys of Bluehill* describe how landscape and nature inform our inner worlds. This inner-outer dialectic connects the materials of language to the language of the natural world ("the forest floats over the land, / the island slides across the sea . . . they are thin as air, as a leaf that has stayed / a century inside a book"). The themes of music, religion, art, language, and nature unwind a fable of being and perception that is unmistakably Ní Chuilleanáin's. From the memory-laden "An Information" and the visionary "The Skelligs," through the haunting "Who Were Those Travellers" on to "Dream Shine" and "The Words Collide," this volume continually draws us into its own extraordinary perspectives on how inner and outer worlds have fluid borders in an almost medieval vision of the blurred lines between nature and culture. Such enigmatic messages land in our hands, for the "you" of the poem is the reader as well as any intended other, and we find that they also are ours to interpret.

In Paula Meehan's recent volumes *Painting Rain* (2008) and *Geomantic* (2016),[29] the poet endeavors to examine the places, public and private, where nature and culture meet; at this intersection she begins to make sense of the suffering of innocents and the powerless, to chart avenues toward liberation, and to salve their psychological and physical wounds by finding poetry in the disappearance and reappearance of the natural world.[30]

In *Painting Rain*, the search for nature is fundamental to the "triangulation" of "landscape, community and selfhood" toward which the volume aspires. The instinctual experience of nature is what Meehan calls "nature rapture," and it triangulates outward to others and to the Other: it is "the holistic vision at the heart" of Buddhism, the "interpenetration of all species and all creatures on the planet." It is the originary and, in many ways, Wordsworthian moment when nature is "integrated" with culture.[31] Trying to portray this integration is like trying to paint the rain, to fix in a standing image what is constantly moving. In terms of the discussion of culture and nature, this paradox is perhaps best contained in the image of the wolf tree (an image Meehan first encountered in an Adrienne Rich poem titled "Slashes").[32]

A wolf tree is a tree that had grown in a meadow but now stands in a forest (the definition of "wolf tree," a tree with lateral branches among trees straight and narrow). *The Oxford English Dictionary* defines a wolf tree as "a tree that is occupying more space than has been allowed for it, so restricting the growth of its neighbours"; clearly, Meehan is playing on the wildness of the wolf as much if not more than its ferocity and rapacity. The combination of wilderness (the idea that the first tree ever to grow, long before human habitation, was naturally a wolf tree) and culture (the fact that husbandry of the land, clearing trees to create meadows for agriculture and then the subsequent reforestation, created many a wolf tree) is fundamental to Meehan's vision. The volume as a whole, the very paper the book is made of, is a symbol of both nature and culture, of Meehan's attempts to find in the suburbs of Dublin the lineaments of the wilderness while recognizing the significance of the nonhuman for our imagination. There is much here to cherish of Meehan's "swinish garden lore" ("Deadwood").

Painting Rain is in many ways an ecovolume that takes us deep into the recesses of nature. It is half panegyric for what is being destroyed and half prophecy of how nature will reclaim us as one of her own even though we reject her. From the first poem of *Painting Rain*, "Death of a Field," we see how nature and culture are locked in a mythological embrace, even in the very names of chemical cleaners ("Ariel," "Flash").[33] "Death of a Field" explains the epigraph by

Meehan's partner and fellow poet Theo Dorgan that "the mysteries of the forest disappear with the forest," or, as Meehan writes: "Who amongst us is able to number the end of grasses / To number the losses of each seeding head?" The field in question is being turned into a housing estate, or as Meehan writes:

> The field itself is lost the morning it becomes a site
> When the Notice goes up: Final County Council—44
> houses . . .
> The end of the field as we know it is the start of the estate.

The word "estate" may cut two ways, signaling what we inherit and what we have destroyed.

Though it is not a major change from *Dharmakaya* (2002), there does seem to be a shift regarding the role of the poet in *Painting Rain*. Meehan as poet is not there to let poetry work its magic in unison with nature, as she was in *Dharmakaya*, but rather to let nature work its magic on her so that she becomes the voice of what will soon be absent. Nature functions on its own transhistorical terms, existing always before and after human history, leaving us, as another poem describes, "dream[ing] leaves" ("Tanka"). The other epigraph to the volume (from *The Diamond Sutra*, "Words cannot express Truth / That which words express is not truth") registers the irony, the impossibility, of this poetic project to state in cultural terms what nature sans culture really means. The poem "On Howth Head" gives us an image of how it might have worked as human history took shape. Gorse is a wild bush that blooms in May, and spring in Irish is called Bealtaine, which comes from Baal's Fire. The "flaming gorse" seeded the previous autumn becomes the fire of the mythic figure of Baal. Perhaps in the end, the closest approximation culture has to expressing nature on its own terms is through myth, which is where human consciousness began.

Meehan's volume is trying to paint the rain, to capture nature on canvas. It is a wolf tree, a nexus of culture and nature, a landscape etched with the palimpsests of the primeval while carrying the traces of human history. It is a tree in the mysterious forest that remembers "when it was the only tree / in an open field . . . when / there was no competition for the light." The wolf tree is "a kind of alpha tree, with a kind of alpha memory" that only the "keenest loneliest eyes" may see. That Meehan originally chose "The Wolf Tree" as her title for the volume makes a great deal of sense, though it is a pity that another poet had already used it for the title of a book.[34] Nevertheless, the present title has its own descriptive power: Meehan is trying to paint what is almost too dark or tangled for recognition, that is, the rain on an obscure day, or the wolf tree in the forest. The use of the line "So much depends" from William Carlos Williams's "The Red Wheelbarrow" emphasizes Meehan's piety before the given object and the natural world, attitudes that she inherits from Williams and Gary Snyder alike.[35]

Like a wolf tree (a tree that had matured in a meadow but now stands in a forest) stretching its arms wide for the sun among trees growing straight and narrow, this volume endeavors to find in the suburbs of Dublin the lineaments of the wilderness and "the original tree." It does so while cherishing the imaginative significance of the nonhuman force that gave birth to us and holds us still in its arms:

> revealed out in your own original domain
> the desert sand moving towards you
> the pressure mounting, the original diamond pain.

Beyond that original diamond, the glint of sunlight in the rain or of sand in the desert, the ur-mother,[36] we can go no further. We must merely marvel at the transformative jewel that has been created from the pain of our origins in the natural realm that predates us—we who are its mythographers, artists, and far too often its destroyers.

Geomantic, Paula Meehan's most recent foray into the world of landscape and nature, provides another example of an earth-centered ecological vision. The very title is evocative of the role of poet in nature, based on the art of geomancy (as the back cover of the Dedalus edition tells us), which comes from the Greek for "earth divination" and means "a method of divination that interprets markings on the ground of the patterns formed by tossed handfuls of soil, rocks, or sand." The title reveals how central the earth is to her poetry and how much she is a geomancer, to employ an obsolete usage of the word. In the poem "The Last Lesson," she signals this usage and the importance of the craft, how the very shaping of the land, the landscape, is a type of poem, as human and natural activity blends into the poetry of form, much as it did in Ní Chuilleanáin's poem "Pygmalion's Image":

> Romantic, geomantic, antic:
> the small green fields, the earth from above,
> the autumn hedgerows, turning, turning,
> turned with winter's white and black magic
> into hieroglyphs of mortal love
> signaling heaven with our yearning.
> The frail glider suddenly mythic
> is stopped a moment as if to prove
> the craft is lighter than the learning.

We return to that mythical sense of our place on earth and the explanation of that place, our genesis in the world, one that precedes history and underlies it as it unfolds. That is the "craft" that is "lighter" than the "learning" or knowledge of place and circumstance. Myth is the language of the illiterate heart. Poems such as "The Poem for Dillon with North Carolina in It" and the last poem, "The Island," set in Greece, illustrate how wide Meehan's interest is in nature as palimpsest of universal suffering.

In these poems there is a sense of the same subconscious connection to nature that appeared in "Admiring the Scenery"—not so much a reflection of our conscious admiration as a demonstration of how interwoven we are in nature's very fabric. In "The Querant," this tapestry becomes the texture of our pain, of our ignorance of its causes, and of our subsumption in natural cycles:

> There's nothing to be learned from the rain
> falling through red, through green neon light,
> nothing to be gleaned on the matter,

> no solace in the sound of the train
> shunting you home in the dark of night.
> Under streetlamps the old boys gather
>
> to talk of the old country, its pain.
> Their childhoods dying in their hindsight,
> with the smell of their fields in summer.

As the title suggests, we seekers are left seeking. Meehan has discussed the importance of John Montague's "Border Sick Call" in her understanding of how nature and our place in it transcends or at least eludes history.[37] In the poem, John Montague's brother Seamus, a doctor, is on sick call across the border between Fermanagh and Donegal. It is snowing, and the place is remote. The natural world seems to dominate the scene so much that history fades from view.

The border between Northern Ireland and the Republic is hazy at the start but grows metaphysical at the end. The political tremors of the Troubles take the poet back to the mythical days of the cattle raids. He notes that the natural world, in this case the cattle, moves across borders "in defiance of human frontiers":

> Border be damned, it was a godsend.
> Have you ever noticed, cows have no religion?
> Sure-footed, in darkness,
> stick-guiding his animals,
> in defiance of human frontiers,
> the oldest of Irish traditions,
> the creach or cattle raid,
> as old as *The Taín*.[38]

Finally, it seems that "the real border is not between countries, but between life and death," and the poet wonders "in what country have we been?" The idea that the borders, political, religious, social, and otherwise, blur into other patterns of our lives is exquisitely captured in Meehan's poem "The Quilt." The "nine squares," the "stripes" and "bows," patterns stitched by the grandmother, which Meehan slept under during "the long and winding nights of childhood," are juxtaposed with the "weathers wheeling past," as is the "aunt's deep breaths" with the "distant thunder." The belief that the living patterns of home repeat those patterns of the wider world is embossed in the length of every poem of *Geomantic*, for every poem is nine lines long, just as the quilt is made of nine squares.[39] Again, we see the poet as agent of geomancy.

Poets such as Mahon, Longley, and Montague in their later stages, Meehan, Ní Chuilleanáin, and Caitríona O'Reilly, Seán Lysaght, Vona Groarke, David Wheatley, among others, mark a sea change, or land reformation, that is new to Irish poetry. It is one where the politics of Irish identity are less important than the tale that nature has to tell. The wilderness is being reclaimed, but the reclamation is not to reformulate Irish history; instead, it is to reformulate the relationship between nature and culture, technology and the human. The very form of *Geomantic* as a volume—its poems centered on the page in the Dedalus edition—makes it seem both earth centered and sea girt. The lands and waters of earth will be central to the story as it unfolds in the extreme terms of climate change—of that there is no doubt. Nature writing now is a question of survival.[40] This question will call upon more than ecopoetry's resources to answer and is a subject for another book, perhaps a book of hours.

Conclusion

The Vision Yet to Come

This book began with a discussion of how the foundations of Irish literary representations of landscape, nature, the Oedipus complex (and with it the importance of family), as well as themes of animal and human, pagan and Christian, can be found in the ancient myths and folktales of Ireland. It explained why they became the basis of the literary renaissance that accompanied the movement toward both cultural and political independence in Ireland. The interest in these themes commenced in the eighteenth century with the antiquarian movement and culminated in the work of Yeats, Gregory, Synge, and Heaney, among others. The themes themselves are apparent in other modes in Irish literature from the earlier periods.

The second chapter examined Swift and Goldsmith, specifically *Gulliver's Travels* and *The Deserted Village*, to understand how, in the former, identity revolves around difficult questions of human beings not as rational animals but as animals capable of rationality, as Swift so brilliantly phrased it. By comparison, Goldsmith described how the spoiling hand of economic change (and implicitly of colonization) defiles the erotic basis of community and the health of the landscape in turn. Irrationality in Swift and despoliation in Goldsmith were signaled in both by the ruptures of nature within home, family, and landscape. In Lady Morgan's *The Wild Irish Girl* and William Carleton's *The Black Prophet*, the original sin of conquest (much like the founding murder of Cain and Abel, or Oedipus's killing of his father) is reflected in the landscape, as well as in nature (both inner and outer). This point is particularly true in the political questions of who should husband the land and thereby quell nature's eruptions and relieve the country of its historical curse.

Such questions continue to manifest themselves in William Allingham's *Laurence Bloomfield in Ireland*, with significant awareness of the growing importance of the Land League. Now nature and wilderness are unequivocally linked to political violence, as figurations of landscape are equated to the careful cultivation of good government. Nature and civilization prove to be diametrically opposed in later literature until for Synge the idea of patricide becomes one of a number of political solutions rooted in the mythological and religious landscape of the West of Ireland. Yeats chose the opposition of flowering lawns and bare hills and stunted trees as his métier, and Heaney saw the bog and other scraggy lands as his emblem for the pitch and toss of Irish history. In Yeats the question of nonhuman and inhuman (animal and divine) forces, which are sometimes one and the same, leads us to consider the relationship of myth and history. In Yeats's view, history hinges on the balance between Oedipus and Christ. Though the pagan and Christian themes that exist in Yeats are already part of Irish myth, they become a conscious part of his literary enterprise, as well as of Joyce and others. Bradley Buchanan notes in *Oedipus against Freud: Myth and the End(s) of Humanism in Twentieth-Century British Literature*:

> The Oedipal tropes that Yeats, Joyce, and Beckett deploy touch on Ireland's political situation, but in the end they explore whether there is a stable human nature for humanism to describe. Yeats accepts the idea of a split in human nature as the very precondition for its existence, and cheerfully drawing on Oedipus as a model, anticipates violent changes both in Ireland's historical circumstances and in the individual lives of humans. Yeats paints a sometimes terrifying picture of the new, Oedipal era he anticipates as the answer to the Christian epoch, but he nevertheless anticipates the antihumanist "Second Coming" that will transform humanity. . . . Joyce offers a more tolerant and novel view of Oedipus and humanity; he envisages Oedipus as a cosmic, eternally recurring human hero (like

> HCE) who contains everyone's tragedy and comedy. . . . For Beckett, neither Yeats's nor Joyce's picture of humanity is wholly satisfactory, but both show how narratives about Oedipal heroes who are supposed to represent humanity as a whole break down into incoherence, uncertainty, and futility, making any firm ideas about human nature impossible. . . . For Joyce and Yeats, an incestuous, parricidal Ireland could be redeemed, rather paradoxically, by being dehumanized (or at least defamiliarized) through language, whereas for Beckett the human condition could not escape its essentially sterile and fatally familiar Oedipal narrative.[1]

Whether it be Synge's use of the myth in *The Playboy of the Western World* or Yeats's in *The Tower* and *The Winding Stair*, the Irish literary renaissance represents in many ways the culmination of the Oedipal theme in Irish literature. The tension between pagan and Christian views becomes more specifically (if not conventionally) Catholic in Joyce, O'Faoláin, Kavanagh, and Heaney. MacNeice, on the other hand, reinterprets the Yeatsian perspective through a Northern Irish Protestant lens, as do Derek Mahon and Michael Longley in differing degrees.

In the penultimate chapter, Seamus Heaney's exploration of landscape, nature, and family provides a conclusive focus of the Oedipal/Christian narrative of this book because it is so much a part of his vision of life and death, culminating his career, as it does, in various confrontations with the ghost of his father. If Buchanan is just in his description of Yeats's terrifying and Joyce's more optimistic view of Oedipus and Christ as heroes (I hope to have shown that though partially right Buchanan, like some other critics, tends to underestimate Yeats's idea of Christianity's role as a redemptive force in the Oedipal triangle), then Heaney is more like Joyce than like Beckett.

The last chapter, "In Defiance of Human Frontiers," enumerates some other possible perspectives on the main themes, particularly the importance of ecological views of nature. Many recent outlooks question the necessity of specifically political meanings in regards to landscape and nature. They question the centrality of the Oedipal and mythological and also question the idea that nature and culture are opposed because they see the Anthropocene era as having undervalued nature as a living organism within which, rather than against which, we must live. Using Deleuze's idea of "becoming-animal," Roberto Esposito explains in philosophical terms what this shift might entail:

> The becoming-animal of the human points . . . to a way of being human that is not coextensive with the person or the thing, or with the perpetual transfer between one and the other that we appear to have been fated to until now. It is the *living person*—not separate from or implanted into life, but coextensive with it as an inseparable *synolon* of form and force, external and internal, *bios* and *zoe*. The third person, this figure that has yet to be fathomed, points to this *unicum*, to this being that is both singular and plural—to the non-person inscribed in the person, to the person open to what has never been before.

The third person of which he speaks sounds very like the inhuman divine, like what or who looks through the sterner eye. In an earlier passage on Simone Weil, Esposito recognizes this aspect as he quotes her: "Everything which is impersonal in man is sacred";[2] however, further in the passage, Esposito separates himself from the mystical aspect of Weil's way of thinking. In the end, the present writer agrees with Weil's mystical conception and with Yeats's idea that God and nature are half unified and half opposed.

The hunting dogs and the wild boar in the painting by James Barry (*The Death of Adonis*) that graces the cover of this book represent the two sides of animal nature and by implication of human nature. On the one side, there is the savage nature of the boar escaping after it has mortally wounded the hunter Adonis; on the other, there is the domesticated hunting dogs howling for their dead master. Venus, goddess of love, reluctantly following the hunts, tried to discourage Adonis from the pursuit of such savage animals. She and her attendant cupids likewise mourn over his death. If one looks closely at the painting, one sees that the blood of Adonis flows down the hill to the autumnal leaves of the same red hue. It is as though the death of Adonis, like the death of Christ, is part of seasonal death and resurrection. The trees moving in sympathy also seem to be grieving over his death, illustrating that, as it had after the Fall and Crucifixion, nature has felt the wound. With Adonis on her lap, Venus plays the role of the Madonna in this pagan *pietà*. The dogs and the boar, like the thieves on either side of the crucified Christ, represent redemption and damnation, respectively. This blending of Christian and pagan themes not only is common in Irish art and literature but has also been commented on in Barry's art.[3] The stone tableau behind Venus reminds one of the artistic origins of the death scene, which Barry has painted and which perhaps points to the immortal world of goddess, cupid, and love.

Adonis is closer to Oedipus in this pagan depiction than to Christ, however, being born of the "ancient crime" of incest and becoming "child of the tree" into which he and the shame of his conception were hidden.[4] In this regard, he reminds us more keenly of the human condition. Although we look for the Kingdom of God on earth "as it is in heaven," we are ofttimes left distinctly on earth without the transcendental analogy we crave, one that we henceforth create or despair of in artistic and literary terms. We live somewhere between opposition to nature, under the sovereignty of the Oedipal taboo, and unity with nature, in that humans like other animals are coextensive subjects of nature rather than its overlords. All the while, we hope that some form of grace or redemption is available to us, that the vision is yet to come.

Notes

Bibliography

Index

Notes

Introduction

1. R. F. Foster, *Modern Ireland, 1600–1972*, 15.

2. Simon Schama, *Landscape and Memory*, 61.

3. Claude Lévi-Strauss, *The Elementary Structures of Kinship*, 65.

4. For a discussion of this question, see Richard Kearney, *The Irish Mind: Exploring Intellectual Traditions*; and Weldon Thornton, *J. M. Synge and the Western Mind.*

5. Quoted in John Wilson Foster, ed., *Nature in Ireland: A Scientific and Cultural History*, 36.

6. For more on this parallel, see Derek Gladwin, *Contentious Terrains: Boglands, Ireland, Postcolonial Gothic.*

7. Julia Wright, *Representing the National Landscape in Irish Romanticism*, 170–71, x.

8. See J. Foster, introduction to *Nature in Ireland*, x.

9. John Wilson Foster, "Nature and Nation in the Nineteenth Century," in *Nature in Ireland*, ed. Foster, 419.

10. Carol Fabricant, *Swift's Landscape*, 10.

11. The relationship of landscape, family, and war has a long history dating back at least to the Romans. See Jessica McCutchean, "Landscapes of War."

12. Michael Viney, "Woodcock for a Farthing: The Irish Experience of Nature," 55.

13. Seamus Heaney, "The God in the Tree," in *The Pleasures of Gaelic Poetry*, ed. Seán MacRéamoinn, 26.

14. See Warren Akin IV, "'I Just Riz the Loy': The Oedipal Dimension of *The Playboy of the Western World*," 55–56.

15. See Bradley W. Buchanan, *Oedipus against Freud: Myth and the End(s) of Humanism in Twentieth-Century British Literature*, 4.

16. J. M. Synge, "The Well of the Saints," in *The Playboy of the Western World, and Other Plays*, 90.

17. Buchanan, *Oedipus against Freud*, 19.

18. See Lee Rozelle, *Ecosublime: Environmental Awe and Terror from New World to Oddworld*, 1.

19. See Tim Wenzell, *Emerald Green: An Ecocritical Study of Irish Literature*, 3. Wenzell also notes that the *Field Day* volumes of women's writing similarly do not address nature writing. The landscape of criticism in this regard has certainly shifted since Wenzell wrote, as hopefully the last chapter here reflects.

1. Stepping through Origins

1. Seamus Heaney, "Feeling into Words," in *Preoccupations: Selected Prose, 1968–1978*, 47. For a more scientific rendering of the same ideas, see Denis Dutton, *The Art Instinct: Beauty, Pleasure, and Human Evolution*. To Dutton, our views of art are not only socially constructed but also traceable to prehistoric tastes for certain types of landscapes and narrative or lyric structures. It is a "universal phenomena—like language, tool-making and [importantly for the connection to Heaney] kinship systems" (64).

2. T. S. Eliot, *The Four Quartets*, 31; Heaney, "Feeling into Words," 47.

3. See Mary Midgley, *Science and Poetry*, but particularly pt. 3, titled "What Kind of World?"

4. In a letter to T. Sturge Moore that is quoted in Richard Ellmann, *The Identity of Yeats*, 234.

5. Dutton, *Art Instinct*, 21.

6. Seamus Heaney, "Kinship," in *North*, 33.

7. Heaney, "Kinship," 39.

8. See Isaiah Berlin, *The Crooked Timber of Humanity*, 172.

9. Seamus Heaney, "The God in the Tree," in *Preoccupations*, 181–89.

10. James Joyce, "Two Gallants," in *A Norton Critical Edition of "Dubliners,"* ed. Margot Norris, 43–45.

11. Thomas Moore, *The Poetical Works of Thomas Moore*, 206.

12. See Johann Gottfried von Herder, "Extract from a Correspondence on Ossian and the Songs of Ancient Peoples" (1773), discussed in Isaiah Berlin, *Three Critics of the Enlightenment*, 202–3. See Wright, *Representing the National Landscape*, for a challenging reading of Herder.

13. The phrase is from Michael Grant, *Myths of the Greeks and Romans*, 374.

14. Seamus Heaney, "Unhappy and at Home," interview by Seamus Deane, *Crane Bag* 1 (1977): 70, quoted in Floyd Collins, *Seamus Heaney: The Crisis of Identity*, 132.

15. Seamus Heaney, *Sweeney Astray*, 17.

16. Seamus Heaney, "In the Country of Convention," in *Preoccupations*, 180.

17. Éilís Ní Dhuibhne, "Midwife to the Fairies," in *Blood and Water*, 29.

18. W. B. Yeats, *Irish Fairy and Folk Tales*, 41.

19. R. Ellmann, *The Identity of Yeats*, 234.

20. Angela Bourke, *The Burning of Bridget Cleary*, 53.

21. William Allingham, "The Fairies," in *Irish Fairy and Folk Tales*, ed. Yeats, 5.

22. Bourke makes this point throughout *The Burning of Bridget Cleary.* For a parallel discussion of similar themes in the myth of *Táin Bó Cúailnge*, see Jeremy Lowe, "Contagious Violence and the Spectacle of Death in *Táin Bó Cúailnge*," 84–100.

23. Bourke, *Bridget Cleary*, 156, 157.

24. Thomas Kinsella, *The Táin*, 224.

25. Kinsella, *The Táin*, 224–25.

26. Patricia Kelly, "*The Táin* as Literature," 87.

27. Bart Jaski, "Cú Chulainn, *gormac* and *dalta* of the Ulstermen," 31.

28. Dáithí Ó hÓgáin, *Myth, Legend and Romance: An Encyclopædia of the Irish Folk Tradition*, 195.

29. W. B. Yeats, *The Poems*, ed. Daniel Albright, 64.

30. Marie Heaney, *Over Nine Waves: A Book of Irish Legends*, 175.

31. M. Heaney, *Over Nine Waves*, 178–79.

32. See Margot Gayle Backus, *The Gothic Family Romance: Heterosexuality, Child Sacrifice, and the Anglo-Irish Colonial Order*; in terms of the Oedipal crisis, linked mostly with female desires and the pre-Oedipal, see 129, 172, and 219.

33. M. Heaney, *Over Nine Waves*, 179.

34. M. Heaney, *Over Nine Waves*, 179.

2. Tumbling Down into the Sky

1. Andrew Carpenter and Lucy Collins, introduction to *The Irish Poet and the Natural World: An Anthology of Verse in English from the Tudors to the Romantics*, ed. Carpenter and Collins, 2.

2. Robert Lloyd Praeger, *The Way I Went*, 385.

3. Estyn Evans, *The Personality of Ireland: Habitat, Heritage, and History*, 88.

4. Quoted in John Elder and Robert Finch, eds., *The Norton Book of Nature Writing*, 145.

5. Jonathan Swift, *Gulliver's Travels*, 253.

6. Fabricant, *Swift's Landscape*, 11.

7. Fabricant, *Swift's Landscape*, 11.

8. Fabricant, *Swift's Landscape*, 17.

9. Julia Kristeva, *Strangers to Ourselves*, 188; Swift, *Gulliver's Travels*, 222.

10. Oliver Goldsmith, *The Deserted Village*, in *The Poems and Plays of Oliver Goldsmith*, 17; all subsequent citations of the poem taken from this edition.

11. Ovid, *The Metamorphoses*, bk. 6, 527–30. The metaphor of prey and predator is apparent throughout Shakespeare's poem.

12. Kristeva, *Strangers to Ourselves*, 191.

13. Kevin Whelan, "The Modern Landscape: From Plantation to Present," in *An Atlas of the Irish Rural Landscape*, ed. F. H. A. Aalen, Kevin Whelan, and Matthew Stout, 67.

14. Quoted in A. N. Jeffares, "Place, Space, and Personality and the Irish Writer," in *Place, Personality, and the Irish Writer*, ed. Andrew Carpenter, 14.

15. Swift, *Gulliver's Travels*, 167.

16. Swift, *Gulliver's Travels*, 168.

17. Catherine Nash, "'Embodying the Nation': The West of Ireland and Irish Identity," 106.

18. Edmund Burke, "A Letter to Sir Hercules Langrishe, M.P., 1792," in *Letters, Speeches and Tracts on Irish Affairs*, 265.

19. Foster, *Modern Ireland, 1600–1972*, 232, 207.

20. R. F. Foster, *The Oxford Illustrated History of Ireland*, 155; W. J. McCormack, *Burke to Beckett: Ascendancy, Tradition and Betrayal in Literary History*, 46.

21. Oliver Goldsmith, *The Vicar of Wakefield*, 1:35.

22. Raymond Williams, *The Country and the City*, 76.

23. Oliver Goldsmith, *The Works of Oliver Goldsmith*, 275.

24. See Michael Griffin, "Oliver Goldsmith, 1728–1774," in *The Cambridge Companion to Irish Poets*, ed. Gerald Dawe, 53.

25. Edmund Burke, "A Letter to Richard Burke, Esq.," in *Letters, Speeches and Tracts*, 350.

26. Peter Fallon and Derek Mahon, eds., *The Penguin Book of Contemporary Irish Poetry*, xxii; Thomas Kinsella, "The Divided Mind," 208–9.

3. Great Hunger, Unspeakable Home

1. "The exploitation and reduction of Irish woodlands was a natural consequence of Tudor military action and the policy of settlement—plantation—that accompanied it. . . . Woodlands, in addition to being the wooden *el dorado* for the English, now become important rallying places and strongholds for the Irish—hence the common use of the word 'fastness' to describe them. Elizabeth I, well aware of the two aspects mentioned above, expressly ordered the destruction of all woods in the country to deprive the Irish of this shelter. . . . The systematic devastation of Irish woodlands followed rapidly on the unexpected defeat of the combined Irish and Spanish forces at Kinsale in 1601. As a result, the substantially forested Ireland of 1600 had by 1711 become a treeless wilderness and a net importer of timber. . . . Thus was introduced a pattern that accelerated dramatically during the sixteenth and seventeenth centuries, when forests were felled indiscriminately for profit and because they were refuges for Irish soldiers (hence the coinage of the term 'woodkerne')." Eoin Neeson, "Woodland in History and Culture," 140–41.

2. Here I am thinking of the anonymous poem in Irish (*Caoine Cill Chais*) titled, in English, "Lament for Kilcash." There have been many translations of this poem; among them number Thomas Kinsella's, Paul Muldoon's, and Eiléan Ní Chuilleanáin's.

3. See Neeson, "Woodland in History and Culture," 145–46.

4. For a discussion of nineteenth-century attitudes toward nature, see J. Foster, *Nature in Ireland*, 409–39.

5. Among the most recent are Joep Leerssen, *Remembrance and Imagination: Patterns in the Historical and Literary Representation of Ireland in the Nineteenth Century*; Backus, *Gothic Family Romance*; Kathryn Kirkpatrick, ed., *Border Crossings: Irish Women Writers and National Identities*; Mary Jean Corbett, *Allegories of Union in Irish and English Writing, 1790–1870: Politics, History, and the Family from Edgeworth to Arnold*; Dáire Keogh and Kevin Whelan, eds., *Acts of Union: The Causes, Contexts, and Consequences of the Act of Union*; Ina Ferris, *The Romantic National Tale and the Question of Ireland*; Jarlath Killeen, *Gothic Ireland*; Clíona Ó Gallchoir, *Maria Edgeworth: Women, Enlightenment and Nation*; and Susan M. Kroeg, "'So Near to Us as a Sister': Incestuous Unions in Sydney Owenson's *The Wild Irish Girl* and Maria Edgeworth's *The Absentee*."

6. Lady Morgan [Sydney Owenson], *The Wild Irish Girl: A National Tale*, 1:136. Subsequent references to *The Wild Irish Girl* will appear in the text parenthetically with volume number and page. Emphasis in the original has been retained.

7. Swift, *Gulliver's Travels*, 280.

8. Burke, "Letter to Richard Burke," in *Letters, Speeches and Tracts*, 350.

9. Katie Trumpener, *Bardic Nationalism: The Romantic Novel and the British Empire*, 141.

10. For examples of this opinion, see Kathryn Kirkpatrick's introduction to *The Wild Irish Girl*; and Corbett, *Allegories of Union*, 21–82.

11. "In *The Wild Irish Girl* and *The Absentee*, Owenson and Edgeworth quietly remind their English readers that behind the violence of the Union lies the crime of incest." Kroeg, "'So Near to Us as a Sister,'" 279.

12. Burke, "Letter to Richard Burke," in *Letters, Speeches and Tracts*, 350.

13. J. W. Foster, "Nature and Nation in the Nineteenth Century," in *Nature in Ireland*, ed. Foster, 413.

14. J. Foster, *Nature in Ireland*, 413.

15. J. Foster, *Nature in Ireland*, 416.

16. "Had we been engaged in any innocent or benevolent enterprise, there was something in our situation just then that had a touch of interest in it to a mind imbued with a relish for the savage beauties of nature." Looking at the burning house, after the gruesome deaths of those within, the narrator significantly observes, "Abstractedly it had sublimity, but now it was associated with nothing in my mind but

blood and terror." William Carleton, "Wildgoose Lodge," in *Stories from William Carleton*, 198.

17. Carleton, "Wildgoose Lodge," 199.

18. Even early commentaries made this clear. As Thomas Flanagan perceptively observes, though nature is not his subject, "The vividness and clarity with which [*The Black Prophet*] reveals a countryside lying under sentence of death give the forcefulness of observed fact to the novel." John Cronin similarly notes that the novel powerfully conveys "the atmosphere of the period: the incessant rain accompanied by warmth which produced rotting crops; the horror of the famine fever; the make-shift, lean-to sheds for the sick and dying by the roadside; the shallow graves which scarcely concealed the diseased corpses; the starving peasants grubbing for nettles and watercress by road and brook; the riots and attacks on provision carts heading for the port with precious food incredibly intended for export." Cronin then complains, however, "Yet when Carleton moves from the fact to the fiction, he can only fumble with sentimental heroines and hackneyed abductions and clumsy flashback to forgotten and tedious rural crimes." Of course, there is a strong element of truth in his complaint, but in the shift from nature to culture, from the wide view to the particular characters, something important is happening. Carleton is trying to uncover the relationship of landscape, culture, and nature. It is important to remember here that nature and landscape are different, that landscape, as Simon Schama notes, is culture before it is nature, that landscape is an acculturated version of nature, but one, I think, through which the effective writers find a lens to magnify the role of nature in culture. One has only to count how many times Carleton, in this novel, uses the landscape as a way of discussing man's nature, how many times the haunting of the natural world becomes a prelude for a discussion of human nature. There is no easy way of sorting out the triangle, or pretending that the lines do not blur, but there is some instruction in tracing it throughout the melodramatic trappings of the plot. Flanagan, *The Irish Novelists, 1800–1850*, 318–19; John Cronin, *The Anglo-Irish Novel*; Schama, *Landscape and Memory*, 61.

19. William Carleton, *The Black Prophet: A Tale of Irish Famine*, 221.

20. Carleton, *Black Prophet*, 2, 3–4.

21. Burke's phrase is from *Reflections on the Revolution in France*: "To love the little platoon we belong to in society is the first principle (the germ as it were) of publick [*sic*] affections" (44). Goldsmith's phrase is from *The Vicar of Wakefield*, 35.

22. Carleton, *Black Prophet*, 122.

23. Flanagan, *Irish Novelists*, 319.

24. Burke, "Letter to Richard Burke," in *Letters, Speeches and Tracts*, 350.

25. Julian Moynahan, *Anglo-Irish: The Literary Imagination in a Hyphenated Culture*, 72.

26. Carleton, *Black Prophet*, 406.

27. Moynahan, *Anglo-Irish*, 72.

28. For a discussion of the historical epistemology, see John Gatta, *Making Nature Sacred: Literature, Religion, and Environment in America from the Puritans to the Present*, 213.

29. Margaret Kelleher, *The Feminization of the Famine: Expressions of the Inexpressible?*, 39.

30. Maud Ellmann, *The Hunger-Artists: Starving, Writing and Imprisonment*, 54; Carleton, *Black Prophet*, 81.

4. Some Fragments Like a Hippogriff

1. Allingham's new preface to the 1890 edition of *Laurence Bloomfield; or, Rich and Poor in Ireland* reveals that his concerns are the same, if not heightened. He is aware both of how Ribbonism has become "Fenianism" and of how the British public's view "retains much, if not quite all, of its old feelings (part apathy, part disgust), towards everything Irish" (iv). He continues to think the Irish are "at present very unfit for self-government" (vii), yet he knows that English rule is misguided and that the Irish question has broader application to the British Empire, that it would "do well to bear in mind that some of the so-called 'Irish Questions' have relation not merely to Ireland and England, but to the Modern World. The modern world is disturbed and discontented to the core; full of vague but profound uneasiness, as though half aroused from trance; full of dim and deep longing for a word of deliverance, for the example of a step into freer and truer life" (x).

2. Backus, *Gothic Family Romance*, 76.

3. William Allingham, *Laurence Bloomfield; or, Rich and Poor in Ireland*. All quotations are from this volume cited in the bibliography.

4. David Burleigh feels Allingham brings impartiality to his work. See "Who We Are: Protestants and Poetry in the North of Ireland," 292.

5. Matthew Campbell also views Allingham's aim as a "rediscovered noblesse oblige." See Matthew Campbell, "Recovering Ancient Ireland," *The Oxford Handbook of Irish Poetry*, ed. Fran Brearton and Alan Gillis, 13.

6. Campbell notes how much more Bloomfield is indebted to the Irish novel than to Irish poetry in "Recovering Ancient Ireland," in *Oxford Handbook of Irish Poetry*, ed. Brearton and Gillis, 13.

7. Yeats detested the poem, calling it "a failed epic." See Herbert F. Tucker, *Epic: Britain's Heroic Muse, 1790–1910*, 412.

8. Allingham himself was haunted by the crime of history and often felt shadowed as a boy by thoughts of bloody insurrection. "I used to fancy and sometimes dream frightfully of a swarm of fierce men seizing the town." Quoted in Alan Warner, *William Allingham*, 44–45.

9. Oliver Goldsmith, *The Deserted Village*, in *Poems and Plays of Goldsmith*, lines 131–36.

10. Seamus Deane, *Celtic Revivals*, 6.

11. See the note from this edition of the poem: "Ireland has individual character. On this point, those interested would do well to read a brief, clear, and sensible little book, *Irish Ethnology*, by George Ellis, Fellow of the College of Surgeons, Ireland. The author of it is himself, no doubt (like the late George Petrie, and many other men whose names are honourable to Ireland), of that compound ancestry which often mingles some of the best Keltic and Teutonic qualities. 'Race' is an interesting subject of study, and a real though very complicated and obscure factor in life; but to found, in regard to this Island, any political argument or idea upon 'race' is, to my mind, a mischievous absurdity" (128).

12. Justin Quinn, *The Cambridge Introduction to Modern Irish Poetry, 1800–2000*, 43.

13. W. B. Yeats, *The Collected Works of W. B. Yeats*, 9:298–99.

14. Tucker, *Epic*, 412; Yeats, *Irish Fairy and Folk Tales.*

15. Donald Torchiana, "God-Appointed Berkeley," in *W. B. Yeats and Georgian Ireland*, 242.

16. Burke, "Letter to Richard Burke," in *Letters, Speeches and Tracts*, 368.

17. W. B. Yeats, *A Vision*, 237.

18. W. B. Yeats, *Complete Plays*, 681–89.

19. "He lash'd the Vice but spar'd the Name." Jonathan Swift, from "Verses on the Death of Dr. Swift," in *Selected Poems*, 88.

20. See J. W. Foster, "Encountering Traditions," in *Nature in Ireland*, ed. Foster, 23–71.

21. Yeats, *The Poems*, ed. Albright, 294.

22. Edmund Burke, *A Philosophical Enquiry into the Origins of Our Ideas of the Sublime and the Beautiful*, 101.

23. Yeats, *The Poems*, ed. Albright, 239.

24. See Samuel Monk, *The Sublime: A Study of Critical Theories in Eighteenth-Century England*, 87.

5. A Sterner Eye

1. W. B. Yeats, "Fighting the Waves" from "Wheels and Butterflies," in *Explorations*, 377.

2. The importance of philosophy in studying Yeats has a long history and remains important today. See, for example, Robert Snukal's *High Talk: The Philosophical Poetry of W. B. Yeats.* "We have seen how the thrust of Yeats's philosophical poems is to develop a critique of abstraction that does justice to the importance of ideas, but which at the same time delivers us from what Whitehead called the fallacy

of misplaced concreteness" (234). The present argument is that the sublime encounter with the inhuman forms a bridge between the transcendental and the empirical, an argument with which Snukal would not agree.

3. This encounter can be extended to the act of reading or writing itself (see concluding discussion of the present essay). See Roberto Calasso, *Literature and the Gods*, 192–93.

4. Jean-François Lyotard, *Inhuman: Reflections on Time*, 2; Theodor Adorno, *Aesthetic Theory*, 24.

5. Yeats, *Explorations*, 377; W. B. Yeats, "Meditations in Time of Civil War," in *The Poems*, ed. Albright, 251.

6. Roberto Calasso, *Tiepolo Pink*, 163.

7. Calasso, *Tiepolo Pink*, 124.

8. Lyotard, *Inhuman: Reflections on Time*, 153.

9. Gilles Deleuze, *Pure Immanence: Essays on a Life*, 31; Lyotard, *Inhuman: Reflections on Time*, 21; Theodor W. Adorno, *Minima Moralia*, 190.

10. In his introduction, Frederiek Depoortere makes clear the importance of this divide in contemporary philosophy between ideas of a transcendent and immanent God. He notes of the genesis of this project: "The original project text mentioned the names of John D. Caputo, Richard Kearney, Gianni Vattimo, Merold Westphal and Slavoj Žižek. My first exploration of these philosophers suggested to me that they can be divided into groups. The first group consists of Caputo, Kearney and Westphal. In the wake of Heidegger's announcement of the end of onto-theology and inspired by both Levinas and Jacques Derrida, they search for a post-metaphysical God, a God who is often indicated as *tout autre* (wholly other). Žižek, on the other hand, does not belong to this group. . . . [H]e does not aim at tracing a post-metaphysical God. . . . [W]ith Žižek, furthermore, Vattimo shares the attention for the event of the incarnation and the conviction that that incarnation amounts to the end of God's transcendence." Depoortere, *Christ in Post-modern Philosophy: Gianni Vattimo, René Girard and Slavoj Žižek*, 1.

11. Yeats, *Explorations*, 451.

12. See Robert Pogue Harrison, *Gardens: An Essay on the Human Condition*, 143–44.

13. John Berger, *Why Look at Animals?*, 18. See also R. G. Collingwood, *The Idea of Nature*, 3–9.

14. See Harrison, *Gardens*, 41.

15. See Harrison, *Gardens*, 39.

16. Harrison, *Gardens*, 144.

17. The most obvious example is these lines from Yeats's "Under Ben Bulben": "Even the wisest man grows tense / With some sort of violence / Before he can accomplish fate / Know his work or choose his mate."

18. Yeats, *Explorations*, 376–77; Bill McKibben, *The End of Nature*, 201.

19. Yeats, *A Vision*, 53.

20. Edna Longley, *Yeats and Modernism*, 109.

21. Yeats, *A Vision*, 105.

22. Bruce Clarke, "The Nonhuman," 145.

23. Yeats, *A Vision*, 105.

24. There is a general critical consensus that "Yeats became a great poet, not merely a post-Victorian lyricist, with the publication of *Michael Robartes and the Dancer* (1921), *The Tower* (1928), and *The Winding Stair and Other Poems* (1933)." Denis Donoghue, "Why W. B. Yeats Matters," *Irish Times*, June 12, 2015. I make no different claims other than to say that *The Tower* and *The Winding Stair* are central to this evaluation.

25. Yeats schematically renders the difference between the two dispensations thus: the "*primary* dispensation look[s] beyond itself towards a *transcendent* [emphasis added] power, it is dogmatic, leveling, unifying, feminine, humane, peace its means and end. Its characteristics are necessity, truth, goodness, mechanism, science, democracy, abstraction, peace." In contrast, the "*antithetical* dispensation obeys *immanent* [emphasis added] power; it is expressive, hierarchical, multiple, masculine, harsh, surgical. Its characteristics are freedom, fiction, evil, kindred, art, aristocracy, war" (*A Vision*, 182). As regards our present sense of historical change, of millennialism, Yeats thinks that the swan will begin an antithetical age. The aesthetic significance here is very important. The feminine aspects of the primary and the beautiful shall give way to the masculine aspects of the antithetical and the sublime. Yeats invokes his readers, "Love war because of its horror, that belief may be changed, civilization renewed." He describes the change in terms that have deep implications for the relationship between morality and aesthetics, as well as between civil and natural law.

26. See Anthony Easthope, *The Unconscious*, 40–44.

27. Easthope, *The Unconscious*, 26.

28. Jacques Rancière, *Dissensus: On Politics and Aesthetics*, 177.

29. Sophocles, *Oedipus Rex*, 44.

30. Yeats, *The Poems*, ed. Albright, 303. All quotations from this volume cited in the bibliography. Much of the following discussion will center around poems that are less frequently discussed, in order to show how Yeats, the great lyric poet, uses the minor lyric form to develop many of his major themes. For the present writer, this point is where pedagogy and research interests combine. Many years of teaching Yeats have led me to understand how these minor poems allow access to the Yeatsian poetic and how they in fact may even be equally central to it, as the lyric is Yeats's primary response to a world from which he felt out of phase. Discussions of the role of the humanities in the university seem also to revolve around how the material world and the spiritual one are bound to lyric expression.

31. Giambattista Vico, *New Science: Principles of the New Science Concerning the Common Nature of Nations*, 377, 504.

32. See Heinrich Heine, "Gods in Exile," in *The Prose Writings of Heinrich Heine*, 268–376.

33. Walter F. Otto, *Dionysus: Myth and Cult*, 108–9.

34. Robert Pogue Harrison, *Forests: The Shadow of Civilization*, 32–33.

35. Harrison, *Forests*, 26.

36. Calasso, *Literature and the Gods*, 192–93.

37. Markus Müller, "Interview with René Girard."

38. Calasso, *Literature and the Gods*, 120.

39. Yeats's words from "The Trembling of the Veil" section of the *Autobiographies* are "After Stéphane Mallarmé, after Paul Verlaine, after Gustave Moreau, after Puvis de Chavannes, after our own verse, after all our subtle colour and nervous rhythm, after the faint mixed tints of Conder, what more is possible? After us the Savage God" (349; quoted in Calasso, *Literature and the Gods*, 138).

40. Yeats, *A Vision*, 28–29.

41. Calasso explains the meaning of this vibration: "Lógos is articulate discourse, a concatenation of meanings. Akşara is the irreducible vibration that preceded meaning, composes meaning, but is not absorbed into it" (*Literature and the Gods*, 161).

42. Calasso, *Tiepolo Pink*, 250.

43. René Girard, *Things Hidden since the Foundation of the World*, 82. Of particular importance is when Girard writes that with the cry "Father, forgive them for they know not what they do," Christ was addressing the idea of the unconscious before it had been theorized (*The Scapegoat*, 110–11).

44. See an early version of *A Vision* for reference to Michael Robartes's comment "general mass, call it Nature, God, the Matrix, the Unconscious, what you will." My thanks to Neil Mann for drawing my attention to this quotation. See Neil Mann, Matthew Gibson, and Claire Nally, eds., *W. B. Yeats's "A Vision": Explications and Contexts.*

45. Calasso, *Tiepolo Pink*, 256 (emphasis added).

46. Colum Power, *James Joyce's Catholic Categories*, 171.

6. Bleeding from the Torn Bough

1. See, in particular, Christine Cusick, "'Clacking along the Concrete Pavement': Economic Isolation and the Bricolage of Place in James Joyce's *Dubliners*," in *Eco-Joyce: Space, Place, and Environment in the Writings of James Joyce*, ed. Robert Brazeau and Derek Gladwin, but the whole volume of essays is incisive and helpful.

2. See Jefferson Holdridge, "'Of the Dark Past': The Brittle Magic Nation of Joyce's Poetics."

3. Richard Ellmann, *James Joyce*, 593.

4. See Anne Fogarty, foreword to *Eco-Joyce: Space, Place, and Environment in the Writings of James Joyce*, ed. Brazeau and Gladwin, xvi.

5. Quoted in Oona Frawley, "Nature and Nostalgia in Irish Literature," 269.

6. Joyce's Epiphany 25 is even more ornate in its gendered counterpoint: "In the colonnade are the girls, an April company. They are leaving shelter, with many a doubting glance, with the prattle of trim boots and the pretty rescue of petticoats. . . . They are returning to the convent—demure corridors. . . . Amid a flat rain-swept country stands a high plain building, with windows that filter the obscure daylight. Three hundred boys, noisy and hungry, sit at long tables eating beef fringed with green fat and vegetables that are still rank of the earth." Joyce, *Poems and Short Writings*, 185. All poems cited are taken from this edition.

7. Seamus Heaney, "Joyce's Poetry," in *Finders Keepers: Selected Prose, 1971–2001*, 388; Eamon Grennan, "The Poet Joyce," in *Facing the Music: Irish Poetry in the Twentieth Century*, 73.

8. Chester Anderson, "James Joyce's 'Tilly,'" 285.

9. Sigmund Freud, "Family Romances," in *On Sexuality: Three Essays on the Theory of Sexuality, and Other Works*, 221.

10. Robert Scholes, "James Joyce, Irish Poet," 263.

11. Joyce, *Poems and Shorter Writings*, 98.

12. See W. B. Yeats's "Her Vision in a Wood" from the sequence "A Woman Young and Old" and Ezra Pound's Canto XLVII.

13. Yeats, *The Poems*, ed. Albright, 66.

14. Oscar Wilde, "Mr. Froude's Blue Book," 136.

15. Lawrence Buell, *The Environmental Imagination: Thoreau, Nature Writing, and the Formation of American Culture*, 49.

16. An extreme version of this aestheticizing attitude toward landscape, this "willed amnesia," is apparent in Richard Murphy's memoir *The Kick*, when his Anglo-Irish mother exclaims, "Do look over there, darling! Isn't that perfectly beautiful? Not a person or a house to spoil the view." Murphy concludes, not without irony, that "this was the ideal of beauty, nature untainted by humanity" (11).

17. James Joyce, *Giacomo Joyce*, 9.

18. See Joyce, *Poems and Shorter Writings*, 289.

19. Heaney, *Finders Keepers*, 388. It is interesting to note that Seamus Heaney and Ted Hughes include "Tilly," "On the Beach at Fontana," and "A Flower Given to My Daughter" in their anthology of poetry titled *The Rattle Bag*.

20. Heaney, *Finders Keepers*, 389.

21. Noted in Rebecca J. West, *Eugenio Montale: Poet on the Edge*, 97.

22. Eugenio Montale, *Tutte le poesie*, ed. Giorgio Zampa, 749–50.

23. Montale, *Tutte le poesie*, 750.

24. R. Ellmann, *James Joyce*, 347. Unlike McCourt, Ellmann emphasizes the amorous inspiration of the poem, which was written in San Sabba near Trieste on September 7, 1913: "As the scullers pulled towards the shore, they began to sing an aria from Puccini's *La Fanciulla del West.* Joyce's poem played lugubriously on the last line, e non ritornero più. . . . This is the melancholy of the lover who anticipates his own failure. Joyce continued his silent, secret wooing of Signorina Popper, always in the presence of another person, into 1914" (347).

25. Julian Budden, "Fanciulla del West, La," in *The New Grove Dictionary of Opera*, ed. Stanley Sadie, Grove Music Online, Oxford Music Online, Sept. 12, 2008, http://www.oxfordmusiconline.com/subscriber/article/grove/music/O00 7114.

26. John McCourt, *The Years of Bloom*, 240.

27. Montale, *Tutte le poesie*, 750.

28. Heaney, *Finders Keepers*, 389.

29. I would like to thank Wanda Balzano for her help with this discussion of Montale's translation of Joyce.

30. Joseph Cary, *Three Modern Italian Poets: Saba, Ungaretti, Montale*, 236–37.

31. McCourt, *The Years of Bloom*, 240.

32. Tim Robinson, *Setting Foot on the Shores of Connemara, and Other Writings*, 107–8. A compass rose is defined as "the card of a mariner's compass (now usu. compass rose) or of a barometer; more generally, a circular pattern showing the points of the compass" (*The Oxford English Dictionary*, 2nd ed., 1989).

33. McCourt, *The Years of Bloom*, 240.

34. Julian Budden et al., "sonnambula, La," in *New Grove Dictionary of Opera*, ed. Sadie, Grove Music Online, Oxford Music Online, Sept. 12, 2008, http://www.oxfordmusiconline.com/subscriber/article/grove/music/O007293.

35. Kate Soper, *What Is Nature? Culture, Politics and the Non-human*, 49. The use of the concept of authenticity "intends to capture the immediacy for us of the 'what is' of human experience as we experience it." Glen L. Sherman, "Martin Heidegger's Concept of Authenticity: A Philosophical Contribution to Student Affairs Theory," 1. Of course, this concept is difficult to capture. As Hans Urs von Balthasar writes: "Being eludes knowledge because it can never be an object of cognition." He proceeds to say that like the light in Plato's cave being is that "by which all is seen but is what cannot be seen itself." In his corrective of Kierkegaard, for Balthasar, anguish, or the anxious awareness of sinfulness, of guilt, is what for the Christian provides authenticity. Balthasar, *The Christian and Anxiety*, 126.

36. James Joyce, "Simples," 72.

37. R. Ellmann, *James Joyce*, 382.

38. Quoted in Soper, *What Is Nature?*, 69.

39. Cited in Grennan, *Facing the Music*, 73.

7. Like Splintered Darkness

1. Hermione Lee, *Elizabeth Bowen*, 55.

2. Bowen writes in *Pictures and Conversations*: "Since I started writing, I have been welding together an inner landscape, assembled anything built at random. But if not at random, under the influence of what? . . . A writer needs to have at command and recourse to, a recognisable world, geographically consistent and having for him or her super reality" (36).

3. Paul Stasi, "'Fumbling along the Boundaries of the Personal': History and Affect in Elizabeth Bowen's *The Last September*."

4. Susan Osborn, "'How to Measure This Unaccountable Darkness between the Trees': The Strange Relation of Style and Meaning in *The Last September*," 35, 53, 55.

5. For a thorough discussion of critical views of the novel, see Osborn, "'How to Measure,'" 34–35.

6. Vera Kreilkamp, *The Anglo-Irish Novel and the Big House*, 8–9; Yena Wang, "The Landscape Representation of the Anglo-Irish Cultural Estrangements in Bowen's *The Last September*." See also Donald Mitchell, *Cultural Geography: A Critical Introduction*, 119.

7. Elizabeth Bowen, *Bowen's Court*, 7.

8. Bowen, *Bowen's Court*, 263.

9. Maud Ellmann, *Elizabeth Bowen: The Shadow across the Page*, 60. For Seán O'Faoláin, see *The Vanishing Hero: Studies in Novelists of the Twenties*, 173–74.

10. Elizabeth Bowen, *The Last September*, 7; all references to this text are taken from this edition.

11. For a discussion of the virginal in the novel, see Jed Esty, "Virgins of Empire: *The Last September* and the Antidevelopmental Plot."

12. Bowen, *The Last September*, 25–26.

13. Bowen, *The Last September*, 59, 37 (emphasis added), 38.

14. For a thorough discussion of this stylistic device, see Osborn, "'How to Measure.'"

15. Bowen, *The Last September*, 41.

16. Bowen, *The Last September*, 58, 131, 63, 67, 66.

17. See Robert L. Caserio, *The Novel in England, 1900–1950: History and Theory*; and renee c. hoogland, *Elizabeth Bowen: A Reputation in Writing*, for the former's discussion of "subversive alliances" (251) and the latter's analysis of "phallogocentric gender and nationalist discourses" (69).

18. Bowen, *The Last September*, 92–93.

19. Bowen, *The Last September*, 119–20, 113.
20. Bowen, *The Last September*, 114–15.
21. Bowen, *The Last September*, 108.
22. Bowen, *The Last September*, 127, 128–30.
23. Bowen, *The Last September*, 167, 173.
24. Bowen, *The Last September*, 178.
25. Stasi writes: "The mill becomes, in this reading, the counterpart to Danielstown, representing two halves of the economic and social conditions that have determined the historical fate of the Anglo-Irish in the time of revolution. For it is not the imagined quantity of love contained in the land's bosom which has created the revolutionary climate of the novel's setting, but rather the grievances of the Irish against the actual use of the not only metaphorical land: on the one hand, the unequal distribution of ownership, figured in Danielstown, and on the other, the prohibition against using the land productively, embodied in the mill. Stasi, "'Fumbling along the Boundaries,'" 732.
26. Bowen, *The Last September*, 179, 180–81, 187.
27. Bowen, *The Last September*, 209, 210, 213.
28. Bowen, *The Last September*, 219–20, 224–25.
29. Bowen, *The Last September*, 225, 229–31, 242–44.
30. Bowen, *The Last September*, 250–51.
31. Bowen, *The Last September*, 259.
32. Bowen, *The Last September*, 282–83.
33. Bowen, *The Last September*, 292–93, 7, 299, 298.
34. Bowen, *The Last September*, 302–3.
35. Patricia Craig, *Elizabeth Bowen*, 51.
36. Bowen, preface to *The Last September*, 98–99.
37. Bowen, *The Last September*, 303.
38. As Stasi writes, one gets the feeling that it is the house itself that is acting on the characters by responding to their affective needs. Stasi, "'Fumbling along the Boundaries,'" 719.
39. Bowen, *The Last September*, 303.

8. Through Tightly Closed Eyes

1. Joost Augusteijn, review of *The Black and Tans: British Police and Auxiliaries in the Irish War of Independence, 1920–1921*, by D. M. Leeson, 939.
2. Seán O'Faoláin, *The Collected Stories*, 49.
3. O'Faoláin, *The Collected Stories*, 50, 52.
4. O'Faoláin, *The Collected Stories*, 64.
5. O'Faoláin, *The Collected Stories*, 54.
6. O'Faoláin, *The Collected Stories*, 59.

7. O'Faoláin, *The Collected Stories*, 62.

8. O'Faoláin, *The Collected Stories*, 62, 63–64.

9. Cf. John Milton, *Paradise Lost*, 9:445; and John Keats's sonnet "To One who has been long in City Pent."

10. O'Faoláin, *The Collected Stories*, 9.

11. O'Faoláin, *The Collected Stories*, 11.

12. O'Faoláin, *The Collected Stories*, 16–18, 19.

13. For a fuller picture of the political implications of the short story, see Paul Delaney, *Seán O'Faoláin: Literature, Inheritance and the 1930s*, 161–64; and Marie Arndt, *A Critical Study of Seán O'Faoláin's Life and Work*, 42–44.

14. O'Faoláin, *The Collected Stories*, 31.

15. Pierce Butler, "Admiring the Scenery: Seán O'Faolain's Love Affair with Landscape," 68.

16. Maurice Harmon, *Seán O'Faoláin: A Critical Introduction*, 81.

17. Denis Sampson, "'Admiring the Scenery': Seán O'Faoláin's Fable of the Artist," 72.

18. Seán O'Faoláin, "Admiring the Scenery," in *A Purse of Coppers*, 67.

19. See Collingwood, *The Idea of Nature*, 3–9.

20. See Tim Robinson, *Connemara: The Last Pool of Darkness Pool*, for an eloquent discussion of our subconscious relation to nature, especially in the early chapters when he discusses Wittgenstein in Ireland. Here is Robinson on the relationship of Wittgenstein to Connemara: "In some future legendary reconstitution of the past it will be Wittgenstein's wrestling with the demons of philosophy that tears the landscape of Connemara" (3).

21. O'Faoláin, "Admiring the Scenery," 77.

22. O'Faoláin, "Admiring the Scenery," 79.

23. O'Faoláin, "Admiring the Scenery," 80; J. M. Synge, *The Aran Islands*, 67.

24. Schama, *Landscape and Memory*, 61, 6.

25. O'Faoláin, *The Collected Stories*, 163–64.

26. O'Faoláin, *The Collected Stories*, 165.

27. O'Faoláin, *The Collected Stories*, 199.

28. Sampson, "'Admiring the Scenery,'" 75.

29. Yeats, *The Poems*, ed. Albright, 6.

9. Solving Ambiguities

1. Louis MacNeice quoted in Edna Longley, *Louis MacNeice: A Study*, 57; MacNeice, *Collected Poems*, ed. E. R. Dodds, 133. All quotations from MacNeice are taken from this volume, cited in the bibliography, unless otherwise stated; the titles of the poems are noted throughout.

2. For a discussion of the importance of this figure, see Jon Stallworthy, *Louis MacNeice*, 1–13.

3. For a discussion of nineteenth-century attitudes toward nature, see John Wilson Foster, "Nature and Nation in the Nineteenth Century," in *Nature in Ireland*, ed. Foster, 409–39.

4. Murphy, *The Kick: A Memoir*, 11.

5. Richard Murphy, personal interview, March 18, 2004.

6. For a discussion of the Irish folk tradition concerning the hawthorn, see Niall Mac Coitir, *Irish Trees: Myths, Legends and Folklore*, 52–57.

7. Louis MacNeice, *The Strings Are False: An Unfinished Autobiography*, 217.

8. Yeats, *The Poems*, ed. Albright, 6.

9. MacNeice is punning on "mitred" to include the sense both that the mountain looks like a bishop's hat and that it is sloped at a forty-five-degree angle in order to "weep" shale.

10. Peter McDonald notes: "The sexual imagery used . . . in *Autumn Journal* adds the implication that a union with history is not to be made by the self in isolation—history cannot be taken, but has to be won." McDonald, *Louis MacNeice: The Poet in His Contexts*, 92.

11. Derek Mahon, *Collected Poems*, 17.

12. William Shakespeare, *Antony and Cleopatra*, 263.

13. "Latin *Rubico*, or *Rubicon*, a small stream that separated Cisalpine Gaul from Italy in the era of the Roman Republic. The movement of Julius Caesar's forces over the Rubicon into Italy in 49 BC violated the law (the *Lex Cornelia Majestatis*) that forbade a general to lead an army out of the province to which he was assigned. His act thus amounted to a declaration of war against the Roman Senate and resulted in the three-year civil war that left Caesar ruler of the Roman world. 'Crossing the Rubicon' became a popular phrase describing a step that definitely commits a person to a given course of action." *Encyclopædia Britannica Online*, s.v. "Rubicon," http://search.eb.com/eb/article?eu=65984.

10. The Rising Sap

1. See Michael Pollan, "Desire: Control/Plant: The Potato," in *The Botany of Desire: A Plant's Eye View of the World*, 181–238.

2. Seamus Heaney, "Strangeness and Beauty: A Review of Patrick Kavanagh's *Collected Poems*," *Guardian*, Dec. 31, 2004.

3. For a complete study of Kavanagh's mysticism, see Una Agnew, *The Mystical Imagination of Patrick Kavanagh*.

4. Antoinette Quinn, introduction to *Collected Poems of Patrick Kavanagh*, xiv; Grennan, *Facing the Music*, 173; Seamus Heaney, "The Sense of Place," in *Preoccupations*, 131, 137.

5. Wes Davis, "From Mossbawn to Meliboeus: Seamus Heaney's Ambivalent Pastoralism," 100.

6. Kavanagh, *Collected Poems of Kavanagh*; all poems are taken from this text unless otherwise noted.

7. Synge, *The Aran Islands*, 45.

8. Lévi-Strauss, *Elementary Structures of Kinship*, 24–25.

9. As Jacques Derrida points out concerning the relationship between nature and culture, there is no scandal "except within a system of concepts which accredits the difference between nature and culture." Derrida, *Writing and Difference*, 283–84.

10. Yeats, *A Vision*, 108.

11. For more on pagan and Christian themes in Synge, see Joy Kennedy, "Sympathy between Man and Nature: Landscape and Loss in Synge's *Riders to the Sea*."

12. C. S. Lewis, "The Weight of Glory."

13. Quoted in Bron Taylor, ed., *Encyclopedia of Religion and Nature*, 270.

14. Rachel Carson, *The Sense of Wonder*, 89–90.

15. Peter Godfrey Smith, *Metazoa: Animal Life and the Birth of the Mind*, 17.

16. William Wordsworth, "The Tables Turned," in *The Norton Anthology of Poetry*, ed. Margaret Ferguson et al., 764.

17. Soper, *What Is Nature?*, 71.

18. Mary Midgley writes, "Man fears his own guilt and insists on fixing it on something evidently alien and external. Beasts Within solve the problem of evil." Midgley, *The Essential Mary Midgley*, 50.

19. Patrick Kavanagh, *Tarry Flynn*, 188–89.

20. Soper, *What Is Nature?*, 93.

21. Soper, *What Is Nature?*, 95.

22. See Genesis 6:4. This passage is controversial and in its suggestion of conjugal relations between angels and humans seems to contradict the teachings of Jesus about the nature of his resurrection (Luke 24–39). Kavanagh follows Yeats, Swedenborg, and Milton in the belief that angels enjoyed a type of sexuality, but in "On Raglan Road" he sees it as potentially a loss of angelic status, which has probably more to do with human melancholy than any other truth.

23. Seamus Heaney, "The Placeless Heaven: Another Look at Kavanagh," in *The Government of the Tongue*, 13.

11. Beneath Tilth and Loam

1. Derek Mahon, "Afterlives," in *Selected Poems of Derek Mahon*, 190.

2. Beckett's ideas of place and landscape have been the focus of numerous studies; *Waiting for Godot* has been described as a post–Great Famine landscape in Joseph Roach, "'All the Dead Voices': The Landscape of Famine in *Waiting for*

Godot." The cylinder of *The Lost Ones* has been seen as a coffin ship sailed during the Great Famine in Wanda Balzano, "Searching for Beckett's Real Worlds in *The Lost Ones.*" *Endgame* is often seen as a postapocalyptic landscape. His landscapes have been seen as "abstract landscapes." For a fuller treatment of the various critical perspectives, see Cóilín Parsons, "Beckett's Abstract Landscapes." For the present purposes, we will think of them as landscapes of unspeakable home, for we can say of many of them what David Lloyd notes of Beckett's ideas of Jack Yeats's landscapes, that they are "images of alienation, suspension, disjunction—anything but representations of the continuity of artist and people, inner and outer, spirit and body." Lloyd, "Republics of Difference: Yeats, MacGreevy, Beckett," 46. The view of *Endgame* as the inside of a skull in James Knowlson's study *Frescoes of the Skull: The Late Prose and Drama of Samuel Beckett* accords well with this breakdown of the subject/object split. Beckett's many works contain obvious references to the landscapes of the Dublin and Wicklow Mountains. These landscapes are often models of escape or paradigms of suffering. There is another side for Beckett that is in line with his well-known rejection of nature in such works as *Endgame* and *The Lost Ones*, among others, though as Greg Gerrard has shown, such a rejection of nature may in fact be a deep form of ecological thinking. See his review of *Out of the Earth: Ecocritical Readings of Irish Texts*, edited by Christine Cusick.

3. W. J. T. Mitchell, "Imperial Landscape," in *Landscape and Power*, 29.

4. All following citations from Derek Mahon and Seamus Heaney are taken from the database "Twentieth-Century English Poetry," Cambridge, Chadwyck-Healey (a Bell & Howell Information and Learning Company), 1999, unless otherwise noted.

5. Seamus Heaney, "Feeling into Words," in *Preoccupations*, 57.

6. Mitchell, *Landscape and Power*, 1.

7. Seamus Heaney, "The Sense of Place," in *Preoccupations*, 131, 137.

8. All quotes of Seán Lysaght's poetry are from *The Wake Forest Series of Irish Poetry*, vol. 2, ed. Jefferson Holdridge.

9. Seán Lysaght, "Heaney vs. Praeger: Contrasting Natures," 69.

10. Robinson, *Connemara*, 146.

11. The full sentence reads: "It is my desire to view nature through nature's eyes and to ignore man as an object for special veneration." Haden Herrera, *Listening to Stone: The Art and Life of Isamu Noguchi*, 76.

12. Mitchell, "Imperial Landscape," 14, 29.

13. Luke Gibbons, "Topographies of Terror: Killarney and the Politics of the Sublime."

14. Helen Vendler, "Second Thoughts: *The Haw Lantern*," 171.

15. Edmund Burke, "A Letter to Richard Burke," in *Letters, Speeches and Tracts*, 350.

16. John Montague, "Like Dolmens Round My Childhood," 22.

17. Quoted in an interview by Dennis O'Driscoll in *Stepping Stones: Interviews with Seamus Heaney*, 309.

18. O'Driscoll, *Stepping Stones*, 471.

19. Seamus Heaney, *District and Circle*, 17, 18, 19.

20. Heaney, *District and Circle*, 21.

21. Michael Parker, "Fallout from the Thunder: Poetry and Politics in Seamus Heaney's *District and Circle*," 380.

22. For the most recent formulations of this perspective, see Jefferson Holdridge and Brian Ó Conchubhair, eds., *Post-Ireland? Essays on Contemporary Irish Poetry*; and Declan Kiberd, *After Ireland*.

23. W. B. Yeats, "The Dedication to a Book of Stories Selected from the Irish Novelists," in *The Poems*, ed. Albright.

12. In Defiance of Human Frontiers

1. Lysaght, "Heaney vs. Praeger," 70.

2. Derek Mahon, "Mythistorema," *Irish Times*, Oct. 7, 2017, collected in *Against the Clock*.

3. Donna Potts, *Contemporary Irish Poetry and the Pastoral Tradition*, 165.

4. All quotations from Moya Cannon are from *Wake Forest Series of Irish Poetry*, 2:47–83.

5. Potts, *Contemporary Irish Poetry*, 164.

6. Part of the following discussion is an elaboration of ideas outlined in my essays "'A Snake Pouring over the Ground': Nature and the Sacred in Eiléan Ní Chuilleanáin" and "The Wolf Tree: Culture and Nature in Paula Meehan's *Dharmakaya* and *Painting Rain*."

7. Eiléan Ní Chuilleanáin, "The Lady's Tower," in *Selected Poems*, 29. All quotations are from this volume unless otherwise mentioned.

8. Peggy O'Brien's footnote to the image of the Brazen Serpent in *The Wake Forest Book of Irish Women's Poetry* is instructive: "A complex, even paradoxical symbol. According to the Bible, it was an artifact with supposed healing properties constructed by Moses in the wilderness for the benefit of the Israelites, who earlier had been attacked by deadly serpents (Num. 21, 4–9 and John 3, 14–15)" (276).

9. E. O. Wilson, *In Search of Nature*, 6.

10. Wilson, *In Search of Nature*, 5.

11. Wilson, *In Search of Nature*, 29, 30.

12. For the relationship between symbolic and real, see *The Oxford English Dictionary*, s.v. "thing": "a. That which is signified, as distinguished from a word, symbol, or idea by which it is represented: the actual being or entity as opposed to a symbol of it; for the sexual connotations." See also "11. c. *euphemism*. Privy member, private parts; usually preceded by possessive pronoun."

13. Ní Chuilleanáin, "The Real Thing," in *Selected Poems*, 68.

14. Midgley quoted in Soper, *What Is Nature?*, 83

15. Jung quoted in Erwin Schrödinger, *Mind and Matter*, 40.

16. The phrases are from Ní Chuilleanáin's "The Brazen Serpent." For a full discussion of Locke and Romanticism, see Ernest Lee Tuveson, "The New Epistemology," in *The Imagination as a Means of Grace: Locke and the Aesthetics of Romanticism*, 25.

17. Schrödinger, *Mind and Matter*, 73.

18. Grennan, *Facing the Music*, 293. The quotation is from Donna Haraway, "Situated Knowledges: The Science Question in Feminism and the Privilege of Partial Perspective," 583.

19. See Daniel Smith and John Protevi, "Gilles Deleuze," in *The Stanford Encyclopedia of Philosophy* (Spring 2020 ed.), ed. Edward N. Zalta, https://plato.stanford.edu/archives/spr2020/entries/deleuze/: "*Anti-Oedipus* is, along with its conceptual and terminological innovation, a work of grand ambitions: among them, (1) an eco-social theory of production, encompassing both sides of the nature/culture split, which functions as an ontology of change, transformation, or 'becoming'; (2) a 'universal history' of social formations—the 'savage' or tribal, the 'barbarian' or imperial, and the capitalist—which functions as a synthetic social science; . . . Capitalism's command is utterly simple: connect deterritorialized flows of labor and capital and extract a surplus from that connection. Thus capitalism sets loose an enormous productive charge—connect those flows! Faster, faster!—the surpluses of which the institutions of private property try to register as belonging to individuals. Now those individuals are primarily social (as figures of capitalist or laborer) and only secondarily private (family members)." The idea of the social versus the familial is of primary interest for this discussion, though the social uses by the poets in question are more broadly and sympathetically conceived than in the capitalist dynamic. In many ways, they subvert that dynamic.

20. Lucy Collins, *Contemporary Irish Women Poets: Memory and Estrangement*, 111, 131.

21. Peter Sirr, "'How Things Begin to Happen': Notes on Eiléan Ní Chuilleanáin and Medbh McGuckian," 450.

22. Eiléan Ní Chuilleanáin, *The Girl Who Married the Reindeer*. All quotations are from this volume and cited in the bibliography.

23. A sympathetic response is also apparent in the work of Nuala Ní Dhomhnaill. See Ní Dhomhnaill's "Caoineadh Mháire Nic Aodha" and the discussion of this poem in Seán Crosson, "Nuala Ní Dhomhnaill: Reclaiming Women's Voice from Song," 62–63.

24. See Thomas Kinsella, *An Duanaire, 1600–1900: Poems of the Dispossessed*, 328.

25. Eiléan Ní Chuilleanáin, *The Boys of Bluehill.* All quotations are from this volume cited in the bibliography.

26. Eiléan Ní Chuilleanáin, *The Sun-fish.* All quotations are from this volume and cited in the bibliography.

27. Jefferson Holdridge, ed., *The Shack: Irish Poets in the Mountains and the Foothills of the Blue Ridge*, 20–21.

28. For a discussion of modern travel, see Wanda Balzano and Jefferson Holdridge, "Tracking the Luas between the Human and the Inhuman."

29. Paula Meehan, *Dharmakaya*, *Painting Rain*, and *Geomantic.* All quotations are from these volumes and cited in the bibliography.

30. Lucy Collins, "A Way of Going Back: Memory and Estrangement in the Poetry of Paula Meehan"; Anne Mulhall, "Memory, Poetry and Recovery: Paula Meehan's Transformational Aesthetics."

31. See Jody Allen Randolph, "Breath, Memory, Elegy: An Interview with Paula Meehan."

32. Adrienne Rich, *The School among the Ruins*, 9.

33. See Randolph, "Breath, Memory, Elegy" and "New Ireland Poetics: The Ecocritical Turn in Contemporary Irish Women's Poetry."

34. See "An Interview with Paula Meehan by Amanda Sperry" on the Wake Forest University Press website, https://wfupress.wfu.edu/an-interview-with-paula-meehan/.

35. See Kathryn Kirkpatrick, "'A Murmuration of Starlings in a Rowan Tree': Finding Gary Snyder in Paula Meehan's Eco-political Poetics."

36. The wolf tree's connections to the mother are not overestimated. The "original diamond" of this poem echoes the cut diamond of "A Change of Life: Hectic," in *Painting Rain*, by Paula Meehan, 66. In an email to the present writer concerning the wolf tree, dated March 1, 2008, Meehan wrote: "They are everywhere, the wolves! The first one I saw was up in the woods around Malahide Castle. It was a copse that had grown up around this tree—the tree itself, an oak, was probably about 100 years old. Mostly I've seen them in old abandoned estates where they might have once been specimen trees and nature just moved in on them. In Ikaria last spring and autumn walking in the Aetheros (the mountains of that island) I saw one on the edge of an ancient forest in a small valley—as usual I had no camera. It was maybe an escapee from the forest and then it started to be surrounded and finally overwhelmed by its own children."

37. Paula Meehan helpfully shared this reference with the present critic in conversation, circa the summer of 2010.

38. John Montague, "Border Sick Call," 409. See also Montague, *A Spell to Bless the Silence: Selected Poems.*

39. The use of the number nine is explained on an unnumbered page of the Dedalus edition: "Comprising eighty-one poems of nine 9-syllable lines, Paula Meehan's extraordinary new collection is both a controlled experiment with the challenge of form and, at once, a free meditation on the nature of memory, community, love, and poetry itself. The linked but not strictly sequential poems act like tarot cards or *i ching* hexagrams, providing moments of clarity and insight during 'the long night's journey into day.' 'The craft,' as one poem observes of a glider riding a thermal, 'is lighter than the learning.' In that sense *Geomantic* is a significant new departure and a major achievement."

40. See Jay Parini, introduction to *Poems for a Small Planet: Contemporary American Nature Poetry*, xv.

Conclusion

1. Buchanan, *Oedipus against Freud*. See, in particular, the chapter titled "Freudful Mistakes in Sphinxish Pairc: Oedipal Humanism and Irish Nationalism in W. B. Yeats, James Joyce, and Samuel Beckett," 93–122.

2. Roberto Esposito, *Third Person*, 150–51, 101.

3. For Barry's "syncretic vision" of pagan and Christian themes, see William Pressly, "James Barry's Syncretic Vision: The Fusion of Classical and Christian in His *Birth of Pandora*." Indeed, the myths of Adonis and Dionysus are often seen as prototypes of Christian themes, while Venus, born of the sea, is similarly compared to Mary, star of the sea.

4. Ovid, *The Metamorphoses*, 277–78.

Bibliography

Aalen, F. H. A., Kevin Whelan, and Matthew Stout, eds. *An Atlas of the Irish Rural Landscape.* Toronto: Univ. of Toronto Press, 1997.

Adorno, Theodor W. *Aesthetic Theory.* London: Continuum, 2003.

———. *Minima Moralia.* Translated by E. F. N. Jephcott. London: Verso, 1974.

Agnew, Una. *The Mystical Imagination of Patrick Kavanagh.* Dublin: Columba Press, 1998.

Akin, Warren, IV. "'I Just Riz the Loy': The Oedipal Dimension of *The Playboy of the Western World.*" *South Atlantic Bulletin* 45, no. 4 (1980).

Allingham, William. *Laurence Bloomfield; or, Rich and Poor in Ireland.* London: Reeves and Turner, 1890. Publication date of the electronic edition is 1992 (Cambridge: Chadwyck-Healey).

Anderson, Chester. "James Joyce's 'Tilly.'" *PMLA* 73 (1958).

Arndt, Marie. *A Critical Study of Seán O'Faoláin's Life and Work.* Lewiston, NY: Edwin Mellen Press, 2001.

Augusteijn, Joost. Review of *The Black and Tans: British Police and Auxiliaries in the Irish War of Independence, 1920–1921*, by D. M. Leeson. *Journal of Modern History* 85, no. 4 (2013).

Backus, Margot Gayle. *The Gothic Family Romance: Heterosexuality, Child Sacrifice, and the Anglo-Irish Colonial Order.* Durham, NC: Duke Univ. Press, 1999.

Balthasar, Hans Urs von. *The Christian and Anxiety.* 1932. Reprint, San Francisco: Ignatius, 2000.

Balzano, Wanda. "Searching for Beckett's Real Worlds in *The Lost Ones.*" *Journal of Beckett Studies* 11, no. 1 (2001): 15–37.

Balzano, Wanda, and Jefferson Holdridge. "Tracking the Luas between the Human and the Inhuman." In *Irish Postmodernisms and Popular Culture*, edited by Wanda Balzano, Anne Mulhall, and Moynagh Sullivan, 100–115. London: Palgrave, 2007.

Beckett, Samuel. *As the Story Was Told: Uncollected and Late Prose*. London: Calder, 1990.

———. *Collected Shorter Plays*. New York: Grove, 1984.

———. *The Complete Dramatic Works*. London: Faber, 1986.

Berger, John. *Why Look at Animals?* London: Penguin, 2009.

Berlin, Isaiah. *The Crooked Timber of Humanity*. Edited by Henry Hardy. Princeton, NJ: Princeton Univ. Press, 1990.

———. *Three Critics of the Enlightenment*. Edited by Henry Hardy. Princeton, NJ: Princeton Univ. Press, 2000.

Bidney, David. "Myth, Symbolism, and Truth." In *Myth: A Symposium*, edited by Thomas A. Sebeok. Bloomington: Indiana Univ. Press, 1970.

Bourke, Angela. *The Burning of Bridget Cleary*. New York: Penguin, 1999.

Bowen, Elizabeth. *Bowen's Court*. New York: Alfred A. Knopf, 1942.

———. *Irish Stories*. Dublin: Poolbeg, 1978.

———. *The Last September*. 1929. Reprint, New York: Random House, 2000.

———. *Pictures and Conversations*. New York: Alfred A. Knopf, 1975.

———. Preface to *The Last September*. 2nd ed. New York: Alfred A. Knopf, 1952.

Brazeau, Robert, and Derek Gladwin, eds. *Eco-Joyce: Space, Place, and Environment in the Writings of James Joyce*. Cork: Cork Univ. Press, 2014.

Brearton, Fran, and Alan Gillis, eds. *The Oxford Handbook of Irish Poetry*. Oxford: Oxford Univ. Press, 2012.

Buchanan, Bradley. *Oedipus against Freud: Myth and the End(s) of Humanism in Twentieth-Century British Literature*. Toronto: Univ. of Toronto Press, 2010.

Buell, Lawrence. *The Environmental Imagination: Thoreau, Nature Writing, and the Formation of American Culture*. Cambridge, MA: Harvard Univ. Press, 1995.

Burke, Edmund. *Letters, Speeches and Tracts on Irish Affairs*. London: Macmillan, 1881.

———. *A Philosophical Enquiry into the Origins of Our Ideas of the Sublime and the Beautiful*. Edited by Adam Phillips. Oxford: Oxford Univ. Press, 1990.

———. *Reflections on the Revolution in France*. Edited by J. G. A. Pocock. Indianapolis: Hackett, 1987.

Burleigh, David. "Who We Are: Protestants and Poetry in the North of Ireland." In *Irish Writers and Politics*, edited by Okifumi Komesu and Masaru Sekine. London: Rowman and Littlefield, 1990.

Butler, Pierce. "Admiring the Scenery: Seán O'Faoláin's Love Affair with Landscape." *Eire-Ireland*, no. 14 (1989).

Calasso, Roberto. *Literature and the Gods.* Translated by Tim Parks. New York: Vintage, 2001.

———. *Tiepolo Pink.* Translated by Alastair McEwen. New York: Alfred A. Knopf, 2009.

Carleton, William. *The Black Prophet: A Tale of Irish Famine.* Shannon: Irish Univ. Press, 1972.

———. *Stories from William Carleton.* Introduced by W. B. Yeats. New York: Lemming, 1978.

Carpenter, Andrew, ed. *Place, Personality, and the Irish Writer.* Dublin: Colin Smythe, 1977.

Carpenter, Andrew, and Lucy Collins, eds. *The Irish Poet and the Natural World: An Anthology of Verse in English from the Tudors to the Romantics.* Cork: Cork Univ. Press, 2014.

Carson, Rachel. *The Sense of Wonder.* New York: Harper and Row, 1965.

Cary, Joseph. *Three Modern Italian Poets: Saba, Ungaretti, Montale.* Chicago: Univ. of Chicago Press, 1993.

Caserio, Robert L. *The Novel in England, 1900–1950: History and Theory.* New York: Twayne, 1999.

Cassirer, Ernst. *Language and Myth.* Translated by Suzanne K. Langer. New York: Dover, 1946.

Clarke, Bruce. "The Nonhuman." In *The Cambridge Companion to Literature and the Posthuman*, edited by Bruce Clarke and Manuela Rossini. Cambridge: Cambridge Univ. Press, 2017.

Collingwood, R. G. *The Idea of Nature.* Oxford: Oxford Univ. Press, 1960.

Collins, Floyd. *Seamus Heaney: The Crisis of Identity.* Cranbury, NJ: Associated Univ. Presses, 2003.

Collins, Lucy. "A Way of Going Back: Memory and Estrangement in the Poetry of Paula Meehan." Edited by Jody Allen Randolph. *An Sionnach* 5, no. 1 (2009): 127–39.

———. *Contemporary Irish Women Poets: Memory and Estrangement.* Liverpool: Liverpool Univ. Press, 2015.

Conrad, Kathyrn A. *Locked in the Family Cell: Gender, Sexuality & Political Agency in Irish National Discourse*. Madison: Univ. of Wisconsin Press, 2004.

Corbett, Mary Jean. *Allegories of Union in Irish and English Writing, 1790–1870: Politics, History, and the Family from Edgeworth to Arnold*. Cambridge: Cambridge Univ. Press, 2000.

Coupe, Laurence. *Myth*. London and New York: Routledge, 1997.

Craig, Patricia. *Elizabeth Bowen*. Harmondsworth: Penguin, 1986.

Cronin, John. *The Anglo-Irish Novel*. Vol. 1, *The Nineteenth Century*. Totowa, NJ: Barnes and Noble, 1980.

Crosby, Donald A. *A Religion of Nature*. Albany: State Univ. of New York Press, 2002.

Crosson, Seán. "Nuala Ní Dhomhnaill: Reclaiming Women's Voice from Song." In *Representing Ireland: Past, Present and Future*, edited by Frank Beardow and Alison O'Malley-Younger. Sunderland, UK: Univ. of Sunderland Press, 2005.

Curtis, Tony. *The Art of Seamus Heaney*. Bridgend: Seren, 2001.

Cusick, Christine. "'Clacking along the Concrete Pavement': Economic Isolation and the Bricolage of Place in James Joyce's *Dubliners*." In *Eco-Joyce: Space, Place, and Environment in the Writings of James Joyce*, edited by Robert Brazeau and Derek Gladwin. Cork: Cork Univ. Press, 2014.

———, ed. *Out of the Earth: Ecocritical Readings of Irish Texts*. Cork: Cork Univ. Press, 2010.

Davis, Wes. "From Mossbawn to Meliboeus: Seamus Heaney's Ambivalent Pastoralism." *Southwest Review* 92, no. 1 (2007).

Dawe, Gerald, ed. *The Cambridge Companion to Irish Poets*. Cambridge: Cambridge Univ. Press, 2018.

Deane, Seamus. *Celtic Revivals*. London: Faber, 1985.

———. *Strange Country*. Oxford: Oxford Univ. Press, 1997.

Delaney, Paul. *Seán O'Faoláin: Literature, Inheritance and the 1930s*. Dublin: Irish Academic Press, 2014.

Deleuze, Gilles. *Pure Immanence: Essays on a Life*. Translated by Anne Boyman. New York: Zone Books, 2005.

De Man, Paul. *Allegories of Readings: Figural Language in Rousseau, Nietzsche, Rilke, Proust*. New Haven, CT: Yale Univ. Press, 1979.

Depoortere, Frederiek. *Christ in Post-modern Philosophy: Gianni Vattimo, René Girard and Slavoj Žižek*. New York: T&T Clark, 2008.

Derrida, Jacques. *Writing and Difference.* Translated by Alan Bass. Routledge: London, 1978.

Docherty, Thomas. "Ana-; or, Postmodernism, Landscape, Seamus Heaney." In *Seamus Heaney*, edited by Michael Allen. Basingstoke: Macmillan, 1997.

Donnelly, Brian, ed. Special issue on Derek Mahon, *Irish University Review* 24, no. 1 (1994).

Dutton, Denis. *The Art Instinct: Beauty, Pleasure, and Human Evolution.* New York: Bloomsbury, 2009.

Eagleton, Terry. *The Ideology of the Aesthetic.* Oxford: Blackwell, 1990.

Easthope, Anthony. *The Unconscious.* London: Routledge, 1999.

Elder, John, and Robert Finch, eds. *The Norton Book of Nature Writing.* New York: W. W. Norton, 2002.

Eliot, T. S. *The Four Quartets.* New York: Harvest Books, 1968.

Ellmann, Maud. *Elizabeth Bowen: The Shadow across the Page.* Edinburgh: Edinburgh Univ. Press, 2003.

———. *The Hunger-Artists: Starving, Writing, and Imprisonment.* Cambridge, MA: Harvard Univ. Press, 1993.

Ellmann, Richard. *The Identity of Yeats.* New York: Oxford Univ. Press, 1964.

———. *James Joyce.* 1959. Reprint, Oxford: Oxford Univ. Press, 1982.

Esposito, Roberto. *Third Person.* Translated by Zakiya Hanafi. Cambridge, MA: Polity, 2012. Originally published as *Terza Persona* by Einaudi (2007).

Esty, Jed. "Virgins of Empire: *The Last September* and the Antidevelopmental Plot." Special issue on Elizabeth Bowen, *Modern Fiction Studies* 53, no. 2 (2007): 257–75.

Evans, Estyn. *The Personality of Ireland: Habitat, Heritage, and History.* Dublin: Lilliput, 1992.

Fabricant, Carol. *Swift's Landscape.* Baltimore: Johns Hopkins Univ. Press, 1982.

Fallon, Peter, and Derek Mahon, eds. *The Penguin Book of Contemporary Irish Poetry.* London: Penguin, 1990.

Ferguson, Margaret, et al., eds. *The Norton Anthology of Poetry.* 5th ed. New York: W. W. Norton, 2005.

Ferris, Ina. *The Romantic National Tale and the Question of Ireland.* New York: Cambridge Univ. Press, 2002.

Flanagan, Thomas. *The Irish Novelists, 1800–1850.* New York: Columbia Univ. Press, 1959.

Flannery, Eóin. *Ireland and Ecocriticism: Literature, History, and Environmental Justice.* New York: Routledge, 2016.

Foster, J. W., ed. *Nature in Ireland: A Scientific and Cultural History.* Dublin: Lilliput, 1997.

Foster, R. F. *The Irish Story: Telling Tales and Making It Up in Ireland.* London: Penguin, 2001.

———. *Modern Ireland, 1600–1972.* London: Penguin, 1988.

———. *The Oxford Illustrated History of Ireland.* Oxford: Oxford Univ. Press, 1989.

———. *W. B. Yeats: A Life.* Vol. 2, *The Arch-poet, 1915–1939.* Oxford: Oxford Univ. Press, 2003.

———. *Words Alone: Yeats and His Inheritances.* Oxford: Oxford Univ. Press, 2011.

Frawley, Oona. *Irish Pastoral: Nostalgia and Twentieth-Century Irish Literature.* Dublin: Irish Academic Press, 2005.

———. "Nature and Nostalgia in Irish Literature." *Proceedings of the Harvard Celtic Colloquium* 18–19 (1998–99).

Freud, Sigmund. *On Sexuality: Three Essays on the Theory of Sexuality, and Other Works.* Translated by James Strachey. Penguin Freud Library, vol. 7. London: Penguin, 1991.

Garrard, Greg. Review of *Out of the Earth: Ecocritical Readings of Irish Texts,* edited by Christine Cusick. *Irish Studies Review* 20, no. 1 (2012): 108–10.

Gatta, John. *Making Nature Sacred: Literature, Religion, and Environment in America from the Puritans to the Present.* Oxford: Oxford Univ. Press, 2004.

Gibbons, Luke. *Edmund Burke and Ireland: Aesthetics, Politics, and the Colonial Sublime.* Cambridge: Cambridge Univ. Press, 2003.

———. "Topographies of Terror: Killarney and the Politics of the Sublime." *South Atlantic Quarterly* 95, no. 1 (1996): 23–45.

Gibson, Matthew. "Yeats and Idealism: The Philosophy of Light." In *Yeats Annual, No. 14.* Basingstoke: Palgrave, 2001.

Girard, René. *I See Satan Fall like Lightening.* Ottawa: Orbis, 2001.

———. *The Scapegoat.* Translated by Yvonne Freccero. Baltimore: Johns Hopkins Univ. Press, 1989.

———. *Things Hidden since the Foundation of the World*. Stanford, CA: Stanford Univ. Press, 1978.

Gladwin, Derek. *Contentious Terrains: Boglands, Ireland, Postcolonial Gothic*. Cork: Cork Univ. Press, 2016.

Gladwin, Derek, and Christine Cusick, eds. *Unfolding Irish Landscapes: Tim Robinson, Culture and Environment*. Manchester: Manchester Univ. Press, 2016.

Glendinning, Victoria. *Jonathan Swift*. London: Pimlico, 1999.

Goldsmith, Oliver. *The Poems and Plays of Oliver Goldsmith*. London: Frederick Warne, 1893.

———. *The Vicar of Wakefield*. Salisbury: Collins, 1766.

———. *The Works of Oliver Goldsmith*. Edited by Peter Cunningham. Vol. 4. London: John Murray, 1854.

Grant, Michael. *Myths of the Greeks and Romans*. New York: Mentor, 1986.

Grennan, Eamon. *Facing the Music: Irish Poetry in the Twentieth Century*. Omaha, NE: Creighton Univ. Press, 1999.

———. "Interview of Derek Mahon." *Paris Review* 42, no. 154 (2000).

Haraway, Donna. "Situated Knowledges: The Science Question in Feminism and the Privilege of Partial Perspective." *Feminist Studies* 14, no. 3 (1988).

———. *Staying with the Trouble: Making Kin in the Chthulucene*. Durham, NC: Duke Univ. Press, 2016.

Harmon, Maurice. *Seán O'Faoláin: A Critical Introduction*. Notre Dame, IN: Univ. of Notre Dame Press, 1967.

Harrison, Robert Pogue. *Forests: The Shadow of Civilization*. Chicago: Univ. of Chicago Press, 1992.

———. *Gardens: An Essay on the Human Condition*. Chicago: Univ. of Chicago Press, 2008.

Haughton, Hugh. *The Poetry of Derek Mahon*. Oxford: Oxford Univ. Press, 2010.

Heaney, Marie. *Over Nine Waves: A Book of Irish Legends*. New York: Farrar, Straus and Giroux, 1995.

Heaney, Seamus. *District and Circle*. New York: Farrar, Straus and Giroux, 2006.

———. *Finders Keepers: Selected Prose, 1971–2001*. London: Faber, 2002.

———. "The God in the Tree." In *The Pleasures of Gaelic Poetry*, ed. Seán MacRéamoinn. London: Penguin, 1982.

———. *The Government of the Tongue*. New York: Farrar, Straus and Giroux, 1988.

———. *The Haw Lantern*. London: Faber, 1987.

———. *New Selected Poems*. London: Faber, 1990.

———. *North*. London: Faber, 1975.

———. *Opened Ground*. New York: Farrar, Straus and Giroux, 1999.

———. *Preoccupations: Selected Prose, 1968–1978*. New York: Farrar, Straus and Giroux, 1980.

———. *The Spirit Level*. London: Faber, 1996.

———. *Sweeney Astray*. New York: Farrar, Straus and Giroux, 1983.

Heaney, Seamus, and Ted Hughes, eds. *The Rattle Bag*. London: Faber, 1982.

Heine, Heinrich. *The Prose Writings of Heinrich Heine*. Edited by Ernest Rhys. London: Walter Scott, 1887.

Herrera, Haden. *Listening to Stone: The Art and Life of Isamu Noguchi*. New York: Farrar, Strauss and Giroux, 2015.

Higgins, Richard. *Thoreau and the Language of Trees*. Berkeley: Univ. of California Press, 2017.

Holdeman, David, and Ben Levitas, eds. *W. B. Yeats in Context*. Cambridge: Cambridge Univ. Press, 2010.

Holdridge, Jefferson, ed. "'Of the Dark Past': The Brittle Magic Nation of Joyce's Poetics." *Irish University Review* (Autumn–Winter 2004): 229–46.

———, ed. *The Shack: Irish Poets in the Mountains and the Foothills of the Blue Ridge*. Winston-Salem, NC: Wake Forest Univ. Press, 2015.

———. "'A Snake Pouring over the Ground': Nature and the Sacred in Eiléan Ní Chuilleanáin." Special issue on Eiléan Ní Chuilleanáin, *Irish University Review* 37, no. 1 (2007).

———. *Those Mingled Seas: The Poetry of W. B. Yeats, the Beautiful and the Sublime*. Dublin: Univ. College Dublin Press, 2000.

———, ed. *The Wake Forest Series of Irish Poetry*. Vol. 1. Winston-Salem, NC: Wake Forest Univ. Press, 2005.

———, ed. *The Wake Forest Series of Irish Poetry*. Vol. 2. Winston-Salem, NC: Wake Forest Univ. Press, 2010.

———. "The Wolf Tree: Culture and Nature in Paula Meehan's *Dharmakaya* and *Painting Rain*." Special issue on Paula Meehan, edited by Jody Allen-Randolph, *An Sionnach* (Spring–Fall 2010).

Holdridge, Jefferson, and Brian Ó Conchubhair, eds. *Post-Ireland? Essays on Contemporary Irish Poetry.* Winston-Salem, NC: Wake Forest Univ. Press, 2017.

hoogland, renee c. *Elizabeth Bowen: A Reputation in Writing.* New York: New York Univ. Press, 1994.

Jaski, Bart. "Cú Chulainn, *gormac* and *dalta* of the Ulstermen." *Cambrian Medieval Celtic Studies* 37 (1999).

Joyce, James. *Dubliners.* London: Dover, 1991.

———. *Giacomo Joyce.* Edited by Richard Ellmann. New York: Viking, 1968.

———. *A Norton Critical Edition of "Dubliners."* Edited by Margot Norris. New York: W. W. Norton, 2006.

———. *Poems and Shorter Writings.* Edited by Richard Ellmann and A. Walton Litz. London: Faber, 2001.

———. "Simples." *Poetry* (May 2017).

Jung, C. G. *Answer to Job.* New York: Meridian, 1960.

Kavanagh, Patrick. *Collected Poems of Patrick Kavanagh.* Edited by Antoinette Quinn. London: Allen Lane, 2004.

———. *The Complete Poems.* Edited by Peter Kavanagh. Newbridge: Goldsmith Press, 1972.

———. *Tarry Flynn.* 1948. Reprint, London: Penguin, 1978.

Kearney, Richard. *The Irish Mind: Exploring Intellectual Traditions.* Dublin: Wolfhound, 1984.

Kelleher, Margaret. *The Feminization of the Famine: Expressions of the Inexpressible?* Durham, NC: Duke Univ. Press, 1997.

Kelly, Patricia. "*The Táin* as Literature." In *Aspects of "The Táin,"* edited by J. P. Mallory. Belfast: December, 1992.

Kendall, Tim. "Beauty and the Beast." *Poetry Review* 86 (Spring 1996).

Kennedy, Joy. "Sympathy between Man and Nature: Landscape and Loss in Synge's *Riders to the Sea.*" *Interdisciplinary Studies in Literature and Environment* 11, no. 1 (2004): 15–30.

Keogh, Dáire, and Kevin Whelan, eds. *Acts of Union: The Causes, Contexts, and Consequences of the Act of Union.* Dublin: Four Courts Press, 2001.

Kiberd, Declan. *After Ireland.* Cambridge, MA: Harvard Univ. Press, 2018.

———. *The Irish Writer and the World.* Cambridge: Cambridge Univ. Press, 2005.

Killeen, Jarlath. *Gothic Ireland.* Dublin: Four Courts, 2005.

Kinsella, Thomas. "The Divided Mind." In *Irish Poets in English*, edited by Seán Lucy. Cork: Mercier, 1972.

———, ed. *An Duanaire, 1600–1900: Poems of the Dispossessed*. Dublin: Dolmen, 1981.

———. *The Táin*. 1969. Reprint, Oxford: Oxford Univ. Press, 1970.

Kirkpatrick, Kathryn, ed. *Border Crossings: Irish Women Writers and National Identities*. Tuscaloosa: Univ. of Alabama Press, 2000.

———. "'A Murmuration of Starlings in a Rowan Tree': Finding Gary Snyder in Paula Meehan's Eco-political Poetics." Edited by Jody Allen Randolph. Special issue on Paula Meehan, *An Sionnach* 5, no. 1 (2009): 195–207.

Knowlson, James. *Frescoes of the Skull: The Late Prose and Drama of Samuel Beckett*. New York: Grove, 1980.

Komesu, Okifumi, and Masaru Sekine, eds. *Irish Writers and Politics*. London: Rowman and Littlefield, 1990.

Kreilkamp, Vera. *The Anglo-Irish Novel and the Big House*. Syracuse, NY: Syracuse Univ. Press, 1989.

Kristeva, Julia. *Strangers to Ourselves*. Translated by Leon Roudiez. New York: Columbia Univ. Press, 1991.

Kroeg, Susan M. "'So Near to Us as a Sister': Incestuous Unions in Sydney Owenson's *The Wild Irish Girl* and Maria Edgeworth's *The Absentee*." In *Anglo-Irish Identities*, edited by David Valone. Lewisburg, PA: Bucknell Univ. Press, 2008.

Larrissy, Edward, ed. *Irish Writers in Their Time*. W. B. Yeats, edited by Stan Smith. Dublin and Portland: Irish Academic Press, 2010.

Le Brocquy, Louis. *The Irish Landscape*. Dublin: Gandon, 1992.

Lee, Hermione. *Elizabeth Bowen*. London: Vintage, 1999.

Leerssen, Joep. *Remembrance and Imagination: Patterns in the Historical and Literary Representation of Ireland in the Nineteenth Century*. Cork: Cork Univ. Press, 1997.

Leopold, Aldo. "The Green Lagoons." *American Forests* 51 (1945).

Lévi-Strauss, Claude. *The Elementary Structures of Kinship*. London: Eyre and Spottiswoode, 1969.

Lewis, C. S. "The Weight of Glory." *Theology* 43, no. 257 (1941): 263–74.

Lloyd, David. "Republics of Difference: Yeats, MacGreevy, Beckett." *Field Day Review* 1 (2005).

Longley, Edna. *Louis MacNeice: A Study*. London: Faber, 1988.

———. *Yeats and Modernism.* Cambridge: Cambridge Univ. Press, 2013.

Longley, Michael. *Snow Water.* Winston-Salem, NC: Wake Forest Univ. Press, 2004.

Lowe, Jeremy. "Contagious Violence and the Spectacle of Death in *Táin Bó Cúailnge.*" In *Language and Tradition in Ireland: Continuities and Displacements,* edited by Maria Tymoczko and Colin Ireland. Amherst: Univ. of Massachusetts Press, 2003.

Lyotard, Jean-François. *Inhuman: Reflections on Time.* Translated by Geoffrey Bennington and Rachel Bowlby. Stanford, CA: Stanford Univ. Press, 1991.

Lysaght, Seán. "Heaney vs. Praeger: Contrasting Natures." *Irish Review* 7 (1989).

Mac Coitir, Niall. *Irish Trees: Myths, Legends and Folklore.* Cork: Collins Press, 2003.

MacFarlane, Robert. *The Wild Places.* London: Penguin, 2008.

MacNeice, Louis. *Collected Poems.* Edited by E. R. Dodds. New York: Oxford Univ. Press, 1967.

———. *Collected Poems.* Edited by Peter McDonald. Winston-Salem, NC: Wake Forest Univ. Press, 2013.

———. *The Strings Are False: An Unfinished Autobiography.* London: Faber, 1965.

Mahon, Derek. *Against the Clock.* Meath: Gallery Press, 2018.

———. *Collected Poems.* Meath: Gallery, 1999.

———. *Selected Poems of Derek Mahon.* London: Viking, 1991.

Malloy, Kelli, and Eileen O'Halloran. "An Interview with Paula Meehan." *Contemporary Literature* 43, no. 1 (2002).

Mann, Neil, Matthew Gibson, and Claire Nally, eds. *W. B. Yeats's "A Vision": Explications and Contexts.* Clemson, SC: Clemson Univ. Press, 2012.

Massey, Doreen. *Space, Place and Gender.* Minneapolis: Univ. of Minneapolis Press, 1994.

McCormack, W. J. *Burke to Beckett: Ascendancy Tradition and Betrayal in Literary History.* Cork: Cork Univ. Press, 1994.

McCourt, John. *The Years of Bloom.* Dublin: Lilliput, 2000.

McCutchean, Jessica. "Landscapes of War." *Acta Antiqua Academiae Scientiarum Hungaricae* 53, nos. 2–3 (2013): 261–74.

McDonald, Peter. "Incurable Ache." *Poetry Ireland Review* 56 (Spring 1998).

———. *Louis MacNeice: The Poet in His Contexts.* Oxford: Oxford Univ. Press, 1991.

———. *Mistaken Identities: Poetry and Northern Ireland.* Oxford: Clarendon Press, 1997.

McGahern, John. *By the Lake.* New York: Vintage, 2003.

———. "The Sky above Us." *Ireland of the Welcomes* 45, no. 5 (1996): 39–42.

McGuckian, Medbh. *Venus and the Rain.* Meath: Gallery, 1994.

McGuinness, Arthur E. "Cast a Wary Eye: Derek Mahon's Classical Perspective." *Yearbook of English Studies*, edited by C. J. Rawson 17 (1987).

McKibben, Bill. *The End of Nature.* New York: Penguin, 1990.

Mead, George H. "Bishop Berkeley and His Message." *Journal of Philosophy* 26, no. 16 (1929).

Meehan, Paula. *Dharmakaya.* Winston-Salem, NC: Wake Forest Univ. Press, 2002.

———. *Geomantic.* Dublin: Dedalus Press, 2016.

———. *Painting Rain.* Winston-Salem, NC: Wake Forest Univ. Press, 2009.

Merton, Thomas. *Raids on the Unspeakable.* New York: New Directions, 1966.

Midgley, Mary. *The Essential Mary Midgley.* Edited by David Midgley. London: Routledge, 2005.

———. *Science and Poetry.* London: Routledge, 2001.

Mitchell, Donald. *Cultural Geography: A Critical Introduction.* Oxford: Blackwell, 2000.

Mitchell, W. J. T. *Landscape and Power.* 2nd ed. 1994. Reprint, Chicago: Univ. of Chicago Press, 2002.

Monk, Samuel. *The Sublime: A Study of Critical Theories in Eighteenth-Century England.* Ann Arbor: Univ. of Michigan Press, 1960.

Montague, John. "Border Sick Call." *Southern Review* (Baton Rouge) 31, no. 3 (1995).

———. "Like Dolmens Round My Childhood." In *Collected Poems.* Winston-Salem, NC: Wake Forest Univ. Press, 1995.

———. *The Rough Field.* Winston-Salem, NC: Wake Forest Univ. Press, 1972.

———. *A Spell to Bless the Silence: Selected Poems.* Winston-Salem, NC: Wake Forest Univ. Press, 2018.

Montale, Eugenio. *Tutte le poesie*. Edited by Giorgio Zampa. Milan: Mondadori, 1984.

Moore, Thomas. *The Poetical Works of Thomas Moore*. London: Frederick Warne, 1904.

Morgan, Lady [Sydney Owenson]. *The Wild Irish Girl: A National Tale*. Vols. 1–3. Cambridge: Chadwyck-Healey, 1999.

Moynahan, Julian. *Anglo-Irish: The Literary Imagination in a Hyphenated Culture*. Princeton, NJ: Princeton Univ. Press, 1995.

Muldoon, Paul. *Poems, 1968–1998*. London: Faber, 2001.

———. *To Ireland, I*. Oxford: Oxford Univ. Press, 2000.

Mulhall, Anne. "Memory, Poetry and Recovery: Paula Meehan's Transformational Aesthetics." Edited by Jody Allen Randolph. *An Sionnach* 5, no. 1 (2009): 142–55.

Müller, Markus. "Interview with René Girard." *Anthropoetics* 2, no. 1 (1996).

Murphy, Richard. *The Kick: A Memoir*. London: Granta, 2002.

Nash, Catherine. "'Embodying the Nation': The West of Ireland and Irish Identity." In *Tourism in Ireland: A Critical Analysis*. Cork: Cork Univ. Press, 1993.

Nash, Roderick Frazier. *Wilderness and the American Mind*. New Haven, CT: Yale Univ. Press, 2001.

Neeson, Eoin. "Woodland in History and Culture." In *Nature in Ireland: A Scientific and Cultural History*, edited by John Wilson Foster. Dublin: Lilliput, 1997.

Ní Chuilleanáin, Eiléan. *The Boys of Bluehill*. Winston-Salem, NC: Wake Forest Univ. Press, 2015.

———. *The Girl Who Married the Reindeer*. Winston-Salem, NC: Wake Forest Univ. Press, 2002.

———. *Selected Poems*. Winston-Salem, NC: Wake Forest Univ. Press, 1975.

———. *The Sun-fish*. Winston-Salem, NC: Wake Forest Univ. Press, 2010.

Nicolson, Marjorie Hope. *Mountain Gloom and Mountain Glory*. Ithaca, NY: Cornell Univ. Press, 1959.

Ní Dhomhnaill, Nuala. *The Fifty Minute Mermaid*. Oldcastle, County Meath: Gallery Press, 2007.

Ní Dhuibhne, Éilís. *Blood and Water*. Dublin: Attic, 1988.

Norris, Margot, ed. *A Norton Critical Edition of "Dubliners."* New York: W. W. Norton, 2006.

O'Brien, Flann. *At Swim-Two-Birds.* Norman, IL: Dalkey Archive Press, 1998.

O'Brien, Peggy, ed. *The Wake Forest Book of Irish Women's Poetry.* 2nd ed. 1999. Reprint, Winston-Salem, NC: Wake Forest Univ. Press, 2011.

O'Connor, Anne, and Anne Markey. *Folklore and Modern Irish Writing.* Dublin: Irish Academic Press, 2014.

O'Driscoll, Dennis, ed. *Stepping Stones: Interviews with Seamus Heaney.* New York: Farrar, Straus and Giroux, 2008.

O'Faoláin, Seán. *The Collected Stories.* Boston: Little, Brown, 1983.

———. *A Purse of Coppers.* New York: Viking Press, 1938.

———. *The Vanishing Hero: Studies in Novelists of the Twenties.* London: Eyre and Spottiswoode, 1956.

O'Flaherty, Liam. *A Tourist's Guide to Ireland.* 1929. Reprint, Dublin: Wolfhound Press, 1998.

Ó Gallchoir, Clíona. *Maria Edgeworth: Women, Enlightenment and Nation.* Dublin: Univ. College Dublin Press, 2005.

Ó hÓgáin, Dáithí. *Myth, Legend and Romance: An Encyclopædia of Irish Folk Tradition.* London: Ryan, 1990.

O'Reilly, Caitríona. *Geis.* Winston-Salem, NC: Wake Forest Univ. Press, 2015.

Osborn, Susan. "'How to Measure This Unaccountable Darkness between the Trees': The Strange Relation of Style and Meaning in *The Last September.*" In *Elizabeth Bowen: New Critical Perspectives*, edited by Susan Osborn. Cork: Cork Univ. Press, 2009.

Otto, Walter F. *Dionysus: Myth and Cult.* Translated by Robert B. Palmer. Bloomington: Indiana Univ. Press, 1965.

Ovid. *The Metamorphoses.* Translated by Horace Gregory. New York: Viking, 1958.

Parini, Jay. *Poems for a Small Planet: Contemporary American Nature Poetry.* Middlebury, VT: Bread Loaf, 1993.

Parker, Michael. "Fallout from the Thunder: Poetry and Politics in Seamus Heaney's *District and Circle.*" *Irish Studies Review* 16, no. 4 (2008): 369–84.

Parsons, Cóilín. "Beckett's Abstract Landscapes." In *The Ordnance Survey and Modern Irish Literature*, 185–218. Oxford: Oxford Univ. Press, 2016.

Pollan, Michael. *The Botany of Desire: A Plant's Eye View of the World.* New York: Random House, 2001.

Pollitt, J. J. *Art and Experience in Classical Greece.* Cambridge: Cambridge Univ. Press, 1972.

Potts, Donna. *Contemporary Irish Poetry and the Pastoral Tradition.* Columbia: Univ. of Missouri Press, 2011.

Power, Colum. *James Joyce's Catholic Categories.* Newberg, OR: Wiseblood Books, 2016.

Praeger, Robert Lloyd. *The Way I Went.* Cork: Collins, 2001.

Pressly, William. "James Barry's Syncretic Vision: The Fusion of Classical and Christian in His *Birth of Pandora.*" *British Art Journal* 14, no. 3 (2013–14): 27–35.

Quinn, Justin. *The Cambridge Introduction to Modern Irish Poetry, 1800–2000.* Cambridge: Cambridge Univ. Press, 2008.

Rancière, Jacques. *Dissensus: On Politics and Aesthetics.* Edited and translated by Steven Corcoran. New York: Continuum, 2010.

Randolph, Jody Allen. "The Body Politic: A Conversation with Paula Meehan." Special issue on Paula Meehan, edited by Jody Allen Randolph, *An Sionnach* 5, no. 1 (2009).

———. "Breath, Memory, Elegy: An Interview with Paula Meehan." Special issue on Paula Meehan, edited by Jody Allen Randolph, *An Sionnach* 5, no. 1 (2009).

———. "New Ireland Poetics: The Ecocritical Turn in Contemporary Irish Women's Poetry." *Nordic Irish Studies* 8, no. 1 (2009).

Rawson, Claude, ed. *Jonathan Swift: A Collection of Critical Essays.* Englewood Cliffs, NJ: Prentice Hall, 1995.

Rich, Adrienne. *The School among the Ruins.* New York: W. W. Norton, 2004.

Roach, Jay. "'All the Dead Voices': The Landscape of Famine in *Waiting for Godot.*" In *Land/Scape/Theater*, edited by Una Chaudhuri and Elinor Fuchs, 84–93. Ann Arbor: Univ. of Michigan Press, 2002.

Robinson, Tim. *Connemara: The Last Pool of Darkness.* Dublin: Penguin, 2008.

———. *Setting Foot on the Shores of Connemara, and Other Writings.* Dublin: Lilliput, 1996.

———. *Stones of Aran: Labyrinth.* Dublin: Penguin, 1995.

———. *Stones of Aran: Pilgrimage.* Dublin: Penguin, 1986.

Rozelle, Lee. *Ecosublime: Environmental Awe and Terror from New World to Oddworld.* Tuscaloosa: Univ. of Alabama Press, 2006.

Sampson, Denis. "'Admiring the Scenery': Seán O'Faoláin's Fable of the Artist." *Canadian Journal of Irish Studies* 3, no. 1 (1977).

Schama, Simon. *Landscape and Memory*. New York: Vintage, 1996.

Scholes, Robert. "James Joyce, Irish Poet." *James Joyce Quarterly* 2 (1964).

Schrödinger, Erwin. *Mind and Matter*. Cambridge: Cambridge Univ. Press, 1958.

Shakespeare, William. *Antony and Cleopatra*. London: Arden, 2002.

Sherman, Glen L. "Martin Heidegger's Concept of Authenticity: A Philosophical Contribution to Student Affairs Theory." *Journal of College and Character* 10, no. 7 (2009).

Sirr, Peter. "'How Things Begin to Happen': Notes on Eiléan Ní Chuilleanáin and Medbh McGuckian." *Southern Review* (Louisiana State Univ.) 31, no. 3 (1995).

Smith, Peter Godrey. *Metazoa: Animal Life and the Birth of the Mind*. New York: Farrar, Straus and Giroux, 2020.

Snukal, Robert. *High Talk: The Philosophical Poetry of W. B. Yeats*. 1973. Reprint, Cambridge: Cambridge, Univ. Press, 2010.

Soper, Kate. *What Is Nature? Culture, Politics and the Non-human*. London: Blackwell, 1995.

Sophocles. *Oedipus Rex*. Translated by Sir George Young. London: Dent, 1906.

Stallworthy, Jon. *Louis MacNeice*. London: Faber, 1995.

Stasi, Paul. "'Fumbling along the Boundaries of the Personal': History and Affect in Elizabeth Bowen's *The Last September*." *ELH* 84 (2017) 715–40.

Stephens, James. *The Crock of Gold*. 1912. Reprint, London: Dover, 1997.

Swift, Jonathan. *Gulliver's Travels*. Oxford: Oxford Univ. Press, 1998.

———. *Selected Poems*. Edited by Derek Mahon. London: Faber, 2001.

Synge, J. M. *The Aran Islands*. 1907. Reprint, New York: Penguin, 1992.

———. *The Playboy of the Western World, and Other Plays*. Oxford: Oxford Univ. Press, 1995.

———. *Plays, Poems and Prose*. Edited by Micheál Mac Liammóir. London: Dent, 1972.

Tangney, John. "Yeats, Spenser, and the Poetics of Wandering." *Literary Imagination* 14, no. 2 (2012).

Taylor, Bron, ed. *Encyclopedia of Religion and Nature*. London and New York: Continuum, 2005.

Thomas, Keith. *Man and the Natural World: Changing Attitudes in England, 1500–1800.* London: Allen Lane, 1984.

Thoreau, Henry D. *The Maine Woods.* New York: Bramhall, 1950.

———. *A Week on the Concord and Merrimack Rivers.* Princeton, NJ: Princeton Univ. Press, 2004.

Thornton, Weldon. *J. M. Synge and the Western Mind.* Gerrards Cross: Colin Smythe, 1979.

Torchiana, Donald. *W. B. Yeats and Georgian Ireland.* Oxford: Oxford Univ. Press, 1966.

Trumpener, Katie. *Bardic Nationalism: The Romantic Novel and the British Empire.* Princeton, NJ: Princeton Univ. Press, 1997.

Tucker, Herbert F. *Epic: Britain's Heroic Muse, 1790–1910.* Oxford: Oxford Univ. Press, 2012.

Tuveson, Ernest Lee. *The Imagination as a Means of Grace: Locke and the Aesthetics of Romanticism.* New York: Gordian, 1974.

Vendler, Helen. "Second Thoughts: *The Haw Lantern.*" In *The Art of Seamus Heaney*, edited by Tony Curtis. Bridgend: Seren, 2001.

Vico, Giambattista. *New Science: Principles of the New Science Concerning the Common Nature of Nations.* 3rd ed. 1744. Reprint, New York: Penguin, 1999.

Viney, Michael. "Woodcock for a Farthing: The Irish Experience of Nature." *Irish Review*, no. 1 (1986): 55.

Wall, Eamonn. *Writing the Irish West: Ecologies and Traditions.* Notre Dame, IN: Univ. of Notre Dame Press, 2011.

Wang, Yena. "The Landscape Representation of the Anglo-Irish Cultural Estrangements in Bowen's *The Last September.*" *Theory and Practice in Language Studies* 8, no. 8 (2018): 1029–34.

Warner, Alan. *William Allingham.* Lewisburg, PA: Bucknell Univ. Press, 1975.

Wenzell, Tim. *Emerald Green: An Ecocritical Study of Irish Literature.* Newcastle upon Tyne: Cambridge Scholars, 2009.

———. *Woven Shades of Green: An Anthology of Irish Nature Literature.* Lewisburg, PA: Bucknell Univ. Press, 2019.

West, Rebecca J. *Eugenio Montale: Poet on the Edge.* Cambridge, MA: Harvard Univ. Press, 1981.

Wilde, Oscar. "Mr. Froude's Blue Book." In *The Critic as Artist*, edited by Richard Ellmann. London: Allen, 1970.

Williams, David G. "'A Decadent Who Lived to Tell the Story': Derek Mahon's *The Yellow Book*." *Journal of Modern Literature* 23, no. 1 (1999).

Williams, Raymond. *The Country and the City*. New York: Oxford Univ. Press, 1975.

Wills, Clair. *Reading Paul Muldoon*. Newcastle: Bloodaxe, 1998.

Wilson, E. O. *In Search of Nature*. Washington, DC: Island Press, 1996.

Wilson, Penelope. "Feminism and the Augustans: Some Readings and Problems." In *Jonathan Swift*, edited by Nigel Wood. London: Routledge, 1999.

Wright, Julia. *Representing the National Landscape in Irish Romanticism*. Syracuse, NY: Syracuse Univ. Press, 2014.

Yeats, William Butler. *Autobiographies*. London: Macmillan, 1961.

———. *The Collected Works of W. B. Yeats*. Vol. 5, *Later Essays*. Edited by William O'Donnell. New York: Scribner, 1994.

———. *The Collected Works of W. B. Yeats*. Vol 9, *Early Art: Uncollected Articles and Reviews Written between 1886 and 1900*. New York: Simon and Schuster, 2010.

———. *Complete Plays*. New York: Macmillan, 1982.

———. *Essays and Introductions*. New York: Macmillan, 1961.

———. *Explorations*. New York: Macmillan, 1962.

———, ed. *Irish Fairy and Folk Tales*. New York: Random House, 2003.

———. *The Poems*. Edited by Daniel Albright. London: Dent, 1990.

———. *The Poems*. Edited by Richard Finneran. New York: Scribner, 1997.

———. *A Vision*. New York: Macmillan, 1965.

Index

Jefferson Holdridge, director of Wake Forest University Press and professor of English at WFU in North Carolina, has written two previous critical books: *Those Mingled Seas: The Poetry of W. B. Yeats, the Beautiful and the Sublime* (2000) and *The Poetry of Paul Muldoon* (2008). He has edited and introduced two volumes of *The Wake Forest Series of Irish Poetry* (vol. 1, 2005; vol. 2, 2010), as well as *Post-Ireland? Essays on Contemporary Irish Poetry*, which he coedited and introduced with Brian Ó Conchubhair in 2017. He is also the author of four volumes of poetry, his most recent being *The Wells of Venice* (2020).